Praise for *Hire With Your Head*

"The POWER approach to hiring detailed in this book is a pragmatic, performance-oriented process that will be invaluable for future searches."

Denny Brown, President, Clarkson University

"*Hire With Your Head* provides a clear, useful, step-by-step description of how to recruit, interview and hire the best people for every role. I recommend it to the CEOs whom I coach and the MBA's whom I teach. I think it will become the standard for excellent hiring."

Ann Graham Ehringer, Ph.D., Director, Family & Closely-Held Business Program, Associate Professor, Marshall School of Business, University of Southern California

"Forget the latest pop-sociological blather. Lou Adler presents practical bottom-line oriented principles for accomplishing the most important task we do: hiring the right person for the job. Highly recommended."

Jack D. Lantz, President & CEO, Unitek Miyachi Corporation

"I serve as a member of the Board of Directors of seven corporations. I have introduced the POWER staffing system to three of them thus far and have seen a dramatic improvement in the quality and longevity of the executives hired. The techniques are easy to implement since they correlate so well with objectives of the corporations."

Howard Oringer, Managing Director, Communications Capital Group

"Lou Adler brings a results and performance focus clearly into the hiring process and has produced a useful and practical guide that will help entrepreneurs and managers alike avoid costly people mistakes. *Hire With Your Head* is the POWER approach to hiring effective employees and is destined to become the people's choice!"

Dr. Alfred Osborne, Director, The Harold Price Center for Entrepreneurial Studies, The Anderson School at UCLA

"Most practical and useable information ever presented over my 30 years in business."

Dale C. Rogers, President, Rogers & Associates

"Case Swayne Co., a developer and producer of specialty sauces and seasonings, has had the good fortune of growing at a CAGR of 20+% for a number of years. This has placed a special demand on us to staff our management positions with high caliber people who thrive in an environment of change and growth. Lou Adler's firm has filled virtually all of our more senior positions. In my experience, I have not dealt with a management recruiter who was more adept at focusing the search, and, most importantly focusing me on the key considerations and criteria to insure we 'hire with our heads.' I attribute much of our competitive edge to our people. Lou has played a vital role in helping us gain that edge. He has redefined recruiting with his POWER staffing."

Keith Swayne, President, Case Swayne Co., Inc.

"Lou Adler's insights regarding focusing on results and measuring objectives instead of emotions is invaluable. A must read for every manager committed to hiring the best."

Louise Wannier, President and Founder, Enfish Technology, Inc.

"From the perspective of the CEO, hiring top employees has always been one of the most critical challenges. Lou Adler has taken this complex process and distilled it to a few manageable, logical, memorable and powerful key practices which should be helpful to anyone looking to hire (or be hired)."

Jeff Weiss, President, Center for Corporate Innovation

"A primary issue facing all our CEO members is the finding and retaining of excellent key people. The hiring effort needs serious attention and Lou Adler's strategies and techniques are systematic and effective. His approach has helped many of our members."

Bill Williams, President, TEC (an international organization of CEOs)

HIRE WITH YOUR HEAD

HIRE WITH YOUR HEAD

A RATIONAL WAY TO MAKE A GUT DECISION

LOU ADLER

John Wiley & Sons, Inc.

New York • Chichester • Weinheim • Brisbane • Singapore • Toronto

This publication is designed to provide accurate and authoritative information in regard to the subject matter covered. It is sold with the understanding that the publisher is not engaged in rendering professional services. If professional advice or other expert assistance is required, the services of a competent professional person should be sought.

Library of Congress Cataloging-in-Publication Data:

Adler, Lou.
  Hire with your head: a rational way to make a gut decision / Lou Adler.
    p.   cm.
  Includes index.
  ISBN 0-471-29294-X (cloth : alk. paper)
  1. Employee selection.   2. Employees—Recruiting.   3. Employment interviewing.   I. Title.
  HF5549.5.S38A35   1998
  658.3'11—dc21   98-16189

Printed in the United States of America

10 9 8 7 6 5 4 3 2

To Chuck Jacob, who got me started; my wife Lorraine, who kept me going; my son Keith, who keeps me inspired; and to every manager who has ever made a hiring mistake.

Contents

Preface

After more than 20 years of placing middle managers and senior executives in all kinds of positions and with all types of companies, I've probably seen every type of hiring mistake. Over and over again. For practice, I've even made them myself. A few stand out as classics. Against my loudest protestations, my good friend Chris didn't hire Sam for the financial manager's spot at a prestigious entertainment company. Sam was nervous in the interview. Ten years later, Sam is a top-performing, senior executive at a rival company. Just a few years ago, the president at an Inc.100 fast-growing company tried to do everything he could to kill a director of marketing deal because the candidate seemed a little brash. Luckily, the president was overruled by his staff. This candidate is now the division president, and the company has doubled its size. After a tough director of manufacturing search in the early 1990s, I was proud to place an articulate, intelligent, and well-read executive from my client's major rival. To my dismay, within a few years half his staff had quit and company performance was declining. Everyone has their own stories just like these. How many people working for you shouldn't ever have been hired? How many good ones got away? History does repeat itself. I wrote this book to keep it from happening again.

Most of the time, we make bad hiring decisions because we decide too soon, we're too emotional, we don't know what we're looking for, or we don't know what questions to ask. Hiring great people is the first step to great management, but the traditional approaches used by most managers are misleading and flawed. The need for new, more timely, and more effective hiring approaches has never been more urgent. Many organizations are being restructured, assignments are often brief, and jobs are changing frequently. It is a pace that is likely to quicken. This book presents a new commonsense approach to hiring and interviewing.

One dilemma always seems to come up. Even with lots of interviews, you'll still never have all the information you need to be certain you have made the right decision. At some point, asking others for advice can often create as much confusion as clarification. More interviews, testing, and reference checking can help, but there quickly comes a saturation level when additional information neither helps nor hurts. There are just too many variables to consider. The difference between what you know and don't know doesn't narrow. This gap is what every hiring manager faces when evaluating a candidate. No matter how exhaustive the process, in the end it always comes down to some degree of gut feeling, instinct, and intuition. Effectively shrinking and crossing this inevitable gap represents the difference between a successful and unsuccessful hire. Over the years, and many hiring decisions later, it will represent the difference between a successful or unsuccessful management career.

The book is written from my perspective as both a headhunter and line manager. My field education on hiring and staffing started early. I became a manager within a few years after entering the workforce, and I was soon hiring MBAs, accountants, engineers, and all types of manufacturing people. My corporate experience consisted of stints at two major Fortune 500 companies at six different operating units. While I was a strong performer, my real success was due to my ability to hire good people. After 10 years as a successful division general manager, I quit the corporate world to begin a one-year trial period as a recruiter. I had hired over 50 people and was heading up a multifunctional team of over 200 people, but I had grown tired of corporate politics and believed I could do better helping others hire top people. There seemed to be a growing market for this ability.

Surprisingly, even though I hired lots of people during my corporate career, not once during those 10 years was I asked to attend some type of hiring or interviewing training program. Instead, a human resources old-timer gave me a simple rule to follow. He said, "Only hire those who can meet the *four A's* standard—articulate, affable, attractive, and assertive—and then recruit like heck." I applied this same rule during my first 10 years in the recruiting business. Since we were contingency recruiters, we were only paid when a candidate we introduced to a client was hired; and in turn, our guarantee of the candidate was short—just 90 days. It was easy to meet this target. Only three of the four A's were required, sometimes even two would do.

Although this method worked for me, it quickly became apparent that the whole hiring process was fundamentally flawed. For one, I knew some great people were being overlooked. I had observed that many talented prospects could not meet this superficial standard, particularly during the stress of an interview. In addition, even managers who were good objective interviewers seldom knew the real requirements for the job under consideration and what it would take to be successful in that position. Because these interviewers would substitute an arbitrary level of experience and qualifications to screen candidates, emotions, biases, and stereotypes would then become the primary selection criteria during the interview. Compounding the problem was the lack of enough good candidates. You can't hire good people unless you are able to meet good people. A successful hiring process has to directly consider this sourcing issue. Finally, I came to the conclusion that few managers knew how to recruit a top person to join the team. Most thought it was a selling proposition. I lost many fees because managers oversold the job, thereby cheapening it and driving candidates away, or they paid too much because they had no leverage. Recruiting has more to do with buying than selling. Candidates must earn the right to a valuable job; they then sell you. A problem at any of these stages was enough to cause the whole hiring process to collapse. Recruiters needed to consider every factor for consistent success in hiring.

I had the chance to begin addressing all these issues in 1988 when my firm converted to a retained or fee-based search firm. Under this arrangement, we were guaranteed a fee for every search, but we had to guarantee the candidate's performance for a year. The guarantee and the need to consistently perform changed everything. With a one-year performance guarantee, we had to be right at least 90% of the time to stay in business. We couldn't afford to do many searches over, and we had to be efficient as well as professional in every phase of the hiring process. It was clear that we needed a new approach to candidate sourcing, assessment, and recruiting. Developing a practical and comprehensive hiring system has driven my efforts since then, but I started identifying the underlying concepts many years earlier.

Since 1978, I've talked with thousands of candidates and worked with almost 500 different hiring managers. As a firm, we've had over 1000 placements in many kinds of positions and in all types of companies. During this time, I've been able to track people in their careers for 5- and 10-year periods, and in some cases, even up to 20 years. Consistent and similar patterns have emerged. Regardless of the work performed, successful people did similar things that unsuccessful people didn't do. For one thing, successful people were repeatedly successful. Success was never a surprise or an isolated event. There was always a past pattern of previous success. Likewise, less successful people somehow always missed the mark in some capacity, whether it was lack of team skills, organizational ability, commitment, or technical competence. I became convinced that measuring past performance was the best predictor of future performance.

We started to develop hiring techniques incorporating performance-based criteria. In addition, we benchmarked managers who consistently hired good people. We talked with applicants and hiring managers about the questions that were asked in interviews and how the answers were evaluated. For these managers, the most striking aspect of hiring successes and failures was that using past performance—not experience, education, personality, or intelligence—as the dominant standard of selection dramatically reduced errors. Managers who consistently hired strong people also were thoroughly familiar with the performance requirements of the job. They knew what had to get done and the type of person needed to do it.

Using actual hiring situations, we were able to further refine and simplify our own performance-based assessment techniques. We've discovered that we didn't need to ask a lot of clever questions to determine competency. An inquisitive, fact-finding methodology was more important. In fact, we've found that we only need to ask a few well-chosen questions to conduct a complete interview. As a result, for the past 10 years, our hiring accuracy has improved dramatically, with mistakes occurring now in less than one of every twenty placements.

To improve our firm's overall effectiveness, we started to integrate all the related aspects of successful hiring into the staffing process. This was the basis of the POWER Staffing system. It became the first program to addresses every aspect of hiring in a practical and easy-to-understand manner:

➤ A **P**erformance-based job description drives the process.

➤ It's complemented by an **O**bjective interview and evaluation process.

➤ A **W**ide-Ranging sourcing plan ensures an adequate flow of strong candidates.

➤ A proactive approach to **E**motional control overcomes the impact of first impressions and personality.

➤ The system is completed when combined with a strong **R**ecruiting program.

With this type of hiring system in place, we can consistently attract the best people on our terms. This five-step integrated hiring process is laid out step by step in the following pages. Over the past few years, we've trained thousands of other hiring managers to use these techniques and they're now getting similar accurate results. The POWER Staffing system is a universal hiring process that can be quickly learned by anyone, and it is applicable for any job, at any management level, and in any type of company.

Despite the field successes, there were still many skeptics. A few months ago, I was trying to convince a major direct mail company to carry this book in their upcoming catalog. The president, while obliging, questioned my credentials. He said there were at least 20 other people and companies trying to push hiring products. Each one was contending that theirs was the latest and greatest. He asked why I thought the approach I was pushing was any better than the others. I asked how many of the others were written or created by a Ph.D. "Everybody, but you," he said. "That's why you need to consider ours," I replied. "A Ph.D. can earn a Nobel Prize by developing a new test or technique that's 70 to 75% accurate in predicting a candidate's subsequent success. We'd be quickly out of business if we're not at least 95% accurate."

We've been a successful executive search and recruiting firm since 1978, and that is how accurate we've been for the past 10 years.

I take great pride in the fact that many people contributed to this effort. As you read the book, you'll note that I freely use both I and we. When I is used, it means I was the person responsible, for good or bad, with the topic at hand. The use of we refers to others in my company, our clients and candidates, and my friends and business associates, with whom I worked in coming to the conclusions described here. I evaluated and modified every idea and concept based on the inputs of others and real-life observations. The conclusions and recommendations are based on real jobs, real people, and real situations. We've also reviewed the academic research to validate the main conclusions. In all cases, common sense prevailed. This is the reason these techniques work so well and are so natural to use. You will also note that we use he and she randomly in case studies and examples. This is simply a convention of style to reduce the need for pronouns. Unless stated otherwise, all the material herein is equally appropriate for use by and for both men and women.

This book needs more of your stories. Please send me your thoughts and comments, and describe your hiring successes and failures. You can also visit our Web site (CJApower.com) for our latest hiring hot tips.

LOU ADLER

Mission Viejo, California
email: lousa@cja-careers.com

Chapter

1

Introduction to Performance-Based Hiring and the POWER Staffing System

Hire smart, or manage tough.
—Red Scott

■ A RUDE AWAKENING—WHAT IT REALLY TAKES TO GET AHEAD

I got the call sometime in the morning on a mid-October day in 1972. It was my first management job, Financial Planning Manager at Rockwell's Automotive Group in Troy, Michigan. I was working on my first presentation to the Group President and VP Finance, due the next day. It was going to be a very long night, but I didn't mind—making a good impression was uppermost in my thoughts. My boss, Chuck Jacob, and the reason for my being in Detroit, was on the phone with a desperate plea. Chuck was a

29-year-old, Harvard MBA whiz kid, just out of Ford Motor Company, trying to prove to everyone that he deserved his position as Controller for this $900 million truck-axle business. He was also my idol. I listened. He was over at the University of Michigan interviewing MBA students for planning analyst positions to fill out our department. We needed these people urgently. The good news—too many had signed up for the interview, and Chuck needed me there to interview the overflow. We were going head-to-head with Ford, Procter & Gamble, IBM, and every other top Fortune 500 company, who wanted the best candidates from this prestigious MBA program. He told me there were stars in this group that we needed on our team. The bad news—I didn't have a minute to spare. I protested, vehemently, pleading 14-hour days, a long night, and a critical presentation the next day. There was a momentary delay. Chuck's response still blasts in my ears today. *"There is nothing more important to your success than hiring great people! We'll somehow get the work done. Get your _____ over here now."* He then hung up.

I was there within the hour. Together we interviewed about 20 people, took 8 of them to dinner that night in Ann Arbor, and hired 3 of the top MBA students within two weeks. I've lost track of Russ, Joe, and Vivek, but I want to thank them and Chuck (who passed away at a too early age) for an invaluable lesson: there is nothing more important for your career and company success than hiring great people. Nothing. Chuck and I got back to the office at 10 P.M. that night and worked together until about 3 A.M. to finish the report. I presented the handwritten version the next day to Bob Worsnop and Bill Panny. Chuck and I apologized for the format and lack of preparation, but told them we were doing something more important. They agreed.

■ BENCHMARKING THE BEST

I learned 50% of what I needed to know about hiring that day. Since then, I've been trying to understand the rest. I'm not quite there yet, but close. For the past 25 years, I've been fortunate to be able to work with other people, like Chuck, who always seem to hire great people, year in and year out. Few have had any formal training. They learned through trial and error. Equally important, I've lived and worked with managers who've made every possible hiring mistake in the book. This is their book, too. It's the collective stories of the good and the bad. What to do and what not to do. You'll find some great techniques in this book, but none are more important than your belief that hiring great people is the single most important thing you can do to ensure your own success.

Many years later, I heard Red Scott's adage, *"Hire smart, or manage tough."* This said it all to me. I've never met anybody who could manage tough enough. No matter how hard you try, you can never atone for a weak hiring decision. A weak candidate rarely becomes a great employee, no matter how much you hope for improvement or how hard you try to train the person. Instead, hire smart. Use the same time and energy to do it right the first time. Brian Tracy of Nightingale-Conant fame said on one of his recent tape programs that effective hiring represents 95% of a manager's success. This may be a little high, but with what I've seen, 70 to 80% seems about right to me. This is still enough to keep hiring in the number one position. Every manager says that hiring great people is their most important task; however, few walk the talk. Although important, it never seems urgent enough until it's too late. When it comes down to the actual hiring process, our words don't match our actions. Test yourself and see how you score as a hiring manager. Rank the performance of every member of your own team. Are most of them top-notch and exceeding expectations? If they are, consider yourself a strong manager. Unless you're hiring people like this 80 to 90% of the time, you need to throw out everything you've learned about hiring and start with a new slate. If you're already in the elite 80 to 90%, this book will show you why and will give you some new techniques that will boost your performance even further.

You might try this same exercise with your next candidate for a management position. It's one of our basic interviewing questions. If you need to hire a good manager, make sure the person has a track record of hiring good people. Ask the candidate to describe his or her hiring successes and failures. You'll quickly discover whether the interviewee is a good manager. Most managers find the hiring process frustrating, time consuming, an over-whelming burden, and error-prone. With this built-in negative bias, it's not surprising we're easy prey to the energetic, attractive, affable, and articulate candidate. This is the one who eventually may fall short of our lofty expectations once on the job. Understanding the importance of good hiring decisions is the first step in overcoming these classic problems.

Many of the techniques we'll present have been developed by observing people who consistently hire top people. This process is called benchmarking, and much of the book reflects this approach. Just do what the best interviewers do, and you'll get similar results. In fact, modeling good interviewers this way is similar to modeling good performers for any type of job. Just find out what the most successful people do that makes them successful, and find other people who can do the same things. This principle of benchmarking is a theme of the book and is at the heart of performance-based hiring. You don't need to be a trained psychologist to hire good people. Psychologists look for the underlying traits of high performers. Why bother? Just look for high performers. They'll possess the necessary underlying traits.

We have observed a crucial factor through our benchmarking: The best interviewers use two different critical thinking skills, one for the hiring decision and another for information gathering. They recognize that the hiring decision must be intuitive, since there's never enough information to match abilities, needs, and interests completely. Instead, they substitute a broader group of 8 to 10 generic and job-specific determinants of success to assess competency. Despite the intuitive component, they recognize that they must use an analytical, fact-finding method to collect as much appropriate data as possible about these traits before making the hiring decision. These great interviewers also have the ability to suspend their personal reaction to the candidate long enough to make an unbiased assessment.

From my observations, weak interviewers (those who make lots of mistakes) appear to fall within three broad categories. First, a large percentage are too emotional. These people make quick judgments largely based on first impressions and personality. Not unexpectedly, their hiring results are random. Second, overly intuitive interviewers short-circuit the process, super-ficially assessing only a narrow group of important traits. Every now and then, they'll hire a star, but more often it's a person strong in only a few areas, and not broad enough to handle the whole job. Finally, the technical interviewers are at the other extreme. These people are good at the fact-finding part of the process, but weak at decision making, believing they never have enough information. As a substitute they overemphasize the need for experience and skills. The result is a solid, but often unspectacular staff. The key is to collect enough of the right facts. Trouble occurs when this delicate balance is broken.

If you've built a group of motivated, team-oriented people and have a clear vision of where you're going, you will achieve success. Top-notch people and clear vision are both prerequisites. Superior employees will leave an environment that lacks purpose and direction, so the game plan is important. But a great game plan without top people winds up being a constant struggle. You'll either have to do the work yourself, or spend your energy constantly pushing your team. This is not management. Spend your energy on building the team and the game plan. This is management. To paraphrase Michael Gerber's *E-Myth*, (New York: HarperCollins, 1986), work on your department, not in it. In this book, we'll show you how to make management more efficient by first building the game plan and then finding the right people to execute it. We refer to the game plan as the performance-based job description. It drives every aspect of management and staffing.

■ HIRING IS TOO IMPORTANT TO LEAVE TO CHANCE

Once you know what the real performance needs of the job are, hiring is relatively easy. When you don't know what's required, you substitute your biases, perceptions, and stereotypes. Great managers and great companies start with great people. And nothing is more important to your personal career or company success than hiring great people. Nothing.

Table 1.1   The Hiring Attitude Survey

Survey Question	Response
Have you ever hired anyone who hasn't worked out?	Yes or No
How important is hiring good people to your personal success?	#1, #2, or Other
Do you really like the hiring and interviewing process?	Yes or No
How accurate is the typical one-on-one interview in predicting subsequent success?	_____%
During the interview, how long does it take to make a "no" hiring decision?	_____ minutes
During the interview, how long does it take to make a "yes" hiring decision?	_____ minutes
How many different assessments are there after interviewing a candidate if there are many interviewers?	_____ different assessments
After someone starts, how long does it take to determine the person's competency?	_____ weeks

Understanding some of the problems with the hiring process is the first step toward developing a workable fix. It starts by understanding your hiring attitude. Take this survey shown in Table 1.1 to see how you compare with other managers.

Where do you stand? We analyzed the answers from a random sample of 3000 managers:

➤ 95% said they've made bad hiring decisions.

➤ 95% indicated hiring is #1 or #2 in importance.

➤ 95% don't like the hiring process.

➤ Just about everybody felt that the interview process wasn't very accurate. Few were surprised to learn that a study conducted by Prof. John Hunter of Michigan State University indicated that the typical employment interview is only 57% accurate.

➤ A "no" decision can be confidently, but not necessarily accurately, made in less than 30 minutes in 90% of the cases.

➤ 90% of managers said a "yes" decision could confidently be made in one to three total hours of interviewing.

➤ There are as many different assessments of the same candidate in a one-hour interview as there are interviewers.

➤ It takes at least three weeks to three months after a candidate starts to determine true competence for most jobs.

It seems that interviewing is a random process that doesn't work too well. It's probably one reason most managers find it frustrating. This is a disturbing situation. Hiring, the most important thing we do as managers, is based—in most cases—on a random process. When you think about it, no other processes in our organizations are random, much less one of this importance. Companies spend hundreds of thousands of dollars, even millions, to reengineer a flawed process that has a 5 to 10% error rate. One with a 20% failure rate would be considered out of control and shut down! Yet the one that is considered most important has a 40 to 50% error rate. This is unacceptable. Something can be done. To begin, shut down the current approach to hiring and start over.

■ WHY YOU SHOULD THROW AWAY EVERYTHING YOU KNOW ABOUT HIRING

The typical interview used by most managers is a flawed way of hiring someone. Emotions, biases, chemistry, and stereotypes play too big a role. The competency of the interviewer is questionable. True knowledge of the job is weak. Candidates give misleading information because they're not asked appropriate questions. Standards fall as desperation grows. Understanding the cause of the problems requires first understanding the hiring process and how it developed.

There are three main factors involved in hiring—the candidate, the interviewer, and the job. The dynamic relationship among these three factors is shown in Figure 1.1. I have observed, based on my involvement with more than 3000 interviewing situations, that most of the hiring decision is dependent on the relationship developed early in the interview between the applicant and the hiring manager. This has to do with chemistry, first

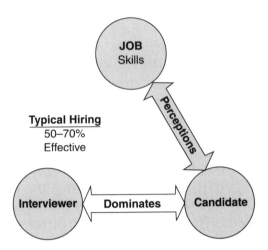

Figure 1.1. The relationship between these three factors determines hiring accuracy.

impressions, emotions, biases, stereotypes, the halo effect (globalizing a few strengths), and the tendency to hire in one's image. In most cases, the true job is poorly understood. Thus biases and perceptions are used as substitutes for real job needs. Even if we know some of the performance requirements, they're still filtered first through this personal relationship bias. This is how randomness enters the hiring process. If you like a candidate, you tend to reduce your performance standards, and if you don't like someone, you don't care whether the person is competent.

Hiring is random because the wrong things get measured. The accuracy of the hiring decision depends directly on whether a candidate is being measured on the ability to get the job or do the job. Getting the job includes things like personality, first impression, handshake, affability, social confidence, assertiveness, appearance, extroversion, and verbal communications. Doing the job includes initiative, team skills, technical competence, management and organizational skills, intellect, and leadership, to name a few. The latter group is harder to measure, so we unconsciously substitute the former and hope for the best. We're all guilty of this, despite our reluctance to admit it. It's been my experience that the "getting to doing" ratio is somewhere around

80/20, maybe 70/30, for most managers. This means that 70 to 80% of the hiring decision is affected by presentation. Figure 1.2 shows what happens when the hiring decision is based more on style than on substance.

When the hiring decision is based more on a candidate's ability to get the job than to do the job, two bad things happen. One, we frequently hire people who fall short of expectations (Figure 1.2, Situation II), and we don't hire people who are strong candidates, but weaker interviewers (III). Two good things can happen, but they're inadvertent. We hire people who are good at both the getting and the doing (I), and we don't hire those weak at both (IV). You don't even need to read this book or take a single training course to get these two parts right. It's all luck. As my former partner once said, "Even a blind squirrel finds a nut every now and then."

When the hiring decision is based primarily on the candidate's ability to do the work everything changes. You still hire those good at both (I), and don't hire those bad at both (IV). More importantly, you also eliminate the other two major hiring errors. You stop hiring those who always fall short of expectations (II), and you start hiring those who are really great, but might be

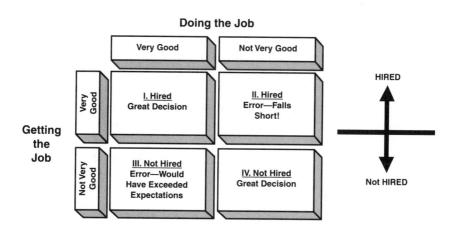

Figure 1.2. What happens when getting the job is more important than doing the job.

a little weak on the interviewing side (III). You need to hire people who are very good at doing the job, not those just very good at getting the job. Making this shift in perspective is what performance-based hiring is all about.

■ SUBSTITUTE THE JOB AS THE DOMINANT SELECTION CRITERION

It is easier said than done. Moving the decision-making process from "getting" to "doing" is hard work and mentally challenging. It takes lots of effort to counteract the natural tendency to judge people on first impression, personality, and a few select traits. You must. You'll quickly eliminate at least 50% of all hiring errors. The lack of real job knowledge represents the balance. Both must be addressed together. Over the past 20 years, I've worked with 700 to 800 hiring managers on many different search assignments. Most interviewers (including me) fall prey to personality bias. A few don't. This select group can suspend their emotional reaction to the candidate until they've determined competency. They also know what real competency looks like. Once they find out if the person can do the work, they then find out if they can work with the candidate. This principle is shown in Figure 1.3.

For most of us, this is neither natural nor easy. Our brains aren't wired this way. It's much simpler to quickly determine whether we like the candidate and then go through some quick questions to determine competency. At CJA, with over 1000 placements made in a variety of positions, from staff accountant to division president, it's been our collective experience that when we conduct hiring as just described, we can predict performance with an accuracy of at least 80 to 90%, for any job, in any company. Based on fallouts, or people being terminated during the first year, the reliability of our search process has been over 95%. When we made mistakes, they could always be traced back to someone having shortcircuited one of the five basic principles of effective hiring. We've combined them all into a new performance-based approach to hiring: the POWER Staffing hiring system.

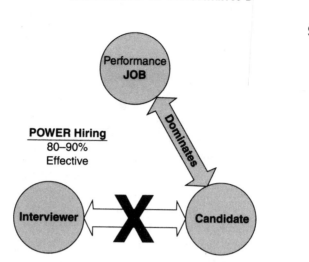

Figure 1.3. Substitute the job as the dominant selection criterion.

■ FIVE STEPS TO GETTING HIRING RIGHT—THE POWER STAFFING SYSTEM

We developed the POWER Staffing system to address all the problems and inconsistencies typically involved in the hiring process. Here's a quick look at each of the components:

1. **P**erformance-Based Job Descriptions. If you want to hire superior people, first define superior performance.
2. **O**bjective, Performance-Based, Evaluations. Past performance is a great predictor of future performance.
3. **W**ell-Ranging Sourcing Plans. You have to see top people before you can hire them.
4. **E**motional Control. Overcome the tendency to make emotional decisions, which you then justify with selective facts.
5. **R**ecruiting Right. Good recruiting is not selling, it's marketing; candidates then sell you.

The "P" in POWER stands for **P**erformance-Based Job Descriptions. It directly affects every other component. I must read hundreds of job descriptions every year. This represents thousands of job descriptions over the past 20 years. Most of them were no more than lists of skills, duties, responsibilities, and required experience. At best, they defined basic competency. Yet in 20 years and over 1,000 assignments, no client has ever asked us to find anything other than a superior candidate. It is our position that if you want to hire superior people you first must define superior performance. Today's job descriptions just don't cut it. We suggest you throw them away and start over. This will represent a first, and major, step in improving your hiring decisions. Once you define superior performance, it becomes much easier to find superior people. If you don't clearly define superior performance, everyone will substitute their own perceptions and stereotypes. This is how the hiring process begins to fall apart. The way most job descriptions are now written prevents you from ever hiring the best.

The "O" in POWER stands for **O**bjective Evaluations. Once performance expectations are defined, the interviewer must use an objective, job-specific approach to determine whether the candidate can do the work. This needs to run the gamut from the one-on-one interview to reference checks, testing, panel interviews, and take-home tests. The interview is only one part of a multistep evaluation process and getting it right is essential to making better hiring decisions. Despite this need for a comprehensive assessment, we'll show how you can distill the one-on-one interview down to four essential questions. With these alone, you can be right 75 to 80% of the time. We'll introduce these questions and then explain how to make them part of a complete eight-question performance-based interview.

The "W" in POWER stands for **W**ide-Ranging Sourcing Programs. This is something most managers ignore or delegate solely to the human resources (HR) department. The quality of the hiring decision first depends on the quality of the sourcing program. If you're only seeing the bottom third of all possible candidates, your hires will come from that group, even if you're great at using all the other techniques. On the other hand if you're only seeing the top 10%, you'll eventually hire one of these great people, even if you're the worst interviewer in the

company. For most organizations, sourcing falls somewhere between these extremes. As a manager, don't assume that your current sourcing programs are adequate. Be proactive. Get involved.
Show your interest. Stay on top of what's going on. A good sourcing
program is a critical component of an effective hiring program,
and it needs to be multitiered. This includes the use of compelling
ads, multichannel sourcing programs, high-tech techniques, and
local and wide-area networking. It also needs to be strategic, not
just tactical. If you only start looking for people when you need
someone, you've just lost a major advantage, time. Desperation is
the second most significant cause of hiring mistakes. Standards always fall as need rises. A good sourcing program has to start at least
60 to 90 days before you need the candidate. If you're effective here,
the rest of the staffing process is relatively painless.

The "E" in POWER represents **E**motional Control. While desperation is the second basic cause of hiring mistakes, it directly
impacts the primary cause of hiring errors—the lack of emotional control. Many hiring mistakes are made based on personality and chemistry. These emotional reactions and gut feelings
are always prevalent. It's been our experience that first impressions and affability are unfortunately more important than competence in deciding to bring back a candidate for a second
interview. The emotional link between the interviewer and the
candidate needs to be broken to conduct an objective interview.
Objectivity is the essential key to reducing hiring errors. We'll
present a range of tips, tools, and techniques to address this critical issue. You'll discover that we're literally programmed to make
major decisions based on first impressions. If positive, we tend to
be less discriminating. If negative, we hold the applicant to a
higher standard, or ignore the person's responses entirely. This
double standard is the primary source of bad hiring decisions.

The "R" in POWER stands for **R**ecruiting Right. Eventually,
you'll meet a candidate you want to hire. Good recruiting skills
then become essential. Recruiting is the process of persuading a
candidate to take the job and then closing all the details. Most
managers believe recruiting is the ability to sell or charm a candidate about the merits and terms of the position. This is the
worst, and least effective, form of recruiting. Emotional control is
a critical need at this point. Once you meet a great candidate,
there is a tendency to start selling. If you oversell, you cheapen

the job. That's why good recruiting is more like marketing than selling. When you create a compelling vision of the job before you know much about the candidate, the candidate is more likely to sell you, instead of the other way around. If you present this same information after you know the candidate, you've lost leverage and your negotiating position. This weakens your hand, since it comes across as selling, not marketing. Once you lose this edge, even closing is more difficult. The candidate, not the hiring manager, will dictate the terms. Recruiting is an essential aspect of a well-developed hiring program. It is the final piece toward building a great team. While not difficult, it requires constant attention. And like just about everything about staffing, it is not what it seems to be.

In the past 20 years, I've sat between hundreds of hiring managers and a few thousand candidates, listening and observing. Sometimes it took few a months to learn about a mistake that could have been prevented. Sometimes a few years. There were thousands of mistakes, although they weren't all recognized as such at the time. Most were small, but these build up to big mistakes, when made over and over again. While less frequent, there were enough successes to establish a pattern. By modeling the successes and avoiding the failures, we discovered a realistic process that can be documented, learned, and applied by anyone wanting to do it right. This is how the POWER Staffing system was developed. Once you try it, you'll know why it works. It's practical, natural, and based on common sense.

■ PUTTING THE PIECES TOGETHER—A ROAD MAP TO THE ORGANIZATION OF THIS BOOK

The organization of this book is designed to present the POWER Staffing system in a logical format. Although it involves five separate stages, many are conducted concurrently. Some of the processes, such as sourcing, take place sooner than others, but you need to know something about the later stages before you can be effective at the early ones. We've organized the book with this learning and implementing process in mind, as shown in Figure 1.4.

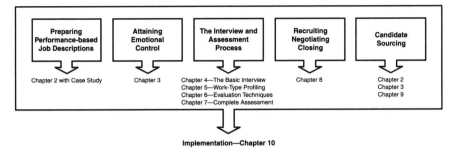

Figure 1.4. The POWER staffing performance-based hiring system.

The hiring process starts by defining superior performance. This allows you to measure substance, not style. Controlling emotions and understanding the performance needs of the job are prerequisites to hiring with your head. Chapters 2 and 3 are devoted to these critical subjects. These two chapters form the foundation of this book. The balance of the book is geared toward the tactics or implementation of the POWER Staffing system.

The complete interviewing and assessment process is presented in Chapters 4 through 7. The basic performance-based interview is introduced in Chapter 4. With this powerful eight-question interview, you can conduct a complete one-on-one performance-based evaluation. With just a few well-chosen questions, you'll be able to learn all you need to make an informed hiring decision. It only takes two questions to assess the core traits of all successful people. With two more questions, it is easy to determine whether the candidate has enough job-specific talent. During the last part of the interview, two questions are used to learn about character, values, personality, and cultural fit. With the eighth and final question, we create supply, demonstrate sincere interest, and learn about candidate motivation. As long as you know what you're looking for, this focused interview is all you'll need to determine if a candidate can do the job.

The candidate assessment starts in Chapter 5 with the introduction of a new concept, work-type profiling. This categorizes work into its four basic components—technical, managerial, entrepreneurial, and strategic. With it, you can easily compare job needs with a candidate's abilities. This will improve job fit and prevent some of the classic mismatches. Additional evaluation techniques including reference checking, testing, and panel interviews are described in Chapter 6. Collectively, they broaden the effectiveness of the performance-based interview. The candidate assessment is pulled together in Chapter 7, which includes checklists covering all important points.

Chapters 8 and 9 deal with effective recruiting and sourcing. Getting the candidate to join the team is critical and we'll describe how to negotiate and close an offer, and what to do when things go wrong. By the time you get to Chapter 9, you'll discover that you've already eliminated 50% of your sourcing problems. You'll be able to broaden the candidate pool by defining the performance needs of the job (Chapter 2) and eliminating your own personal biases (Chapter 3). Chapter 9 presents a grab bag of sourcing tips, techniques, and methods you can quickly use to find the top 10%. Remember you need to see the best before you can hire them.

In the final chapter (Chapter 10) a step-by-step implementation program is presented. Four distinct stages have been developed ranging from a basic process to an integrated, comprehensive system. Each is easy to learn and apply. By taking this stepwise approach, impact and acceptance are immediate. With the guidelines presented, you'll be able to implement those components of the POWER Staffing program that best meet your company's needs.

With the introduction of the POWER Staffing system, every manager now has a chance to hire great people, using the same techniques as the most seasoned hiring pros. POWER Staffing is as much about good management as it is about good hiring. You can't separate the two. They go hand in hand. You become a better manager in the process of hiring better people. Hiring better people, in turn, makes you a better manager.

To *Hire With Your Head,* you need to combine emotional control with good fact-finding skills and intuitive decision making. This whole-brain thinking provides the critical balance to match job needs, the interviewer's personality, and the candidate's abilities and interests. This needs to be combined with sourcing. Without enough good candidates, everything else is futile. Once you start meeting strong candidates, good recruiting skills become essential. Recruiting starts at the beginning, not the end. It must be part of an integrated interviewing and assessment process to work effectively. This is the strength of the POWER Staffing system. It brings all the critical hiring processes together. While each step is easy to use separately, its effectiveness lies in the integration. This is the challenge. Eliminate or ignore any aspect and the whole process collapses. Do them all and you'll get consistent great hiring results.

WHY HIRING IS NUMBER ONE

✔ There is nothing more important to a manager's personal success than hiring great people. Nothing.

✔ Management is easy as long as you clearly know the performance needs of the job and hire great people to do it.

✔ *"Work on your department, not in it."*—Michael Gerber.

✔ Hiring is too important to leave to chance.

✔ Hiring is the only major process in a company that is random. Any other process that is this unreliable would have been scrapped long ago.

✔ The key to better hiring decisions: "Break the emotional link between the candidate and interviewer and substitute the job as the dominant selection criterion."

✔ Hiring is a whole-brain activity. Collect enough unbiased facts to make an intuitive decision.

✔ Measure a candidate's ability to do the job, not get the job. Determine whether you like or dislike the candidate after you've determined the person's competence. Substance is more important than style, but sometimes it is hard to tell the difference.

✔ Great hiring requires more than just good interviewing skills. The POWER Staffing hiring system is the first to bring it all together into an integrated, systematic process.

✔ *"Hire smart, or manage tough."*—Red Scott.

Chapter

Performance-Based Job Descriptions

Begin with the end in mind.
—Stephen Covey

■ IF YOU WANT TO HIRE SUPERIOR PEOPLE, FIRST DEFINE SUPERIOR PERFORMANCE

Everyone wants to hire superior people. Yet the criteria that most managers use to define the work, write ads, filter resumes, and interview candidates are based on a profile that defines, at best, basic competency. At its worst, it can exclude superior candidates from even applying. In this chapter, we show that skills and experience-based job descriptions are misleading and can preclude the hiring of top people. We then explain how to assess a candidate's competency by using the performance needs of a job to source and filter candidates, as well as conduct a comprehensive interview. These performance needs also form the core of the new employee transition program: how you'll manage, motivate, and conduct regular follow-up; and how you'll review, reward, and promote the candidate. Effective hiring starts by preparing a performance-based job description. This sets the foundation for better hiring decisions and the performance management concept underlying the POWER Staffing hiring system.

About two years ago, I gave a half-day presentation to a business group in northern California. An HR representative from one of these companies called me recently and asked if we could help prepare some performance objectives for some of their new positions. After arriving on site, I was pleasantly surprised to find that the company had already prepared performance objectives for every major position. They had switched to a performance-based hiring system after experiencing some disastrous hiring incidents using more traditional methods. Later, the president told me that the results so far indicated that everyone using the process had dramatically reduced hiring errors. At a personal level, he indicated his hiring effectiveness had increased dramatically. Previously, without knowing the performance needs of the job, he said he had relied on gut feel and emotions in making hiring decisions, and was wrong more often then right. He told me he hasn't made a hiring mistake since switching.

■ USE THE SAME CRITERIA FOR EXTERNAL HIRING AS YOU DO FOR INTERNAL MOVES

Whose performance is more predictable—a person you know, moved internally, or an outside hire? It's obviously the internal candidate. And even if an internal person is promoted, the predictability of his or her subsequent performance is very high, about 80 to 90%. For a lateral transfer it's close to 100%, if the jobs and environment are roughly similar. Performance predictions for the external hire are only around 55 to 70% accurate in most situations. The internal move is much more accurate because we really know the person's past performance, attitude, work habits, intelligence, leadership and team skills, ability to learn, management style, potential, and commitment. These are all educated guesses for the unknown outsider. This comparison is shown in Figure 2.1.

The decision-making process between the outside and inside hiring are fundamentally different. Each uses different selection criteria. Our objective is to develop a method for outside hiring

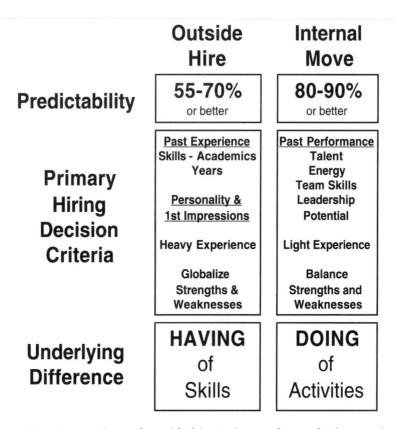

	Outside Hire	**Internal Move**
Predictability	**55-70%** or better	**80-90%** or better
Primary Hiring Decision Criteria	<u>Past Experience</u> Skills - Academics Years <u>Personality & 1st Impressions</u> Heavy Experience Globalize Strengths & Weaknesses	<u>Past Performance</u> Talent Energy Team Skills Leadership Potential Light Experience Balance Strengths and Weaknesses
Underlying Difference	**HAVING** of Skills	**DOING** of Activities

Figure 2.1. Comparison of outside hire to internal transfer/promotion.

that more closely approaches the accuracy of the internal hiring decision. One notable point in the comparison is the level of experience required in both decisions—the internal person always has less experience. We tend to overvalue experience, academics, and specific skills when hiring from the outside, and these same highly valued criteria are always minimized when promoting or moving someone internally. A promotion or lateral transfer is always a developmental move for the employee to gain new skills and experiences. Yet this is not an option for an outside candidate, with experience always being the primary selection criterion. It is obvious that the level of experience does not determine ability, yet it is the primary filter used to screen potential outside candidates. We've all met people with lots of experience who aren't top performers. Likewise, we've all met top performers with little experience. In this way, the traditional experience-based approach excludes some of the best candidates.

The second decision criterion for hiring an external candidate is personality as measured during the interview. Like past experience, personality measured during the interview is also a poor predictor of subsequent performance. We infer too much to the "interview" personality. A person can be outgoing, positive, and friendly in the interview, and underperform once he is hired. Another, more quiet candidate, can be a star when in her element on the job. At work, personality is measured through performance. Likable, outgoing, articulate people don't get ahead if they don't perform, unless they are unusually political. But even these people need to perform if they expect to keep their position or get promoted. Likewise, those who get ahead based on true merit aren't always the most outgoing and initially warm people. That's why many top performers aren't always the best interviewers.

This fundamental flaw in the hiring process often leads to disastrous results. For outside hiring, we use experience and personality as a substitute for on-the-job performance. Within five minutes of the interview, these two poor predictors of performance dominate the hiring decision process. From this bias, most interviewers then globalize strengths and weaknesses. Lots of experience, a strong personality, and a few other traits, and we incorrectly assume the candidate can handle the job. Someone a little quiet and without this experience is automatically considered incompetent. This substitution is unwarranted, unnecessary, and logically flawed. For someone we know, it's a completely different story. For these people, we take a balanced look at strengths and weaknesses. For the internal move, experience and personality are appropriately subordinate to performance. If an employee's performance and potential are high, we'll establish a development program to improve skills and allow movement to another level. This possibility is rarely considered for an outside hire. Personality- and experience-based hiring doesn't give the same results as performance-based hiring.

➤ Focus on the DOING, Not the HAVING

Since the internal move is more predictable, our goal is to apply this same decision process when making an external hiring decision. There is an underlying difference between the internal and external move that makes this transition possible. The internal decision is very DOING oriented. It's dynamic, based on what a person has accomplished. A person's actual past performance dominates the decision. The external decision is very HAVING oriented, based largely on a candidate's background. This is a poor substitute for the work that needs to get done. The underlying logic behind the external hiring decision is that a high enough absolute level of experience, skills, academics, and personality will be sufficient to meet the performance requirements of the job. This fundamental premise is based on flawed logic. A candidate can *have* all of this and not be able to *do* the job. Conversely, there are lots of people who can do the job without having any of these attributes. Just consider all the people who've been successfully promoted or laterally transferred. It is what people do with their skills, experiences, and abilities that determines success, not the absolute level of these skills, experiences, and abilities.

By changing the focus to DOING rather than HAVING, the basic approach to hiring can be altered and accuracy dramatically improved. This DOING approach eliminates the logical flaws inherent in most hiring decisions, and gets at the true characteristics of top performers.

■ IDENTIFY THE CRITICAL SUCCESS FACTORS OF EVERY JOB—SMART OBJECTIVES

We must redefine job descriptions to reflect what needs to get done rather than what a candidate needs to have. This is an outcome-oriented, rather than an input-oriented approach that allows the external hiring decision to more closely parallel the internal move. Performance-based job descriptions define what needs to get done, not the skills and experience the candidate needs to have. It has been shown that the ability to achieve measurable objectives is a better predictor of future performance than the candidate's level of skills and experience. Comparable past performance is a leading indicator of future performance. We want to be able to use this basic concept when hiring candidates from the outside.

Many companies are now moving away from skills-based job descriptions, recognizing their inadequacies. Microsoft describes in the November 7, 1996, issue of *Fortune* magazine how they have changed their applicant selection criteria. They now consider performance and potential over experience and skills. In Tracey and Weirsema's book *The Discipline of Market Leaders* (Amsterdam: Addison-Wesley, 1997), they describe Intel's new approach to hiring. David House, at the time a senior VP with Intel, mentions that job descriptions now include the expected deliverables the candidate must provide in the first 12 months. Intel believes this is a better indicator of subsequent performance than skills and experience. EDS and Cypress Semiconductor are long-time users of performance-based hiring systems.

After preparing about 500 different performance-based job descriptions and tracking subsequent performance, I've concluded that every job has five to six critical performance factors that ultimately determine success. It doesn't matter whether the job is an entry-level position or the CEO of a Fortune 500 company. These performance factors are different for every job, but they fall within similar categories such as effectively dealing with people, achieving objectives, organizing teams, solving problems, and making changes. This concept is demonstrated in Figure 2.2. Defining and prioritizing the most important of these critical success factors form the DOING portion of the performance-based job description.

In preparing the performance-based job description, we develop two or three performance objectives in each of these eight categories to make sure all job issues are considered. The preliminary list could have as many as 15 to 20 (or more) of these performance objectives. These are then ranked in order of importance and narrowed down to the top five or six, which will be used for candidate selection purposes.

We want to make these performance objectives as SMART as possible to help clarify our expectations. By SMART we mean **S**pecific, **M**easurable, **A**ction-oriented, **R**esult, and **T**ime-based. Creating an objective this way is a great way to improve understanding. When performance objectives are too general, they're subject to many different interpretations. Also, broad objectives sometimes cover too many issues. This is why being specific is so important. If you can't quantify objectives, your employees never

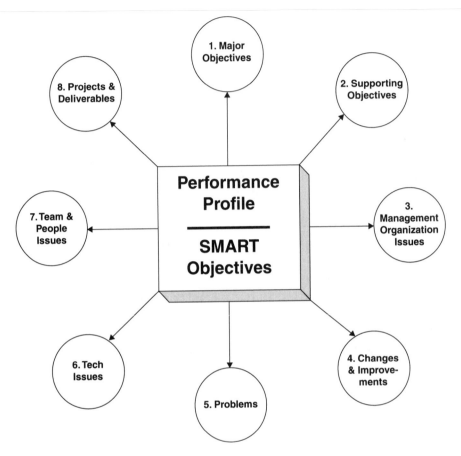

Figure 2.2. Develop measurable performance objectives for each of these categories. Prioritize the most important. These represent the critical performance requirements for the position.

know when they have achieved them. Therefore, objectives should be measurable, either in percentages or in absolute terms; for example, *reduce machine downtime by 10%.* The action orientation requires the objective to include words like *build, improve, create,* or *prepare* that address the change needed. By describing the result or the deliverable and the anticipated time frame, you further clarify the objective. An example of a SMART objective that would fall under the Changes and Improvement category would be: *Within 90 days, upgrade the performance reporting system for tracking rep sales by addressing productivity and performance to quota.* SMART objectives written this way eliminate the ambiguity of the traditional job description.

■ HOW TO WRITE SMART OBJECTIVES

This approach works for all types of jobs. It's most effective if you can prepare and prioritize these SMART objectives with the interviewing team. Everyone has their say, they'll all know the real needs of the job, and their assessments will be more comparable. Getting everyone on the same page this way has value beyond the interview. They'll all have a vested stake in the candidate's subsequent success. They will take the whole interviewing process more seriously. Ask the hiring manager, or team, to describe what the person taking the job must do to be successful in each of the major performance criteria categories. Depending on the job, some will be more important than others. The action verb is the critical part of the SMART objective. Specific action verbs like *create, build, change, improve, establish, develop, design, analyze, identify, prepare, conduct,* and *lead* are good choices. They're much better in describing the work that needs to get done than passive verbs like *have* and *be responsible for* found in most job descriptions. Start off the SMART objective with an action word that can help you focus on the required result.

Following are some examples of SMART objectives for each category for a product marketing manager of a software company.

1. *Major Objectives.* This includes all the major requirements of the job: setting up a new department, developing new products, increasing sales, and so on. For the software product manager position, it could be: "Develop and launch the new Internet buying program within 15 months."

2. *Supporting or Sub-Objectives.* Include some key steps needed to meet the major objectives. Often these are more important then the primary objective itself, since they describe the critical milestones and processes for achieving that objective. Here's a supporting objective related to the product

manager's primary task of launching the new product line: "During the first quarter, identify the size and buying patterns of the user community." Here's another; "Prepare the marketing requirements specification for review within 120 days."

3. *Management and Organization Issues.* Consider all the team and management requirements needed to be successful in the job. Often these are minimized or ignored. You want to consider the size, scope, and complexity of the management challenge. "Identify key resource requirements including team members and budget needs and prepare a detailed plan of action within 45 days of starting," is a classic example.

4. *Changes and Improvements.* What do you want changed, upgraded, or improved? Take everything into account—systems, methods, processes, and people. Consider anything that could be done better and include it on the job spec. Here's one for the product manager: "Improve the project tracking system to better identify critical constraints and bottlenecks."

5. *Problems.* Include any existing problems or those likely to be encountered. Minor ones don't matter, but the major ones do. Lack of time, resources, or special situations fall within this category. One the product manager needed to consider: "During the first quarter develop some alternate PR plans to penetrate the direct mail channel, since our current agency has missed some critical dates."

6. *Technical Issues.* Focus more on the application, expected outcome, or use of these technical skills than on an absolute level. Instead of asking for five years of hardware design plus a BSEE, it's better to request that a new engineer "Lead the design effort on a new optical switching system." One for the product manager could be: "Complete the database interface requirements to ensure efficient on-line ordering by June." This is much better than stating the product manager needs to have at least five years' experience writing marketing requirements for software products.

7. *Team and People Issues.* Some of this might have been covered in the management category, but also include

any special interpersonal needs or problems, or cross-functional team issues. Dealing with another department or dealing with customers is an important component of many jobs that is often ignored. Here's one for a cost accountant: "Develop a new team approach with manufacturing to upgrade the cost and productivity reporting system." The previous product manager had had problems with an egocentric development manager. The objective became "Develop a new communications approach to deal with a very dominant, yet talented, software manager." This was better than saying, "Have good interpersonal skills and a balanced ego," which is an ineffective classic found on most job descriptions.

8. *Projects and Deliverables (Strategic/Creative, Tactical).* This is a grab-bag category for everything else not yet considered. Think about the creative and strategic needs of the job. This could address long-range planning issues or developing new approaches or concepts. Also consider any tactical issues or projects not previously considered. Since this is so broad, you could even start the performance objectives process with this category. For the product manager, a tactical project was,"Prepare the budget request to corporate including pro forma sales forecasts, workforce and expense needs, and capital requirements." A strategic objective was, "Develop a long-term marketing plan based on competitive analysis and technical trends." A creative one could have been, "Lead the design effort on developing new graphic user interfaces."

Sometimes, you won't have all the information necessary to complete each performance objective. In this case, make sure you have at least the action verb and the specific task identified. This is a good start. Complete SMART objectives are the best, since they clarify it all—a specific and measurable task, the expected result, the action verb, and a time limit. Performance objectives written like this are the best way to clarify job needs and improve communications. This will be critical when the candidate starts since it will help guide the transition and track subsequent performance. In some cases, you won't know the time frames or specific needs. In other instances, you'll want to negotiate these with the candidate or let the person determine them after starting.

While you should strive for a complete SMART objective, keep in mind the need to be flexible based on these circumstances. The primary and mandatory shift needs to be from having to doing; that's why the action verb is critical. You'll obtain a still higher level of insight by including the measurable result and the time factor. This improvement in understanding is shown in Table 2.1. Columns 1 and 2 represent the transition from HAVING to DOING. Columns 2 to 3 represent the change from a partial SMART objective to complete understanding.

Table 2.1   Using SMART Objectives to
Transition from HAVING to DOING

The HAVING	The DOING	
Classic Having Requirements	Partial SMART Objective Action Verb and Specific Task	Complete SMART Objective
Responsible for financial reporting.	*Upgrade* the monthly financial reporting package.	Within 120 days, *upgrade* the monthly financial reporting package to include product line profitability analysis.
Have 3–5 years' manufacturing experience controlling expenses.	*Reduce* operating overhead by $30,000 per month.	*Reduce* operating overhead by $30,000 per month within 6 months.
Have 10 years telemarketing industry experience.	*Improve* the performance of all telemarketing sales personnel.	During the first quarter, *improve* the performance of all telemarketing sales personnel by 6% through new training and tracking tools.
Have a BS Engineering and 5–8 years in the plastic molding industry.	*Lead* the design effort on a new high-volume injection molding facility.	Immediately *hire* three new designers and *lead* and complete the design effort on a new high-volume injection molding within 9 months.

Complete and agreed on SMART objectives enable everyone on the selection team to determine candidate competency and better understand real job needs. This will be critical during the interview and evaluation process. It's important to recognize that these SMART objectives are more than just a list of MBOs (Management by Objectives). MBOs are not deep enough. They just cover the broad top-level outcomes. For hiring purposes, SMART objectives need to consider each of the eight performance criteria categories previously noted. When these are narrowed down and put in priority order, everyone involved knows what the job entails. The ability to consistently hire great people is predicated on understanding these real performance issues.

■ COMPLETING THE PERFORMANCE-BASED JOB DESCRIPTION WITH SMART OBJECTIVES

Look in this week's classified ads if you want proof that most job descriptions just list skills, duties, and responsibilities, and describe required experience. This approach excludes strong candidates with related, but not identical experience and overvalues factors that have been shown to be misleading predictors of success. Job descriptions built around performance-based SMART objectives minimize these problems.

Our goal is to better understand the expected outcomes of a job, not the inputs. This is the fundamental difference between performance and experience-based job descriptions. A candidate who can achieve the performance objective obviously has enough experience and skills. The person couldn't achieve it, or something similar, otherwise. Therefore it's better to spend the time in the interview determining what the candidate achieved that was most comparable, and how he or she went about it, rather than the amount of education and experience the person has. The process starts by preparing a thorough performance-based job description.

Once you get the hang of it, it only takes about 30 minutes to an hour to prepare job specs this way. On a strictly time comparison, you'll more than offset this with more productive interviews. The benefits of this approach in hiring better people go far beyond time savings. The SMART objectives will serve as the basis

POWER Staffing™ Objectives Worksheet

Creating the Performance (SMART) Objectives

©1997 by Lou Adler, from his book *Hire With Your Head*. Part of the POWER Staffing™ "best practices" worksheet series, summarizing great hiring tips from some of the top managers in the US. Call 1-800-559-2559 for more hiring hot tips and tools.

Position:	Department:	Hiring Manger:	Date:

Instructions for Creating the Performance Criteria for Any Position

- ☐ Every job has five or six major things that need to get done (performance objectives) for the new employee to be successful.
- ☐ Make all objectives **SMART** - Specific, Measurable, Action Oriented, Result-based, Time Bound.
- ☐ Ignore job spec. Use macro approach to develop performance objective for each major area of job. Follow template below.
- ☐ Use micro approach (over) to convert traditional experience/skill spec to performance. Find out what's done with each criterion.
- ☐ Use benchmark approach (over) by finding traits and capability of people now in the job known to be competent.
- ☐ Prioritize the top 5-6 performance objectives and include on performance-based job description.
- ☐ ANCHOR and VISUALIZE each SMART objective to determine competency (over and Fact-Finding Worksheet).

Determine Performance Objectives using the Macro Approach

Job Factor	Example of HAVING vs. DOING	Comments and Descriptions	SMART Objectives
Major Functional Objectives	Misleading: Have 10 years OEM sales experience. BETTER: Increase OEM sales by 15% in year 1 and build new team.	Objectives need action verb (e.g., increase, change, improve) and measurable objective (e.g., 10% in 90 days).	
Subordinate Objectives	Misleading: Have good planning skills. BETTER: In 90 days submit plan and hire 3 people.	Include the sub-steps necessary to achieve key objectives. Ask for examples.	
Management & Organizational Issues	Misleading: Have good management skills. BETTER: Assess and rebuild the team within 120 days.	Provide measurable objectives to determine quality of management skills needed.	
Changes and Improvements Necessary	Misleading: Be an agent of change. Better: Upgrade the client contact tracking system before the next promo.	Be specific regarding the needed changes and upgrades. It's easier to compare applicant's accomplishments this way.	
Problems to Be Solved	Misleading: Be a problem solver. BETTER: Work with IS to eliminate customer service bottleneck before May.	Describe actual problems needing work and then ask applicants how they would solve them.	
Technical Skills in Actual Situation	Misleading: Have good PC skills. BETTER: Develop PC-based tracking system by June.	Provide specific example of how technical skills will be used. It's better to have open discussion of real work	
Team Skills in Actual Situation	Misleading: Have good team skills. BETTER: Jointly develop inventory reduction plan with sales and manu-facturing.	Describe situations that demonstrate good interpersonal/team skills and get similar examples from the applicant.	
Deliverables-Tactical, Strategic &Creative	Misleading: Have good strategic thinking and planning skills. BETTER: Develop a long range product plan.	Cover anything that hasn't been addressed above. Also describe actual examples of creative and strategic projects.	

CJA-The Adler Group, Inc.   *"Are You POWER Hiring℠ Yet?"*   Dallas • San Jose • Los Angeles
17852 17th, #209, Tustin, CA 92780 • 714/573-1820 • FAX 714/731-3952 • 800/559-2559 • www.cja-careers.com

of the transition program when the candidate starts, so they need to be prepared anyway. You'll use them to get the new employee up and running in the new job. If done at all, most of the time these objectives are prepared just before the new employee starts working. When they're prepared before the interviewing process, they become the foundation of the assessment process. In addition, they'll have value after the transition program. Then you'll also use them to track the employee's performance, give reviews, and recommend promotions.

■ THREE DIFFERENT WAYS TO PREPARE SMART OBJECTIVES FOR ANY TYPE OF JOB

There are three ways to develop these SMART objectives. Each depends on the type of job under consideration. This is shown in Table 2.2.

All three of these techniques can be used together to prepare a complete performance profile for the position. They're described in more detail in the following sections. The POWER Staffing Objectives Worksheet on page 30 will help guide you through the Macro approach to this process. Use the template on page 304 in the Appendix for the other two techniques.

➤ The Macro Approach

Jobs with lots of projects, like the software project manager's position discussed earlier, are generally the easiest to prepare. Use the macro approach in this case. Put aside the traditional job description and ask what the candidate must do to be successful in the job. Each of the eight performance criteria categories needs to be considered. This is the technique we use in preparing most management or project-type performance-based job descriptions. A time line can help clarify this process. Consider the job needs over a one- to two-year time horizon, starting with the first 30 days. Break the job into appropriate time segments and determine what the candidate must do or achieve at each point. First, get the two to three top projects or deliverables and make them SMART objectives. Then determine what interim steps need to

Table 2.2   Three Ways to Prepare SMART Objectives

Method	Description	Example
Macro or The Big Picture Approach *Ask: "What will the person hired need to do to be successful?"*	Get measurable objectives for each major factor in the job. Cover technical needs, management issues, team issues, projects, needed changes and problems.	• Launch three new products within the next 12 months. • In the next 90 days, upgrade the planning system for manufacturing.
Micro Approach *Convert skills into actions.*	Determine what needs to be done with each skill or experience. Develop a measurable objective that demonstrates competency.	• Use PCs to develop a new project tracking system. • Have enough experience to design three new products per year.
Benchmark the Best!	Compare the best people already in the job and select traits that best predict success. Avoid the traits of the underperformers.	• Prepare complex spreadsheets for long periods looking at pricing and cost issues. • Use initiative in dealing with customer return problems and making quick decisions.

occur along the way. Identify the first problem, challenge, or issue the person will face. It could be something like "break the bottleneck in order processing," or "determine the status of a major project."

Next, move out to the 90-day and then to the six-month mark. Figure out what the person must achieve during this time frame. It could relate to staff assessment or rebuilding, or closing a few major deals. Finally, ask what major things should have been accomplished after a year. These are the major objectives of the position. You need to develop lots of SMART objectives. Get everyone involved. After you have listed all the objectives, review each one and put them in priority order. The top five or six are all you really need to define the performance requirements of the job. Don't overlap. Each SMART objective should cover a different aspect of the position. You want to address a broad diversity of ability covering each critical game-breaker issue.

Figure 2.3 shows an example of this macro approach combined with a time line. The overriding SMART objective is to set up a new distribution facility over the next year, a few interim objectives are to coordinate with the design group to complete the physical layout of the site by a certain deadline, and negotiate a contract with the software vendor to meet critical system needs. Understanding these subobjectives is often the difference between success and failure on the job. By identifying them early, you'll eliminate major hiring and performance problems later on.

In addition to the time line, it's important to directly consider some of the tactical and managerial needs of the position. Tactical has to do with obtaining short-term results, either individually, as a team member, or as a manager. Here's an example of an individual tactical objective for a salesperson, "Improve the ratio of closes/calls by 15% by developing improved selling techniques." This gets at specific behaviors and traits much better than the classic, "Have good sales and closing skills coupled with 5 years' experience selling office products."

It's always better to describe the management objective, rather than the level of experience. For most management positions, the

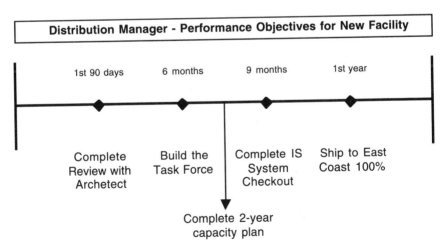

Figure 2.3. Use a time line to help guide your thinking as you develop the interim or sub-objectives needed to meet a major objective.

classic job description just lists the years of management experience required. It's better to describe what the manager needs to do
to build, develop, or manage the team. For example, "During the
first 60 days, establish an employee development program to support a 20% increase in order processing," is a clear tactical management task. During the interview, ask the candidate to give real
examples of comparable accomplishments. Generalities regarding
these types of tactical tasks can get you into lots of trouble if you
assume managerial competency based on years of experience.

Many jobs require strategic or creative skills. You can get at
these by describing the outcomes expected from these conceptual,
long-range planning, or creative skills. Some examples are "Archi-
tect a new system protocol," "Create a new technology to support
high-speed data switching," "Develop a long-range planning system," "Create a new marketing promotional program," and "Prepare a five-year global manufacturing plan." The verbs used in the
SMART objectives need to describe the creative or strategic nature
of the work. When you prioritize all the SMART objectives, the importance of these conceptual skills will stand out.

What to Do When You Don't Know What You Want the Person to Do

Every now and then, you'll want to hire someone that you know
you need, even though you have little idea what the person is supposed to do. In this case, make the creation of these little understood or unknown requirements the primary performance
objective. Basically, you will make writing the performance-based
job description a job objective. Suppose you need someone to take
your existing product line into a new distribution channel where
you have little experience. An appropriate SMART objective in this
case would be, "During the first month prepare and implement a
plan of action identifying all the key requirements for a direct
marketing channel for the xyz product line." Let the candidate tell
you what the needs of the job are, the appropriate resource requirements, and the time line. During the interview, the candidate
needs to describe comparable accomplishments and discuss how
he or she would implement the program if hired for the job.

One of my clients had a product that could potentially be
used in the managed health care industry. They wanted to hire a
VP level person to head the new program. The primary SMART

objective for the position was to "Prepare a five-year business plan within six months." The second one was to "Build the team needed to launch the business." The CEO, while aware of some of the issues, needed a leader to take charge of this new opportunity and define what really needed to get done. In fact, during the first interview, the president and the candidate who ultimately got the job, spent two hours together developing a detailed operational plan for this new business. This was after reviewing some of the candidate's accomplishments in setting up similar ventures. So before even starting the job, the candidate and the CEO were doing real work together. The CEO later told me that the candidate exhibited the same insight, organizational skills, and approach to problem solving on the job that he did in the two-hour session. This is the fundamental benefit of performance-based hiring. Candidates don't just talk about work, they sometimes actually demonstrate their skills during the session.

You can't be expected to know everything about every job under your watch. By delegating this "need to know" to a subordinate, you've just created another performance objective. Higher level jobs often have such needs. Setting up a new business, developing a new system, or creating a new product, fall within this category. If a job now has little structure, you need to find people who are real leaders—those that can build the teams and create the structure. This approach allows you to modify the job description to reflect the true performance needs of the job.

The macro approach tends to be open-ended. It starts by asking, "what does a person taking this job need to do to be successful?" Be careful to cover everything included in the eight performance categories. Once you've gone through this process a few times, it gets easier. This is the critical step in understanding the real nature of work. Not only will it help you hire better people, but once hired it'll also make you a better manager. You can minimize two of the most common management problems by improving communications and clarifying expectations this way.

➤ The Micro Approach

The micro approach can be used for all job types. It converts each job requirement or skill described on the traditional job description into an outcome, by asking what's done with the skill. After you've made your first pass at preparing a performance-based job description using the macro approach, review the original job spec to see if you've left anything important out. We don't want to completely ignore experience, education, and skills; instead, we convert each required skill, trait, or behavior into a specific outcome. For example, rather than saying the candidate must have strong personal computer skills, it's better to state that the candidate must be able to upgrade the performance reporting package using personal computers. This gets at the use of the skill in accomplishing the task, rather than the skill itself. The use or application of the skill is easier to measure than the absolute level of the skill. Our goal is to convert each "having" based skill into a "doing" based activity.

This is a great approach to use for technical positions. Rather than state that a job requires three years of tax accounting, it's better to specify, "upgrade the state sales and use tax reporting system by June." This gets at the application of the skill in a real situation and more accurately defines the work that needs to be performed. For a technical design position, something like "develop two new electro-mechanical devices to handle the measurement of fluid flow in high speed oil lines" is better than "Have three years' experience in fluid flow controls and product design." During the interview, you'll get examples of real comparable designs to determine competency.

Behaviors and personality traits can be treated the same way. Everyone wants good interpersonal skills, but this is job and culture dependent. It's better to convert the behavior into an outcome. For example, rather than saying "work well with engineering," you'll gain more insight with "develop a means to deal with a very technically oriented engineering manager in developing product launch plans." Asking the candidate to describe comparable situations will get directly at this issue during the interview. Another behavior classic is to "have good team skills." It's better to describe the actual team situation and then ask the candidate for comparable examples of team accomplishments and the role played in persuading and leading others. "Lead the process improvement team for order entry to reduce cycle time by two days by August," is a good SMART team objective.

Sometimes, preparing SMART objectives changes the very nature of the job or eliminates a criterion altogether. In Table 2.3,

Table 2.3   Comparing Skills Converted to Performance Objectives

Original Skill-Based Criterion	Skill Converted to Performance Objective	Comments
1. Strong one-on-one selling skills.	Set-up training program for new sales staff to penetrate national accounts.	The person needed to be a great sales manager and trainer, not an individual salesperson.
2. Very creative at the product level.	Take the lead on coordinating the introduction of three new products per year.	The person didn't have to be creative at all. He just had to coordinate the activities of creative people.

two original skills-based objectives for a director of sales and marketing have been converted to their performance equivalents. In each case, we asked the hiring manager what the person would do with each skill. The results were startling.

The skills-based criteria were not representative of the work that was required. This client had been looking for months to fill this position, yet no one could agree on what was required. It's not surprising. When you convert skills and experiences to outcomes, you clarify real needs.

Most job descriptions fall short because they rely on an underlying absolute level of skills, years of experience, academics, and required behaviors. This shortcut approach ignores the real need and gives the hiring manager a false sense of security. Also, specifying an arbitrary level of skills and experience can inadvertently exclude a strong candidate. By converting skills and experiences to outcomes, you completely and easily eliminate the problem. After you've done this using the micro approach, just incorporate the SMART objectives created into your master list. You might not use them all, but you won't eliminate something important this way.

➤ The Benchmarking Approach

Building a performance profile is relatively easy for a task or project-oriented job. It's a bit more challenging for a process, transaction-oriented, administrative, or entry-level position. In these cases, the benchmarking approach works best. Examine the best performers in the job to determine what makes them effective. These criteria then become the basis of the assessment. Just determine what the best people do that make them best, and look for these same traits, skills, and behaviors in the people you hire. Also study the worst people, discover what they do that makes them poor performers, and avoid these traits, skills, and behaviors in the people you consider.

Some examples will help in understanding this approach. We had a client in the jewelry business with a lot of turnover in their polishing department. It turned out that the best employees had a great eye for detail work, they could quickly determine which pieces were good and bad, and they tended to stay in each previous job for more than two years. Turnover was dramatically reduced using these selection criteria. For a receptionist, the ability to handle lots of calls politely, and accurately transfer them to the appropriate party was the key performance need of the position. For an entry-level accountant, the ability to learn new processes quickly and be detail-oriented became the dominant selection criteria. The ability to handle rejection, make lots of calls, and be persuasive were the performance issues for a telemarketer. The key in all these situations was to find out what made others successful in the job, and look for these same traits in the candidates interviewed. During the interview, get examples of when the candidates used these traits to get results.

Identifying typical problems is a good way to establish performance objectives for entry-level positions. For a waitress, a typical problem is a mistake on an order and an irate customer. Handling these effectively is essential for success. Get examples of similar past situations and find out how these were handled. Look for a pattern. Describe a problem you have recently encountered and ask the candidate how she would have handled it. Don't accept superficial answers. Get at the logic and thinking behind the response. It's easy for the person to say she would have replaced the order, but it's less easy to describe how she would have calmed the customer, made amends, and balanced the needs of the group waiting for the new meal to arrive. You don't have to be an industrial psychologist to understand this type of behavior. By getting examples of past performance, you'll be able to observe the underlying behavior in action.

When to Use the Benchmarking Approach

You can use this benchmarking technique for all kinds of positions, but it works best for jobs that follow a routine or a standard process. Southwest Airlines uses this approach to hire flight attendants. Through benchmarking, they developed an ideal set of traits, behaviors, experiences, and skills. They also came up with a profile to avoid. During the selection process, they match applicants to the profile by getting examples of related accomplishments. Marriott uses a similar approach to assess service personnel. We're working with Xerox on developing a profile for their document center managers. Promising candidates for this position need to be able to accurately prepare work orders; prioritize job runs based on size, need, and job complexity; and maintain real-time quality control. Once the performance criteria are established, the interview can be structured to assess these abilities.

■ FINE-TUNING YOUR LIST

When you prepare your list of SMART objectives using the macro, micro, and benchmark methods, you may have more objectives than you need. Some may be redundant or unnecessary. Pare the list down to the essentials. Then put them in order of importance. These SMART objectives have two purposes: One is to serve as a guideline for selecting candidates; the other is to transition and manage the new employee after starting the job. As a selection tool, the list can be shorter, just broad enough to cover the major performance objectives of the job. During the interview, you will be asking candidates to provide examples of comparable accomplishments. If two objectives require similar attributes, like managing a group, one example will suffice.

■ ADDRESSING THE DIVERSITY ISSUE

The preparation of performance-based objectives is a useful means to address the important diversity issues now facing companies.

Diversity should be considered from two perspectives. First, it requires giving equal consideration to all potential candidates, either male or female, regardless of their racial, religious, ethnic backgrounds, or physical challenges. Second, diversity should address the increasing need to effectively work with these same people in the workplace, both as customers and as co-workers. Both issues can be directly addressed with the performance-based hiring approach.

You eliminate the first diversity issue when the dominant selection criterion is the candidate's ability to meet the performance needs of the position. Under these circumstances, achieving the SMART objectives drives the selection process. This is the most fair, legal, and appropriate way to overcome the typical diversity problems. If a candidate can meet the performance needs of the job, he or she deserves the opportunity, regardless of background, religion, or any physical challenges. Conversely, if a candidate can't meet these requirements, background, gender, or physical condition should be immaterial in the selection. In the case of physical challenges, the United States has created the Americans with Disabilities Act (ADA) to address possible inequities. Under these circumstances, some workplace modifications might be necessary to assist the candidate in meeting the required performance objectives. The key to fairness is that all the performance objectives be required. As long as all candidates are measured against the same SMART objectives, performance-based job descriptions are the most fair and legal means to determine job competency.

With workforces and customers becoming more diverse, it's also important to directly consider these issues in the preparation of the SMART objectives. For marketing or sales positions, this might mean directly mentioning the need to effectively deal with a variety of ethnic backgrounds in the performance objective. Rather than just say, *"Increase market share by five points,"* it's better to expand this to say, *"Increase market share by five points, half coming from the Hispanic community."* We often have manufacturing positions that require management of multiethnic labor groups. In this case, the SMART objective should include this important need. For example, *"Install a total quality management program addressing all the needs of a diverse labor team."* This sets up the requirement for applicants to be proficient, or at least sensitive to the cultural differences and needs of these important work groups. If you want to create a diverse workforce, a performance objective might be, *"Over the next two years, establish a multiethnic workforce and training program that gives every employee an opportunity to grow."* By incorporating these requirements directly into the SMART objectives, companies can begin directly considering these important diversity issues directly in the interviewing and evaluation process.

■ PERFORMANCE-BASED JOB DESCRIPTIONS IMPROVE EVERY ASPECT OF HIRING AND MANAGEMENT

There are a number of related benefits using performance-based job descriptions. For one, it will make you a better manager. The performance-based job description is really the manager's game plan. If you don't want to prepare this, you're overlooking an important aspect of management. Just preparing it will make you a better manager, and you'll be able to hire better people as a result. The following sections describe other important benefits.

➤ The Bottom Line Benefits of a SMART Approach to Defining Performance

➤ You can use performance-based job descriptions to write ads and screen candidates. When you write ads based on the having, rather than the doing, they come across as boring, and you can exclude great candidates. Screen resumes on comparable accomplishments, not skills, experience, academics, and industry. You'll interview better candidates this way. One of our clients, a restaurant chain in southern California, started looking outside the restaurant industry for managers and serving staff, as a result of focusing on doing rather than having. Within six months, they were fully staffed with outstanding people, a first in seven years. A major portion of your sourcing issues will disappear when you eliminate the artificial barriers to entry. Compromise on experience, not performance.

➤ Performance-based job descriptions help in recruiting. Candidates will exclude themselves if the job is too much of challenge, or not big enough. You'll attract those who see the job as an important career move. They will clearly understand the importance of the job using SMART objectives as the expected standard of performance. Asking for examples of comparable accomplishments during the interview allows the candidate to clearly understand the job and the opportunities. Top people get turned off when the interviewer focuses more on past experience than on past performance.

➤ The performance-based approach is also more fair and legally sound. If a person can demonstrate the ability to meet the performance needs of the job, he or she deserves it. Performance-based hiring is color-blind. If the person who can do the job should get it whether that candidate is old or young, female or male, black or white, or physically challenged. This is a very important point. Focusing on performance, minimizes our biases and prejudices.

➤ The performance-based job description can be used as a natural transition program for the new employee since you've discussed job expectations during the interview. Expect to reprioritize and renegotiate the performance objectives after the candidate starts. You want to get buy-in. This will help clarify expectations between you and your new employee from the beginning. Lack of clear expectations is one of the biggest causes of employee turnover and poor performance. This is a great way to eliminate a serious potential problem.

➤ The SMART objectives form the basis of a complete performance management system. You'll be able to use these to monitor performance throughout the year and conduct more meaningful annual reviews.

➤ Performance-Based Job Descriptions Work for Every Position from Contract Temps to Chairman

This is a universal process. Performance-based job descriptions are applicable for any position, in any type of company, and for any level. The macro and micro approach are great for staff and management positions. The benchmark and micro approaches are perfect for technical, administrative, or process oriented positions.

It's an equally useful approach for project work with consultants or outside contractors. You can use the same methods to create the list of prioritized SMART objectives, but the time frame will typically be less than a year. A frequent problem with these temporary workers is that expectations are not clearly defined up front. As a result, lots of time is wasted. Clarifying the SMART objectives should be the topic of the first meeting. If you quantify work in detail, it eliminates much of the confusion in hiring contractors who are unfamiliar with your company's jargon and ways of doing business.

➤ Create SMART Objectives to Get Teams Up and Running Faster

The following objective should be the first SMART objective on every team's list:

Primary SMART Objective for the ABC Project Team

By the end of this meeting, create a list of prioritized deliverables identifying all the major objectives of the team. Include resource requirements, assign responsibilities, prepare a reasonable time line, and identify the major bottlenecks.

The first time a team meets, it should prepare its list of SMART objectives. The process alone will improve understanding and communications among the team members. Include what you don't know and what you need to find out. Use the POWER Staffing SMART Objectives Worksheet to define all the other major objectives. Post them all on the wall. Don't ignore anyone or prejudge anybody's input. Pare the list down to the most important items and then put them in priority order. By the end of the meeting, you'll have established the team's focus.

➤ SMART Objectives Save Time

"It takes too much time." This is the biggest complaint we hear when first describing the SMART objective process. It doesn't. It

saves time. The list of performance objectives is essentially what you'd discuss with the new employee on her start date. Why wait? Discuss it three weeks sooner during the interview process. The preparation of these objectives is a basic part of the management process. A manager who chooses not to do it, is abdicating an essential aspect of the job. Since you need to do it anyway, our suggestion is to just do it sooner.

You'll save time by clarifying expectations during the interview, eliminating unqualified candidates sooner, and reducing the likelihood of hiring a weak candidate. The time involved in managing an under-performer is far greater than the time it takes to prepare one of these performance-based job descriptions. The cost and time involved in eventually dismissing a person you should never have hired in the first place would justify any time added to the evaluation process.

Once you learn the technique, preparing performance-based job descriptions takes about 30 minutes or less. The first time, it could take an hour or more. Double that with a group prioritizing and deciding. In this case, you improve communication, get buy-in early, and increase understanding of the real job needs. If this group will be involved in the interviewing process, this is added time well spent. The quality of their assessments will increase many times over. During a seminar, I asked a facilities manager who complained loudly about the time element to list the five biggest problems he wanted his new plant engineer to address once he came on board. He put the list together in less than 10 minutes! We waste time not knowing what we want our people to do. If you want to save time, preparing performance-based SMART objectives is an effective alternative.

■ A REAL-WORLD CASE STUDY

➤ Creating a SMART Performance-Based Job Description

In this section, we'll complete a performance-based job description for a customer service director by preparing the SMART objectives. To make sure we cover everything and listen to everyone's input, we want to consider every aspect of the job and we might actually develop 15 to 20 performance objectives. Eventually, we will narrow them down to the top five or six. The short list will then be put into priority order to form the critical performance drivers for the position. With this framework, we'll have the ability to more accurately benchmark a candidate's competency against the real performance needs of the position. The macro approach will be the primary one used in this exercise. The completed worksheet is shown on pages 46–47 for this job description.

Using the time line to determine the *Major Functional* objectives, we concluded that the customer service department was in trouble; fixing it required defining the scope of the problem (item 1, the customer survey) and then reducing customer complaints dramatically (item 2). Rebuilding the staff (item 3) was also considered critical to job success and was included here even though it could also have been in the management category.

The *Supporting or Subobjectives* required the quick identification of the cause of the problems and the system constraints (items 4 and 5). Drilling down this way gets at some of the key process steps necessary to achieve the primary objective. Both objectives uncovered this way eventually made it to the final list.

Management and Organizational issues are often ignored in job specs, yet these are frequently the most important in determining ultimate success or failure. This is true in our example. The customer service department needs better trained or new supervisors to improve performance and reduce turnover (items 6 and 7).

When we looked at necessary *Changes and Improvements,* it was clear that support services, methods, and procedures were a problem. There was a breakdown in the communications link between the home office and the field support team that needed to be improved immediately (item 8). The process of handling defective parts also required some procedural changes (item 9).

One of the key *Problems* that needed to be solved was to reduce the level of backorders. These were way too high (item 10). This is a problem that must be fixed by coordinating with other departments. The improvement in customer service (item 11) incorporates this serious backorder problem and quantifies it more clearly. This one eventually made the short list of critical SMART objectives.

CASE STUDY
Customer Service Director for Ajax Parts, Inc.
The SMART Objectives Worksheet

Performance Category	Performance Objectives
1. Major Functional Objectives	1. Conduct customer satisfaction survey during the next quarter.
	2. *Reduce customer complaints by 75% during the first year.*
	3. *Restaff the customer service group to support 25%/year growth.*
2. Subordinate Objectives	4. *Within 45 days, determine the major bottlenecks and establish corrective action plan.*
	5. *By June, conduct complete process review of the department identifying key staff and systems issues.*
3. Management and Organizational Issues	6. Upgrade supervisory capabilities and skills.
	7. Reduce turnover from 40% to less than 10% during the first year.
4. Changes and Improvements Necessary	8. Improve the communications between the home office and field sales support to ensure timely customer response.
	9. By July, develop quick return/replace parts program.
5. Problems to Be Solved	10. Work with material control to eliminate backorders on critical parts (target January).
	11. *Increase customer service to 99% from 93% within 6 months.*
6. Technical Skills in Actual Situation	12. *Lead the user team on the upgrade for the order tracking system, including developing the EDI and bar-coding specs*
7. Interpersonal and Team Skills in Actual Situation	13. Within 6 months, improve the morale and productivity of the department by reducing turnover and complaint handling time.

CASE STUDY *(continued)*	
Performance Category	**Performance Objectives**
8. Deliverables—Other Tactical, Creative, and Strategic Projects	14. Take a management lead on organizing multifunction task force in developing company-wide customer service improvements.
	15. *Take the lead on a new IS system to be functional within 18 months.*
	16. *Develop a series of interim solutions to reduce backorders, improve returned material re-placements, and improve commu-nications with the field support team. Present action plan to management within 90 days.*

We identified *Technical Competence* by defining the outcomes or projects that depended on the required technical skills. In this case, we needed someone with strong systems to upgrade the order tracking system (item 12).

The required *Interpersonal and Team Skills* were determined using a similar outcome-oriented approach. Good team leadership skills were defined as the ability to reduce turnover and complaints within the group (item 13). During the interview, we'll get past examples of similar performance from someone who has done this before and obviously demonstrated good team leadership skills, at least as defined for this job.

The catchall category, *Projects/Deliverables,* was used to think about the tactical, strategic, and creative needs of the job one more time. It forced us to reconsider the short-term tactical needs of the position. This department was in trouble, and while it had to be rebuilt, some short-term, Band-Aid changes needed to be made immediately. Thus item 16 required the interviewing team to examine the candidate's ability to address these important immediate problems.

We developed 16 SMART objectives. We don't need this many for the Performance-Based Job Description, five or six will do. For selection purposes, you only need the top five or six SMART objectives as long as each one covers a different issue. One might cover management needs, and the other technical issues. Another might deal with the ability to deal with pressure and scarce resources. Still others might address problems, strategic needs, and interpersonal issues. Breadth is important. You'll need many different types of comparable examples of performance to make an accurate hiring decision and these SMART objectives will be used to guide your questioning. You'll still use the complete list of SMART objectives after the candidate starts, so keep the worksheet.

To narrow the list down, we first underlined the most important ones. Some of these were combined and rewritten to eliminate redundancies. After lots of negotiating, the following five represented the final performance criteria for this position. This was an invaluable process. Everyone involved clearly knew the performance requirements of the job before interviewing candidates.

In this case study, we didn't need to use the micro or benchmark to create these SMART objectives. We identified all the important performance objectives using just the macro approach. But in the end, we did compare the original and traditional skills-based job requirements for this position with the performance objectives, as shown in Table 2.4. The difference is startling. Using the original criteria, there is little chance the company would have been able to find a suitable candidate, whereas the performance-based criteria clearly define superior performance.

CASE STUDY
SMART Objectives for Customer Service Director

1. *Improve customer service from 93% to 99% within 12 months. This will reduce customer complaints by 75% during the first year.*
   This was item 11 on the preliminary list and was considered the most important of all the objectives. It was combined with item 2. Everything else that needed to get done was geared toward achieving this goal. This was a major objective and the candidate taking the spot had to demonstrate examples of dramatically improving a high transaction process service through process reengineering.

CASE STUDY *(continued)*

2. *Rebuild the customer service department to support a 25% per year growth rate. This includes training or replacing of supervisors, an improvement in productivity, reduction in turnover, and complete process reengineering of the group.*

   This is a critical management task, item 3 on the original list. Since it had to do with management and team skills it was combined with items 6 and 13. It includes the process and people issues necessary to support the high expected growth. The ability to build strong teams in a rapidly growing situation is essential to success in this job. The interviewing team needs to find lots of examples of team building. It doesn't have to be only in customer service, though.

3. *Take a management lead on organizing a multifunction task force in developing companywide customer service improvements. This will support the 18-month IS conversion program now underway incorporating new technologies such as EDI, bar coding, and Internet catalog and ordering.*

   We've combined items 12 and 15 covering technical, management, and long-range issues. Cross-functional teams and good distribution systems are the critical success factors in this SMART objective. To validate competency on this one, the candidate must provide some examples of leading similar system-related changeovers.

4. *By June, conduct a complete process review of all aspects of the department identifying key staff issues, system problems, and bottlenecks. Coordinate with major customers addressing their needs and begin a corrective action plan immediately.*

   This is a combination of items 4 and 5, both subobjectives. It's a critical step that must be accomplished successfully or else the rest of the project stumbles. The person taking the job must be able to get into the process to ensure that key issues and problems get addressed right away.

5. *Develop a series of interim solutions to reduce backorders, improve returned material replacements, and improve communications with the field support team. Present action plan to senior management within 90 days.*

   This was item 16. This includes lots of short-term issues that need to be dealt with immediately. Sometimes a process-oriented person might not move as fast as necessary. This was put on the critical list to ensure that everyone knew of its importance and that the candidate selected was comfortable with this kind of pace.

Table 2.4 Comparing the Experience-Based and Performance-Based Job Descriptions for the Customer Service Director, Ajax Parts, Inc.

Original Experience-Based Criteria	New Performance-Based Criteria
Ten years' customer service experience in a distribution environment.	Improve customer service from 93% to 99% within 12 months. This will reduce customer complaints by 75% during the first year.
Good management and interpersonal skills.	Rebuild the customer service department to support a 25% per year growth rate. This includes training or replacing of supervisors, an improvement in productivity, reduction in turnover, and complete process reengineering of the group.
The ability to interface with other functional departments. Good knowledge of systems, order tracking, and customer service systems.	Take a management lead on organizing a multifunction task force in developing company-wide customer service improvements. This will support the 18-month IS conversion program now underway incorporating new technologies such as EDI, bar coding, and Internet catalog and ordering.
A BS degree.	(Eliminated from job spec—desirable, but not necessary to meet performance needs of job.)
Good interpersonal skills, high energy, and strong communication skills.	By June, conduct a complete process review of all aspects of the department identifying key staff issues, system problems, and bottlenecks. Coordinate with major customers addressing their needs and begin a corrective action plan immediately.
Responsible for department of 10 people, coordinating order status, handling of returned materials, and handling customer complaints in a timely matter.	Develop a series of interim solutions to reduce backorders, improve returned material replacements, and improve communications with the field support team. Present action plan to senior management within 90 days.

■ PUTTING THE JOB DESCRIPTION TOGETHER

From a practical standpoint, the SMART objectives and a position organization chart (the list of subordinates with titles) form the essentials of the position. Together, they clearly describe the performance and organizational aspects of the job that drive success. These will be used as the comparative benchmark to assess candidate competency. Using the following completed job description for the Customer Service Director on pages 52–53 as a sample, we want to show you how you can integrate your existing job descriptions with this performance-based approach.

This job description is just a suggested format. It's appropriate to use any form that best fits your company's needs. Nonetheless, the SMART objectives combined with the organization chart should represent 80 to 90% of your assessment. If you don't have either of these, you might want to include them as attachments to your existing job descriptions. The other sections of the job description meet company and legal needs, and guide some of the compensation issues, but do little to help you determine candidate competency.

Don't throw away the original complete list of SMART objectives, even though you'll only include the most important on the performance-based job description. You'll then be able to use the full list as a management tool after the candidate starts. For most jobs, this can form the basis of the new employee transition program. For some of the more senior positions, you'll want to review and rework the list of SMART objectives with the new employee.

It's always better to get agreement on these objectives, than to dictate performance. For one thing, new circumstances will always develop and priorities will shift. With mutual agreement, the performance-based SMART objectives can then become a invaluable management tool to track and review performance. This review process is also a great way to improve communications and understanding between the supervisor and new subordinate.

Here's a quick review of each section of the preceding performance-based job description we developed for the Director of Customer Service for Ajax Products, Inc.

CASE STUDY

Sample Performance-Based Job Description

Position: Director,   **Company/Division:** Ajax Products, Inc.
            Customer Service

Hiring Manager/Position: Kathy York, VP Marketing

Position Summary

Ajax Products is a mid-size distributor and manufacturer of automotive parts and accessories. Growth is projected to be 25% per year over the next few years due to an aggressive product development effort now underway. The Director, Customer Service will be responsible for rebuilding the customer service department, organizing the group to handle the anticipated growth, and leading many of the efforts toward upgrading the customer service activity. The key to success in this position is to ensure a companywide focus on improving all aspects of customer service. This includes direct support, new systems, and better handling of complaints. The person selected will be responsible for customer service, order processing and tracking, returned goods, warranty sales, and technical support. The company's future growth depends on establishing new procedures in all aspects of customer service, especially on-line ordering and tracking.

Organization Chart

The position supervises 24 people through three supervisors.

Titles of Direct Reports	Subordinate Staff	Key Duties— Major Responsibilities
Customer Service Manager	12	Handles telesales and customer rep group—clerical/administration.
Warranty and Returns Supervisor	7	Physical responsibility for spares, warranty, and returns—warehouse.
Technical Support/ Applications	5	Tracking, updating product usage, and approved applications. Technical product focus.

CASE STUDY (continued)

SMART Objectives

1. Improve customer service from 93% to 99% and reduce customer complaints by 75% within 12 months.
2. Rebuild the customer service department to support a 25% per year growth rate. This includes upgrading supervisors, a reduction in turnover, and a complete process reengineering of the group.
3. Take a management lead on organizing a multifunction task force in developing companywide customer service improvements. This will support the 18-month IS conversion program now underway incorporating new technologies like EDI, bar coding, and Internet catalog and ordering.
4. By June, conduct a complete process review of all aspects of the department identifying key staff issues, system problems, and bottlenecks. Coordinate with major customers addressing their needs and begin a corrective action plan immediately.
5. Develop a series of interim solutions to reduce backorders, improve returned material replacements, and improve communications with the field support team. Present action plan within 90 days.

ADA Requirements

The key physical requirements for this position include the ability to travel to the company's five warehouse locations around the country, use of standard office equipment including PCs, and movement within a standard office and distribution warehouse.

Basic Experience

The candidate selected for this position needs to have 5–10 years in a high volume distribution operation with a track record of implementing process-based changes. Experience must include a strong systems background, especially in the area of automated order systems, including bar coding and EDI. This should include knowledge of alternative system configurations and approaches. The ability to build and develop strong teams of at least 15–20 people is essential. The person needs to be able to handle the demands of a fast-growing company and provide direction to other functional departments in the area of improving customer service.

The Position Summary

This is the classic job description format used by most companies, but we've expanded on it to make it more descriptive of the company environment. We've also incorporated some of the performance objectives. This allows anyone reading it to better understand the dynamics of the position. When you just list skills, duties, and responsibilities, you miss the real nature of the job. The approach we use will help when you advertise for the job and filter potential candidates to interview. By making the position summary as characteristic of the job as possible, you minimize the possibility of excluding good candidates who get turned off by a dull description and won't even respond.

Organization Chart

It's good to draw an organization chart or at least describe it as shown. Include direct reports and subordinate staff. Include the titles and main responsibilities of each position. This is important, since it addresses the types of management skills necessary to efficiently direct the group. It also helps clarify the importance of individual contributor versus management skills. This area is often ignored during the interview. Most interviews focus too much on individual skills and accomplishments, even when the job is management oriented. Also, think about any organizational changes that are required and include them in the SMART objective list. This could include rebuilding or training, supporting growth, addressing new responsibilities, or downsizing.

During the interview, ask candidates to draw their organization charts. Then find out how they've improved, built, and managed their team. Compare this management development activity to the job needs. Also, address span of control and any personnel issues likely to be encountered. Comparing a candidate's span of control to the job needs is one of the best predictors of performance we've seen. Lots of bad hires are caused by ignoring this critical issue. Many hiring errors can be prevented by including a detailed organizational chart with the job description.

SMART Objectives

We transferred this list from the SMART Objectives worksheet. Don't forget to review these SMART objectives and their relative importance with everyone on the interviewing committee. Just by using the SMART objectives as a benchmark and getting interviewers to write down their evaluations improves accuracy and reduces emotional errors.

ADA

This refers to the Americans with Disabilities Act. From the SMART objective list, identify all the physical requirements of the job. Include lifting, traveling, use of equipment, and mobility kinds of tasks. If they're not required, don't include them. For example, lifting anything other than a briefcase is not required for most office jobs. According to the ADA act, you don't have to compromise your performance standards as long as they're essential. You do have to provide a reasonable level of accommodation (ramps, access devices, larger screens) for those that can otherwise meet the performance objectives. If physically challenged candidates can meet these performance objectives with some reasonable level of accommodation, they deserve the job. And be thankful you've found a great candidate. Conversely, if they can't meet these requirements, or you found someone who is better at meeting them, this approach will allow you to justify your decision. Make sure this is documented and get specific legal advice if you have any questions. This area is constantly being evaluated in the courts, so it's important to have the latest advice.

Basic Experience

This section is also part of the classic job description. It includes education, level of experience, and specific technical requirements. It's the "having" part of the job description, we want to minimize. In fact, for screening purposes specify the absolute minimum requirements only. Couple this screening with the need to meet at least one of the key performance objectives plus a track record of performance with good companies. This way you'll be seeing some strong candidates, even if they're not a direct hit. In the ad, rather than stating that an MBA and BSEE (for example) are required, it's better to state that they're preferred. This way you won't exclude good candidates by being too narrow. Remember that candidates can have all of these and still not be successful. Also strong people can be successful without any of this background. They bring energy, general talent, ability to learn, leadership, and team skills into play, and this is what you really want. These are the real prerequisites of success. They're often overlooked when too much focus is given to experience and background.

The completed performance-based job description for the customer service director takes into account all of the advice we recommend. Even with limited interviewing experience, anyone using this description as a guide through the assessment will do a better job. By clarifying expectations this way, everyone on the assessment team is better prepared. We suggest that every interviewer summarize their assessments about a candidate against the benchmark of this performance-based job description. The key to good interviewing is to get a comparable example of a past accomplishment for each SMART objective. This alone will dramatically improve accuracy. Interviewers will naturally become more objective since a standard of performance has been established. There's a tendency to substitute emotions and biases as the selection criteria when we don't know what the job requires. While this type of job description has a great many benefits, this is the most important.

■ PERFORMANCE-BASED HIRING—IT STARTS WITH THE "P" IN POWER

If you want to hire superior people, first define superior performance. This sets the foundation for a shift from an experience-based selection process to one based on performance. When you create SMART objectives based on what a person needs to DO, rather than HAVE, interviewing accuracy increases dramatically. Ads are more compelling and meaningful, and it becomes easier to screen and filter candidates. Unqualified candidates are eliminated early, and strong candidates, previously excluded for the wrong reasons, now have a chance. In the experienced-based selection process, well-qualified candidates often get excluded from consideration because their background isn't an identical match. It doesn't need to be.

Performance-based hiring provides a great alternative to traditional skills based hiring because past performance is the best indicator of future performance. Every aspect of hiring is improved when superior performance becomes the selection standard. When performance isn't the foundation, the candidate's personality and interviewing skills become poor substitutes. A clear understanding of superior performance is the first step in hiring superior people.

PERFORMANCE-BASED JOB DESCRIPTIONS

✔ Focus on the DOING not the HAVING to improve hiring accuracy. It's what a person does with their skills that determines success, not the skills alone.

✔ Experience and personality are poor predictors of subsequent performance. It's better to define and use the real performance needs of the job to screen and interview candidates.

✔ Every job has five to six success factors that ultimately determine success. Once developed, they form the basis of the selection decision. Cover them all. They range from dealing with people to meeting technical and business objectives, organizing teams, solving problems, and making changes.

✔ Create a series of SMART objectives (**S**pecific, **M**easurable, **A**ction Oriented, **R**esult, and **T**ime-based) covering each category and then put the top five or six in priority order.

✔ Use the macro approach to create SMART objectives. Just ask the hiring manager what the person taking the job needs to do throughout the first year to be successful in the job.

✔ Use the micro approach to create additional SMART objectives. Convert each required skill or experience into an active task by asking what the person needs to accomplish or do with each skill.

(continued)

(continued)

✔ For entry-level or process-oriented positions, benchmark the best (and worst people) already doing the job. Use this to create performance objectives for any type of position.

✔ The performance-based job description establishes the framework for better hiring and better management by clarifying the expectations for the job. This helps in selection and subsequent management. Everyone involved is on the same page.

Chapter 3

Emotional Control

It ain't so much the things you don't know that get you in trouble. It's the things you know that just ain't so.

—Artimus Ward 1834–1867

■ TO GET IT RIGHT DON'T DECIDE TOO SOON— DELAY THE HIRING DECISION 30 MINUTES

A few months ago, the CEO of a fast-growing marketing company cornered me before I was to speak at his trade group breakfast seminar. He had an interview with a VP candidate the next day and wanted a few quick tips on hiring. In response, I gave him the most important secret of hiring success. I told him not to make a hiring decision in the first 30 minutes of the interview. More hiring mistakes are made in the first half-hour of an interview than at any other time and if he could just delay his decision, favorable or unfavorable, by 30 minutes he'd eliminate 50% of his hiring mistakes.

The Shortest Course in Interviewing

Wait 30 minutes before making any decision about a candidate's ability to do the work.

First impressions based on emotions, biases, chemistry, personality, and stereotyping cause more hiring errors than any other single factor. Style, or the lack of it, has more impact on the hiring decision than substance. We hire people with appealing style and are often quickly disappointed. We exclude some great people who don't seem to have it, and never learn the extent of our loss. In this pivotal chapter, we explain how to get past the deceptive impressions we all tend to use for hiring decisions. Using our head means that we must first understand why we sometimes do not use our head at all.

Once we accept or reject a candidate, the evaluation essentially stops. For many this happens within 5 or 10 minutes. Then new information, even if it conflicts, has less value than the original. We go through the motions of asking more questions, but in many ways the inquiries are self-serving. We either use the new facts that surface to support our initial assessment or ignore them if they don't. It's difficult to change such opinions once they are formed. By some estimates, it takes two or three times the original amount of data to change an initial opinion about a candidate. An article in the *Wall Street Journal's National Business Employment Weekly* (March 12, 1992) stated that 70% of the hiring decision is made based on these initial impressions. Figure 3.1 displays this principle.

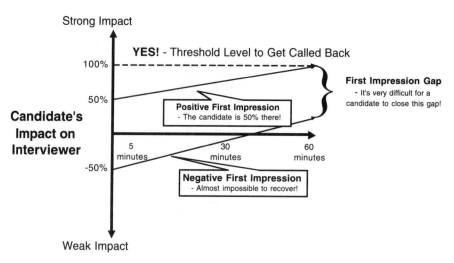

Figure 3.1. First impressions—limited value but lasting impact.

The chart shown in Figure 3.1 assumes a candidate needs to get to the threshold level of 100% to be considered a viable candidate. If the first impressions are positive, the candidate can quickly move up to the 50% position in just a few minutes, without doing much. It's easy to get to a "Yes" from this point. In fact, the interviewer often will help the candidate along by minimizing or ignoring contradictory data and overvaluing confirmative data. A weak first impression can cause an almost instantaneous drop to a minus 50% position. It's almost impossible for a candidate to recover from this hole. We ask tougher questions and minimize or ignore positive information. Staying objective and getting lots of facts to make a well-informed hiring decision is hard work. Why bother, when we can apparently get 50% of the answer in less than five minutes? It's much easier to take these intuitive and emotional shortcuts. Only much later, we discover we're on the wrong path.

One of our clients, the president of a small retail store chain, recently told me a revealing story. He and all of his managers had attended one of our workshops and wanted to implement the ideas in their company. When we spoke, the implementation was just beginning. After only a few months of use, they had experienced a significant improvement in hiring accuracy and a reduction in turnover.

More important to the president was the deeply personal impact the program had on him. He said that prior to understanding how his emotions affected his judgment, he always made quick hiring decisions based on personal biases and stereotypes. Most of these had to do with physical appearance, ethnic background, affability, and intelligence. He would exclude anyone who fell outside this narrow range of acceptability, and he felt that he could confidently make this important decision in less than five minutes. After implementing our program, the president has found that many of the candidates he would have previously discounted are actually outstanding performers. He has since hired a few who have quickly proven themselves to be stars.

This is powerful and revealing testimony. It took courage for the president to admit this to me, and even more for him to be honest with himself. But this understanding has changed his whole outlook on the hiring process. Most of us are guilty of the same offense. It's the biggest obstacle we need to overcome if we want to make better hiring decisions.

■ HOW EMOTIONAL TRIGGERS AFFECT YOUR JUDGMENT

The key to effective hiring is to move beyond this type of emotional reaction to the candidate and substitute the job as the dominant selection criterion. Emotions play a powerful role in the interviewing and assessment process. Very little of this input has a positive effect. We're wired to make bad hiring decisions. Recognition and reprogramming therefore need to take place before clear and accurate decision making is possible. Hiring doesn't need to be a random process, but first the dynamics of how emotions affect the hiring decision need to be understood. These are powerful forces that, when unchecked, always lead us astray. Once we recognize them, we can apply some effective countermeasures to keep our emotions at bay.

Our hardware (the brain) and firmware (built-in emotional response software) is designed to tell friend from foe within seconds. This is the fight-or-flight response. Once the choice has been made, our rational brain briefly stops functioning. Within a few minutes—if we discover our fears or desires are unfounded—our brain begins to restore some degree of rationality, and the response is completely neutralized within 30 minutes. By this time, however, many of us have already made the yes or no hiring decision. We're now poisoned. During the first 30 minutes, we've collected enough facts to support our initial flawed impressions, good or bad. A facsimile of this internal switching mechanism is shown in Figure 3.2. It's important to be aware of the physiological symptoms of this switch as it moves to the "on-yes" or "off-no" position. In both cases, it short-circuits our rational thinking brain. Once this is understood, reprogramming can begin.

➤ The Positive "Yes" Response

If you've ever felt a wave of positive feelings after just meeting a candidate, you're caught. When you think you're going to enjoy

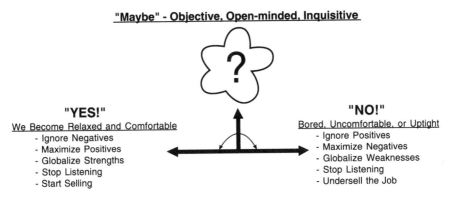

Figure 3.2. Our emotional switch causes predicatable responses.

the interview, you know you're in trouble. This relaxation response is the first clue to an emotional and premature buy-in. At this moment, you've made the buying decision, and your course is now predetermined.

The relaxation response causes us to ignore negative data, globalize strengths, begin selling, and stop listening. Lack of skills will be dismissed as unimportant or something easily learned. You'll be thinking about how you can convince the candidate this is a great job, and only superficially listen to the person's answers. You won't ask tough questions covering real job needs. You'll assume that the candidate can do all these tasks because he possesses a few apparently important characteristics. In fact, you'll go out of your way to find easier questions to ask, and you'll even unknowingly give your favorite candidate the answers. This approach not only gives the interviewee the upper hand, but you waste time considering candidates who are more fluff than substance.

On a recent search assignment, I interviewed a professional, outgoing, and confident person for a VP Human Resources position. We clicked immediately. We had good give-and-take throughout the interview, but the candidate's answers particularly with respect to strategy while solid, seemed rehearsed, not insightful. I glossed over this caution flag and didn't press the issue further. I accepted these and other general responses too easily, swayed by a great first impression and self-confidence. I did not want this candidate to fail my normally rigorous questioning pattern! The day before, I had met a solid pro for the same job, but first impressions, while adequate, were not spectacular. This person's responses to the same questions were both insightful and engaging. Nonetheless, I spent another few minutes asking questions to ensure complete understanding. The candidate passed with flying colors. I've been interviewing candidates daily for over 20 years, and I still have to fight these first impression biases. If we like someone, we don't push hard enough. Good candidates are hard to come by, and we don't want them to fail. Unfortunately, they often do once they get on the job.

➤ The Negative Response

Some candidates bother you right from the start. Your buying switch just moved to the closed position. You grit your teeth and begin thinking of how you can end the interview as soon as possible. Sometimes boredom sets in. If you listen at all, you'll ignore all positive data as being a fluke or unrepresentative. Weaknesses will be magnified as rationalizations to your astute interviewing skills, and you'll instantaneously judge any idea as worthless or ill conceived. If the candidate still seems formidable (or has been highly regarded by someone else), you'll undersell the job, as something beneath the person's qualifications. This is in the vain hope that they'll exclude themselves, without making you the bad guy. About a third of the time, you'll exclude a great candidate from consideration this way.

I almost eliminated a candidate who came to my office a few months back interviewing for a GM spot. The man looked tired and worn out. I was immediately put off and regretted setting up the interview. He had a solid resume, however, and came highly referred. It took me about 20 minutes to fight through my negative filters, and I'm glad I did. For 30 years, this guy had been running on all eight cylinders, building and turning companies around. Maybe that's why he looked so tired—he had achieved so much at every level of his career. In retrospect, I can't believe I had the gall to dismiss a talented person like this because he looked old and tired. You might wonder how many great people got away from you this same way. None of us want to be judged this way, deeming it callous and unfair. Yet we're all guilty of it.

It's important to fight through this difficult time. Understanding your emotional triggers brings your biases to the conscious level. Recognition is the first step to emotional control. As soon as you feel the buying trigger closing on a yes or no decision it's time to become proactive with your own emotions. You need to fight to keep this emotional switch open as long as possible. It's the key to an accurate, unbiased assessment.

➤ The View from the Other Side of the Desk—The Candidate's Response

This emotional response is not one-sided. When considered from the applicant's perspective, staying the buyer and remaining open-minded has even more importance. It gives candidates a chance to recover from their own emotional reaction. For some (even very good) applicants, the emotional turmoil of an interview is similar to asking someone for a date, making a public speech, meeting the CEO, asking for a raise, or making a cold call to solicit business. These are anxious times for even the stouthearted.

When the ego is on the line, this type of nervousness leads to dry mouth, constricted voice patterns, shallow answers, forgetfulness, and an increased level of perspiration. Even smooth salespeople can fall prey to these unkindly bodily effects. Caused by a surge of adrenaline, it's another example of the fight-or-flight emotional response unveiling itself at an inopportune time. If it's a temporary condition, these physical effects will dissipate in about 15 to 30 minutes. It's been our experience that about 30 to 50% of all candidates (strong and weak) get somewhat nervous during an interview. Nervousness reveals itself in many ways, none very positive. Table 3.1 lists a few traits of the nervous candidate, and the typical interviewer's reaction.

The problem with these assessments is that they're all wrong. Once these conclusions are drawn, it's easy to find facts to support them. That's the real problem. This is why the first 30 minutes of an interview are so important. Once you can get past the superficial aspects of the interview, you'll find some great candidates sitting across the desk from you. You don't have to change any aspect of your current sourcing program to find these future stars. About

Table 3.1   Interpreting the Behavior of Candidates

Nervous Trait	Likely Interpretation
Shallow responses, dull, slow-witted	Not very intelligent, no sense of humor, lack of judgment.
Sweaty palms and/or brow	Weak, too soft, nerdy, couldn't make a presentation to a customer or executive.
Twitching	Too nervous, uncomfortable with people, not a team player.
Too chatty	Dumb and superficial.
Lack of confidence	Not aggressive enough.
No eye contact	Untrustworthy.
Say stupid things without thinking of consequences	A real jerk, weak team player, insensitive to others.
Lack of warmth	Arrogant.
Superficial questions	Wrong priorities, no character.
Dry throat, strained voice, coughing	Lacks confidence, not a lot of insight, unprepared.

25 to 35% of the people I interview take at least 15 to 40 minutes to lose their stage fright and become their real selves. It is well worth the effort: From this pool, you'll find some great people that others have overlooked.

Recovering from negative first impressions is difficult for both the candidate and the interviewer. Good interviewers know this can happen and work with the candidate to get through it, especially if an interviewee otherwise appears strong. Understanding the physiological reactions will help you through these rough periods. If these unusual conditions persist for more than 30 minutes, personality characteristics other than nervousness could be involved, and it's best to move on to other candidates.

We don't want to minimize the importance of interpersonal skills. Personality and cultural fit are important to job success. We just want to delay the measurement until both the candidate and interviewer are past the emotionally charged first 30 minutes of the interview. Then objectivity can prevail.

■ UNDERSTANDING YOUR INTERVIEWING STYLE IS THE FIRST STEP TO REPROGRAMMING

We all have a tendency to hire in our own image. In his landmark book *Up the Organization* (New York: Knopf, 1984), Robert Townsend, said, "Hire complementors, not reflectors." This is great advice. When we clearly know the performance requirements of the position, this natural tendency is just as naturally put aside. When we don't know the job, we substitute our perceptions, biases, and stereotypes about successful performance as the selection traits of choice. Not surprisingly, they're mirror images of ourselves. Even if you're a star, you want diversity on the team. There are other equally bright stars who might just not want to do it your way.

We can gain some insight into our own image when we become aware of our emotional triggers. These are the traits that quickly cause our positive/negative switch to engage. We've observed they reveal one of the three basic interviewing styles—the emotional, intuitive, and technical. Each comes to a hiring decision from a different perspective, and with varied results. The most effective style is a combination of all three.

Fill in the Emotional Triggers and Hiring Hot Buttons Worksheet with your own hiring triggers— those traits that quickly turn you on or off about a candidate. Include in the "Yes" column

Emotional Triggers and Hiring Hot Buttons Worksheet

"Yes" Criteria w/Time	"No" Criteria w/Time
Example: Friendly—3 minutes	Example: Too Quiet—5 minutes

List positive and negative traits and attributes and time it takes in the interview to observe.

attributes that get you excited about a candidate, and in the "No" column list traits that bother you. Also show approximately how long it takes you to get a sense for each. When completed, compare these with the "Yes" and "No" criteria in Table 3.2.

Table 3.2 lists the different hiring criteria categorized by interviewing style. Review the table to determine your hiring criteria (shown in the "yes" and "no" columns) and interviewing style. Once you know your style, you'll have the ability to modify it to improve your interviewing effectiveness.

The criteria you select will determine your personal interviewing style. Most of us are a combination of the emotional and either the intuitive or the technical interviewing style. These are the wrong combinations. For the best interviewing results, we need a combination of the intuitive and the technical styles.

The hiring decision itself needs to be intuitive, since you never have enough information to make a 100% accurate decision. You just can't gather enough information in a few hours to make a foolproof decision about performance. Intuitive thinking therefore needs to be used to compare aspects of the candidate's abilities and interests to job needs. But to do this right requires more detailed information than the typical intuitive interviewer wants to seek out. This is where the technical style comes in. The technical interviewer is conservative and skeptical and naturally does a good job of data collection. While this time intensive, fact-finding approach is important in data gathering, however, the interviewer usually is not collecting the right data. That's why the best of the intuitive and technical styles need to be combined. At the same time, emotions also have to be held in check, or you'll get biased results.

Achieving this ideal combination depends on your dominant style. Review the following tips. By bringing these issues to the conscious level, you'll be in a better position to understand how your hiring decisions are being affected by your interviewing style.

➤ The Emotional Style

➤ If you're EMOTIONAL, you tend to globalize competency, or the lack or it, based on a few observed superficial traits.

Table 3.2 Recognizing Your Hiring Criteria and Interviewing Style

Interviewing Style	Description	"Yes" Criteria	"No" Criteria
Emotional	Makes decision based largely on first impressions, personality, appearance, emotional reactions, and feelings about the candidate. Other factors might include academics, personal biases, stereotypes, and racial or gender issues.	Time: less than 5 minutes • Poise and social confidence • Affable • Articulate • Positive Appearance • Extroverted • Good chemistry	Time: less than 5 minutes • Poor eye contact • Weak handshake • Poor appearance • Nervous—Distant • Short answers • Introverted • Bad chemistry
Intuitive	Decision based on gut feelings and having a few critical traits. Decision is then globalized—with them the candidate can do everything and without them, nothing. More general factors include character, religion, values, appropriate style, and location where raised.	Time: 5–15 minutes • Intelligence • 1 or 2 great talents/skills • Verbal Communications • Assertive • Initiative	Time: 5–15 minutes • Not enough intelligence/talent • Not enough confidence • Shallow answers • Lack of energy
Technical	Decision based on possession of strong skills, experiences, and methodologies. The yes is long, but the no is quick.	Time: over one hour • Lots of relevant experience • Similar process thinking • Strong skills • Great technical capability	Time: 5–15 minutes • Not enough experience • Not enough education • Not enough skills • Difference in approach

You tend to make judgments quickly (within a few minutes) based on first impressions, personality, and appearance. Emotional interviewers have the most random results and make lots of hiring mistakes, since there's little logic involved. To overcome this, you first need to delay the hiring decision. Get lots of examples, facts, and details to validate your initial first impression, good or bad. This will make you a more technical fact-finder. Collecting the data involves the left or analytical side of the rational brain. Force yourself to do this. Keep written notes. The actual hiring decision needs to be a right-brain or intuitive process. This is where creative or "out-of-the-box" thinking takes place. Since no two jobs are exactly alike, you need to compare two sets of related, but not identical information, to make a hiring decision. This is tough enough, but if you're making a purely emotional decision, your short-circuiting the rational decision-making process. It's a fundamental problem that affects most of us some of the time.

➤ The Intuitive Style

➤ If you're the INTUITIVE style, you tend to globalize strengths and weaknesses based on only a few, normally important, traits. This takes about 5 to 15 minutes. Not surprisingly, sometimes these traits are very similar to those that have made you personally successful. This is where the "hire in your own image" problem comes into play. While these traits may (or may not) be important, you still need a more balanced and complete perspective. Intuitive interviewers often hire some stars, but they just as frequently hire those who can't meet all the needs of the job. The key is not to overvalue a few traits such as intelligence or assertiveness at the expense of others. Neutralize your biases and conduct a complete assessment. You need to be more analytical in collecting relevant data. Using a technical fact-finding approach may enable you to find some weaknesses not initially considered or some offsetting strengths. In fact, you might find some of these missing traits when you look again in more depth. Candidates don't need to be just like you to be successful. In the long run, it's probably better if they're not.

➤ The Technical Style

➤ If you're a TECHNICAL interviewer, you're too conservative and too much of a box checker. It takes you at least one to two hours to come to a favorable decision. You tend to overvalue years of specific experience, degrees held, specific areas of technical competence, and thinking skills. Technical interviewers have the ability to build solid, if unspectacular, teams, with few mistakes. This approach often excludes fast-track candidates who want to grow. You automatically exclude them because they don't have enough experience (yet). They also exclude themselves, since they don't want to do the same work over again. While this analytical style is good for data collection, it's not good for hiring, since the wrong data is being collected. You need to base the hiring decision on traits that better predict performance, not on an absolute level of skills, education, and experience. It's better to determine competency by finding out what a candidate has already accomplished. Find comparable achievements and ask about the process used to attain them, even if different from the ones you need. Don't immediately dismiss a candidate without all of the prerequisites. These people might be some of these stars. Finally, find out what was accomplished without lots of experience to determine motivation and ability to learn. You'll discover that this is a much better predictor of success than identical experience.

The Tracking System Worksheet on page 72 will help you identify your hiring criteria and emotional triggers on a real-time basis. Fill it in after each interview. Once you know how you're making hiring decisions, you will be in a better position to use some of the specific countermeasures presented in the following section.

Tracking System Worksheet to Uncover and
Control Your Emotional Triggers

Candidate and Position	Yes No	Time	Why Yes or No?	Job Spec	Planned IV?	1st Impression	2nd–1st Impression

Here's the information you need to track for each candidate interviewed.

➤ In the "Yes/No" column, just indicate whether you liked or disliked the candidate.

➤ Under "Time" show in minutes how long it took to reach the yes/no decision.

➤ In the "Why?" column, include the two to three prime reasons you based your yes/no decision.

➤ Under "Job Spec," just put a yes or a no to indicate whether you used a performance-based job description.

➤ In the "Planned IV (interview)"column, put a yes or a no to show whether you used a performance-based interview or, at minimum, a series of preplanned questions.

➤ Under "1st Impression," note whether it was positive or negative, and why.

➤ Under "2nd−1st Impression," note your comments about the candidate's visual impact when you reexamined it after about 30 minutes into the interview. (For more on this, see the following section.)

If you fill in this worksheet for your next 6 to 10 interviews, some patterns will begin to emerge. This is a simple technique to uncover some important issues about yourself. It will also go a long way in helping improve the quality of your hiring decisions.

■ BREAKING DOWN WORK INTO MORE MANAGEABLE AND MEASURABLE PIECES

Understanding how we make hiring decisions can reinforce the importance of knowing your interviewing style. It starts by recognizing that work can be subdivided into components, some more easy to measure than others, and some more important. Unscrambling this is part of the solution to more effective hiring.

In a broad sense, all work-related behavior can be divided into three trait categories—performance, character, and personality and presentation-type traits. Performance-based traits have to do with getting the work done—technical competency, initiative, organizational ability, leadership, and team skills, to name a few. Character represents the deep rooted traits of honesty, reliability, and integrity. Personality related traits include affability, social confidence, speech patterns, attitude, physical presence, and poise. These three trait groups are shown in Figure 3.3.

Consider your top people. Those who are most effective are strong and well-rounded in all three of these trait categories. Conversely, we've all met people who are strong in one, but weaker in another. Their overall performance suffers in some way. To get the best candidates, we want strength in all three categories, not just one or two. Applying this concept to the hiring decision requires that the candidate meet all job needs—the performance

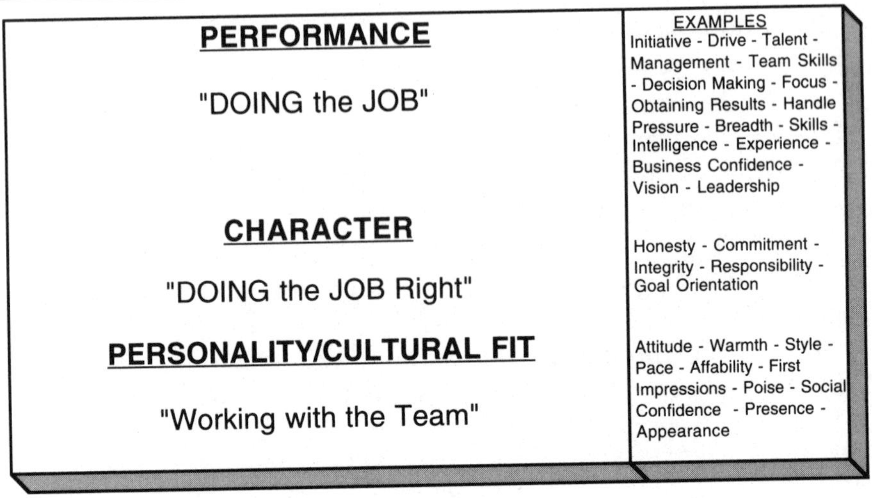

PERFORMANCE "DOING the JOB"	EXAMPLES Initiative - Drive - Talent - Management - Team Skills - Decision Making - Focus - Obtaining Results - Handle Pressure - Breadth - Skills - Intelligence - Experience - Business Confidence - Vision - Leadership
CHARACTER "DOING the JOB Right"	Honesty - Commitment - Integrity - Responsibility - Goal Orientation
PERSONALITY/CULTURAL FIT "Working with the Team"	Attitude - Warmth - Style - Pace - Affability - First Impressions - Poise - Social Confidence - Presence - Appearance

Figure 3.3. Work-related behavior groups.

needs, character needs, and personality needs—to be successful. We call this the basic hiring formula:

Basic Hiring Formula = Performance + Character + Personality

While performance, character, and personality are all essential to an accurate assessment, they're not all equal in importance nor are they evaluated the same way. This is part of the reason the hiring process can quickly fall apart. Sorting through these factors is a critical step in developing a workable hiring system.

► Personality

It is difficult to obtain an accurate assessment of all three trait groups during the interview. During the interview, personality is much easier to measure than performance. It can be measured to some degree in as little as a few minutes, and in reasonable fashion in an hour. An equivalent measure of performance is more difficult. Even on the job it can take anywhere from three weeks to three months.

While easier to measure, personality has little predictive value. For one thing, personality in the interview is not always the same as personality on the job. Candidates put their best forward in the interview. Seemingly nice people can be gruff, pouty, and real pains under the normal pressure of the job. We also inadvertently overvalue personality traits and assume someone who is affable, has a strong handshake, and is poised and socially confident will have good team skills, high initiative, and strong leadership ability.

On a 1995 *60 Minutes* segment, the reporter applauded a three-week program that taught minority candidates how to be upbeat, confident, articulate, and assertive in an interview. This bothered me because it elevated the value of the superficial over the substantive. In most situations, sadly, this is usually all it takes to impress interviewers. Combine a great opening with a polished resume, solid academics, and some reasonable company experience, and the interview can be over within a few minutes. If the company's need factor is great, even those with lesser credentials can pass this hurdle with a great first impression.

Conversely, nervousness, a weak handshake, poor eye contact, or a mismatched tie can quickly lead a candidate to the scrap heap. Personality, while important to on the job success, is a poor predictor of subsequent performance. You can have personality, charm, and style in the interview and be a dud on the job, and be a dud in the interview and be great on the job. Deciding too soon based on these false indicators is the number one cause of hiring errors. Figure 3.1 describing the impact of first impressions on decision making reinforces the point.

You might want to try this exercise out for yourself to get a sense of how personality affects us. In a recent seminar, I asked the 75 attendees to count everyone they've ever worked with closely that they truly didn't like. Most had fewer than half a dozen, a few percentage points of the total, at most. I then asked what percentage of candidates they've interviewed that they felt they couldn't work with or didn't like. This ranged from 30 to 40% on the low side to 80% on the high side. This is a shocking result. It means there are few people we don't like once we get to know them, yet we hold these very same people to much higher standards during the interview. Don't measure the candidate based on his or her ability to be a best friend or lover. Hold the person to a more reasonable standard, that of a co-worker. This is an important distinction. Don't be too quick to include or exclude anyone on the basis of the candidate's interviewing personality.

➤ Character

Having strong character doesn't imply great performance (remember Jimmy Carter). And not having it doesn't mean the lack of great performance (consider most other politicians, lawyers, and your favorite used-car salesman). True character is harder to measure than personality, but for most it doesn't have the same emotional tug as personality, so we don't have to worry too much about it affecting our judgment. Like personality and cultural fit, character, while important for on-the-job success, is a poor predictor of subsequent performance.

➤ Performance

Performance, on the other hand, is different. Most would agree that past performance is a strong predictor of future performance. Top performers tend to remain top performers given reasonably similar job situations, and weak performers remain weak if the jobs are comparable. Of the three trait groups, past performance is the best predictor of subsequent performance.

To reflect the importance of performance we need to change the order in which we measure each of the three traits. Here's a modified version of the hiring formula reflecting this change.

Performance First! Hiring Formula

Measure performance first—then determine if character and personality enhance or detract from that performance.

This hiring formula is represented graphically in Figure 3.4. Most of us tend to make an emotional decision early in the

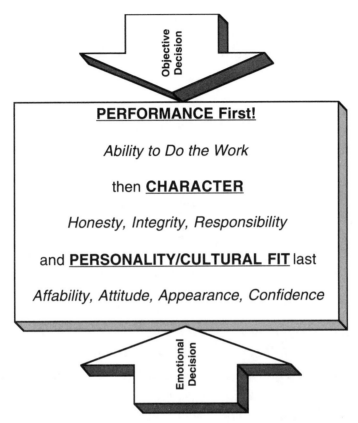

Figure 3.4. The top down approach: Increase hiring accuracy—measure performance first!

interview based on a few traits, and then use the balance of the interview to find facts to support this decision. This is the bottoms-up approach. It's much easier to make an intuitive or emotional judgment early in the assessment process and then seek out information to support this view. You'll always be able to find enough. This is why different interviewers can have so many different readings of the same candidate.

When you first assess the candidate's ability to meet the performance needs of the job, your evaluation will be more accurate. The key is to first determine whether the candidate can do the work, then determine whether you like the person. While performance, character, and personality are all prerequisites of a good hiring decision, you need to measure performance first if you want to conduct an accurate interview. This is the top-down approach, which puts substance first and style second.

■ HIRING ACCURACY DEPENDS ON YOUR PERSPECTIVE—TOP-DOWN VERSUS BOTTOM-UP

You can normally tell if the hiring decision was top-down or bottom-up by listening to the comments made about the candidate after the interview. Don't ignore your own comments in this assessment, either. A few examples will help you understand this. Here are some typical negative comments from an interviewing team. Each is a clue that personality was more prized than performance.

- ➤ *"Too arrogant. Not a leader."*
- ➤ *"Too stuck in his ways. Probably won't listen."*
- ➤ *"A little too quiet. I would have difficulty working with him."*
- ➤ *"I'm not sure he's a team player."*
- ➤ *"I don't think I could learn anything from him."*
- ➤ *"His experience is all with big companies. We're a small company. I don't think there's a fit."*
- ➤ *"He's smart, but kind of distant."*

These were all real comments about one of my candidates for a director of sales and marketing spot for a small medical device manufacturing company. When you hire on personality and presentation, the assessments are superficial and the results random. When we measure the ability to get the job, rather than do the job, different interviewers have a diversity of opinion about the same candidate.

Negative opinions also carry more weight than positive opinions. One or two confident naysayers are all it takes to eliminate a promising candidate. In fact, a wide diversity of opinion regarding competence is a reliable indicator that the interviewing team didn't know the real requirements of the job. Question these hiring decisions. They're probably wrong.

Following are some other comments to watch out for. They're more positive, but are equally indicative of making a decision based more on getting the job than doing the job.

➤ *"I like her. I think she can do the job."*
➤ *"A real go-getter—confident, affable, and real positive."*
➤ *"Great personality. A real team player. Just what we need."*
➤ *"Really fits with the company culture."*
➤ *"Smart and assertive. That's what we need around here."*

These are also all true statements. I'm sure you've heard similar ones before. And while these are nice attributes, they don't indicate competency. When everyone likes the candidate for personality reasons, raise the caution flag. This is another reliable indicator of a bad interview. It means the assessment of performance was compromised.

We want to base the hiring decision primarily on performance, and it's certainly all right to eliminate a candidate who can't do the work. But make sure that the decision to exclude a candidate is based on a performance first, or top-down assessment. You'll know you and your team have reached emotional maturity if the "yes/no" comments are based on ability to do the work, rather than personality traits.

In the case of the candidate for the director of sales and marketing noted at the medical device manufacturer, the president intervened before the candidate was eliminated. He did not believe the negative assessments were warranted. I was there in the meeting and I can still hear his comments:

This young man is one of the finest people I've ever had a chance to meet. His accomplishments in every job he has held have been spectacular. I'd like you to meet him again. We can't afford to lose a star, because he's a little quiet in the interview.

The candidate was reinterviewed and hired. Within six months, he was the general manager. After 60 days on the job, the comments from his peers and subordinates on the interviewing team were effusive. To a person, they agreed that this quiet young man was a superstar. He still is. The president spent three hours in the first interview and knew talent when he saw it.

When you focus on doing the job rather than getting the job, the whole approach to the interviewing and assessment process is different. In this case, a performance-based assessment overrode one based on personality and prevented a major mistake. These accurate assessments don't happen often enough.

The following comments reflect a performance-based assessment. Because they are more insightful, they're longer and each comment is based on collected facts, not opinions or feelings:

➤ *"She anticipates problems, understands customer needs, and is very detail oriented."*

➤ *"A strong team player. He provided numerous examples of going out of his way to support others to ensure that the team's projects were completed on time and budget."*

➤ *"This person has made an impact in every job. She has built solid teams, set up development programs for each staff member, and can weed out the weaker players."*

➤ *"This candidate is technically top-notch. We worked on a couple of problems together, and I could tell that he knew the issues involved, was logical, understood the impact on the other systems, and was real inquisitive."*

➤ *"What a great salesperson. We discussed specific major accounts and I could tell that this candidate knew how to prospect, cold-call, present our complex product, negotiate, and close big orders."*

When the assessment is based on the ability to do the work, the assessments are always more uniform and more accurate. It requires some mental reprogramming to get to this stage. The first step is to remember and use the performance-first hiring formula. This is especially true just before and during the early part of the interview. Post the formula somewhere on your desk. It will help you through the emotional first stage of the interview.

■ GETTING THROUGH THE FIRST TREACHEROUS HALF HOUR OF THE INTERVIEW

In this section, we describe 10 tactics to help you safely through the first half hour. Each one helps overcome the natural tendency to focus more on personality than performance. Most of these techniques don't require any preparation, but they do take some mental gymnastics. Make a copy of Table 3.3 for quick reference and reread it just before the interview. This review will help you restore balance when your mind starts to stumble. The following sections explore these techniques in detail.

➤ Fight with Yourself to Remain Objective

The assessment stops once you decide on the candidate's competency. You'll never have enough data to come to a valid conclusion if this happens in the first thirty minutes of the interview. One way to overcome this is to keep track of your initial emotional responses to the candidate. In your notes, describe the candidate's first impression and your reaction to it. As soon as you feel uncomfortable, bored, or relaxed and casual, write down when this occurred and the cause. A quick note like "++/5min/energy" is your clue that within five minutes you felt good about the candidate because of their enthusiasm. "−2min/nervous" means a negative response due to applicant nervousness. These notes help you recognize your interviewing style and biases. If you do this for every interview, you'll soon be able to catch yourself and add a few minutes to each successive interview before you decide. You need to take some action to fight the tendency to reach a quick decision. The process of note taking will bring the triggering process to the conscious level so you can deal with it. I've been interviewing candidates for 25 years, and even today, I have to fight the tendency to make a decision within 10 minutes. It's a constant battle, but worth it. About 50% of the time, my impressions of a candidate are completely different after a half hour than after 10 minutes. In the second half of the interview, just as many good candidates falter, as weaker candidates strengthen.

Table 3.3   Ten Great Reprogramming Techniques

Reprogramming Technique	Comments and Description
1. Fight with yourself to remain objective.	Recognize when you feel relaxed or uncomfortable. Fight to keep the buying switch in the "maybe" decision. This way, all information has equal value.
2. Conduct a 20-minute phone interview.	When you talk to someone on the phone first, you automatically minimize the impact of personality and first impressions.
3. Don't start the interview right away.	Go on a tour, see a demo, but get into a give-and-take discussion. This will help minimize emotions and set up the framework for a good dialogue.
4. Use a preplanned structured interview.	Write down a few performance-oriented questions to ask right away, whether you like the candidate or not.
5. Measure first impressions again after 30 minutes.	After 30 minutes, revisit first impressions. Compare with the original and evaluate your reaction. This will help restore balance.
6. Change your frame of reference.	If you like the candidate, be skeptical and ask tougher questions. Be more interested in and more open with those you don't particularly like.
7. Listen 4 times more than you talk.	The interview is not casual conversation. It needs to be a fact-finding expedition. Get a page of notes for each accomplishment.
8. Treat the candidate as a consultant.	We always listen more to those who are experts or have a superior position. Treat candidates the same way to elicit more open responses.
9. Talk about real work.	Discuss problems and related business issues. Accuracy will increase if the interview is more like a problem-solving session than an inquisition.
10. Use panel interviews.	You'll save time and minimize emotional re actions, since there's less of a one-on-one relationship.

➤ Conduct a 20-Minute Performance-Based Phone Interview

A major European orchestra recently reinstated black curtain auditions because it was the only way the evaluation team could conduct an objective evaluation of the performer. With this approach, they never see or meet the candidate until after the audition. Before the black curtain, the competency of the women was always inferior to the men. Afterward, they were equivalent.

A preliminary phone interview is the interviewer's black curtain. It helps minimize emotions when you meet the candidate face to face since you already have some measure of true performance. This is a great way to get instant objectivity. You won't be as swayed by a weak first impression. Candidates also feel better. They're less nervous knowing that they've already passed muster on some critical aspects of the job. Preplanned phone interviews are a key component of any effective hiring system. Try it out a few times and compare the quality of your assessment with and without a phone interview.

I was a guest speaker at a real estate seminar in early 1997. The group's president had heard me speak at one of her company functions the year before. Her introduction illustrated the importance of the phone interview. She told the group that while she used all aspects of the POWER Staffing program, the most important to her was the phone interview. With this screening tool alone, she was able to reduce the number of personal interviews by over 50%. In addition, she said that about 80% of those she did personally interview were extremely competent. She indicated that first impressions were much less influential now. Already knowing the candidate through the phone interview helped establish a bond that minimized the emotional aspect of the first impression. Now, she'll never meet a candidate without first conducting a phone interview. This is the easiest technique to apply and one of the most powerful suggestions presented in this book. It will also save you enough time to try out all the others.

➤ Don't Start the Interview Right Away

Don't begin the interview until both you and the candidate know each other better. Do something different. A few of my clients take a 30-minute facility tour before the interview starts. During this tour, they make it a point to visit areas that are related to the job. This could be a factory problem, a system's installation, the CAD design room, a product demo, or an area where new marketing tools are being developed. A tour isn't the only possible delaying move. Anything that allows the interviewer and the candidate to get into a normal business discussion is appropriate. Reviewing financial results or discussing a relevant newspaper article can have the same impact.

Whatever you do in this delaying phase, it's important to solicit questions. These are often revealing. Their quality reveals both insight and inquisitiveness. By putting the candidate at ease this way, you go a long way toward minimizing the impact of first impressions and your own personal biases. The objective of this normalizing session is to establish open, nonjudgmental, two-way communication. Don't use it to give a 15-minute spiel about your great company. Just by delaying the inevitable, this approach often increases candidate nervousness.

➤ Use a Preplanned Structured Interview

When the questions are preplanned, they allow you to overcome the normal impact of the first impression, good or bad. Ask the same questions whether you like or dislike the candidate. In fact, ask the same questions of all candidates so you can compare answers. After 30 minutes of this type of questioning, the emotional impact will have been neutralized. With preplanned questions, you won't have wasted any time, and you'll have some valuable insight into both yourself and the candidate. Those candidates that initially seemed great often lose their glow, and those without one sometimes really shine. Observing this change will reveal some of your built-in biases. Once these are identified, they're much easier to control.

➤ Measure First Impressions Again after 30 Minutes

Measure first impression traits again when you're no longer emotionally caught up in them. Do this whether you like the candidate or not. After 30 minutes, ask yourself why you initially liked or disliked the candidate. Compare your initial impression to your second and more objective delayed assessment of that first impression. They'll usually be different. Determine why. Was it you or the candidate? If the second check of first impression is worse, raise the caution flag. Ask some tough questions. Revisit some of the questions asked earlier in the interview. If the candidate's first impression has improved or has become less important, you might have a very competent candidate who just doesn't do well early in the interview. Start the interview over if you've inadvertently dismissed this candidate. We often meet great people who don't interview well. These are the pleasant surprises.

Retesting first impressions is a good technique to practice. Because the emotional pull of first impressions is so strong, it requires constant vigilance to get past them. When you work at it though, you'll discover many weak first impressions were due only to initial nervousness. You'll also discover that many great first impressions often hide weak performance.

➤ Change Your Frame of Reference

Do the exact opposite of what you feel like doing. This will counteract your initial emotional response to the candidate. For those you like, get tougher. Give the benefit of the doubt to those you don't like. This is another critical step in your reprogramming. At the moment, you feel yourself sliding into a yes or no decision, you must take action. Changing your frame of reference is the first step. For those you like, make a mental assumption that they can't do the work and begin asking tougher questions. Something like *"Can you describe in detail the steps you used to implement the change and the critical challenges you had to overcome?"* works for most situations. This approach will offset the positive emotional bias and provide more balance to the assessment.

I'm reprogrammed now. Whenever I see an affable, articulate, assertive, and attractive candidate, I raise my guard. I assume I'm going to be conned. I become the cynic and assume the person can't do the work. A smooth-talking, highly educated marketing manager comes to mind. This guy was a good consultant-type, great business insight, and strong persuasive skills. The position required a line manager though, and while he could talk a good game, I didn't think he was the best candidate. I asked him to give me specific details of how he would implement his programs, rather than discussing their strategic impact. These answers were shorter and more shallow, clearly indicative of a person out of his element. This was a very strong and competent applicant, but not suited for this role. We tend to ignore this factor when we meet people we really like.

The same approach can be used for those you don't like. As soon as you move toward the no decision, for whatever reasons, take some opposing action. Go out of your way to prove that the candidate can do the work. Listen more, become less judgmental, and get the candidate to be more open. Try this. Lean forward and say something like *"That's really interesting. Can you explain the steps you had to go through to achieve that result?"* Be friendly and sincere. By getting the candidate to open up and talk more, some of the initial nervousness will soon abate. Your goal is to get specific examples of past accomplishments to judge a candidate's ability. There are some excellent candidates sitting across the desk from you who might not have great interviewing skills. It takes work to find them, but it's well worth the effort.

➤ Listen 4 Times More Than You Talk

We all talk too much and we don't learn anything while we talk. It's better to ask questions. Interviewing is a fact-finding exercise, not a social conversation. When we like candidates, we either begin selling the job or enter into some casual dialogue. Either way, we never learn whether the candidate can do the work. The way to get candidates to open up is by asking more questions, not by talking. I met a candidate recently for a senior level marketing position in the automotive after-market. I had worked in this industry in an earlier life and we had many common acquaintances. I realized after 30 minutes that I hadn't learned anything about this person's ability to achieve results. While I liked him personally, it was time for a shift. I told him I needed to know specific details about what he accomplished at each past job. At that moment, the interview changed from casual cocktail conversation to a serious interview.

A good interview takes work. If you can't fill out a page of notes to validate each of the candidate's accomplishments you haven't done enough fact-finding. At the beginning of the interview, don't spend more than two or three minutes describing the company. Start asking questions right away. Don't feel compelled to editorialize or comment about your reactions or feelings. These are unnecessary. Listen four times more than you talk. Don't judge the candidate's answers during the response. Stay objective and don't interrupt. Also, don't be thinking about something clever to ask next. Listen to the responses and write your notes. Through fact-finding, you'll always come up with an appropriate trail of thought to follow, or you can always ask for another example.

➤ Treat the Candidate as a Consultant

As the interviewer, you hold power over the candidate. This is even more true if you're also the hiring manager. This balance of power needs to be changed to ensure an open discussion. You can achieve this by mentally treating the candidate as a consultant during the interview.

We tend to listen more and are less judgmental with people we consider to be superior to us in some way. This is why we're more deferential toward experts, customers, and supervisors than toward suppliers and subordinates. If we treat candidates as superiors, you'll notice that they open up more and their answers are longer and more insightful. We do this all the time when we take advice from lawyers, doctors, consultants, and customers. It works equally as well with candidates.

Be sincerely interested in their answers. Ask follow-up questions that demonstrate your active listening. Ask for advice on real job-related problems. Provide positive feedback to the candidate. Something like, "that makes a lot of sense," is appropriate. Don't worry about overselling. It won't come across that way unless you talk too much. These affirmations will spark the candidate to tell more without much prompting. (This is not a bad strategy for managing subordinates, either.) You'll be amazed at how well this simple technique can open the floodgates to communications and valuable information.

➤ Talk about Real Work

If you can make the interview more like real work, accuracy will soar. One big flaw of the interview is the need for spontaneous responses. Treat the interview more like a problem-solving session than an inquisition. Work through a relevant problem during the interview. Ask how the candidate would handle a typical issue that's likely to come up on the job. These could be specific problems, business objectives, people or management problems, or a technical matter. Go on a tour of the facility. When you come to a problem or important issue, ask the candidate for advice on how to address it. Feel free to use the white board. Allow questions. A give-and-take discussion is more like "real talk" than Q&A interview talk. Not only does it provide great insight into an applicant's ability to visualize an objective, but style and personality are naturally revealed during the response since the candidate is more relaxed.

Here are a few typical problems that can be turned into good interviewing discussions:

- ➤ *Sales.* Difficulty closing an important account.
- ➤ *Accounting.* Tracking down a reconciling item.
- ➤ *Manufacturing.* Eliminating a bottleneck.
- ➤ *Customer Service.* Dealing with an irate customer.
- ➤ *Systems.* Designing a new interface.
- ➤ *Engineering.* Overcoming a technical challenge that has everyone stumped.
- ➤ *Marketing.* Getting some quick competitive analysis completed.

However, talk is sometimes cheap, so there is a caveat. Ask the candidate to describe some comparable past accomplishments. This adds a foundation of reality to the candidate's responses. There are many people who can describe how they would accomplish a task, but can't actually do it. Conversely, there are many people who can't adapt their experiences to different environments. This approach will uncover the few that can do both.

➤ Use Panel Interviews

This technique is not only one of the best interviewing approaches ever advocated it has the double benefit of minimizing emotions.

It's not appropriate at the first interview since it's too intimidating for the candidate. For the second round, though, it's a great way to minimize the personality-based interviews common to people who have less stake in the candidate's success. A panel interview with three or four people is also a good way to save time and involve more people in the assessment process. It will increase objectivity by allowing the panel members more time to evaluate the answers without having to continually think of what to ask next.

The panel interview can be an even more powerful tool if you give the one or two finalists a take-home problem to present to a panel. This takes some extra time so give the candidates a few days to make sure they are sincerely interested in the job. The problem or minicase should represent a real issue and should take at most a few hours to study and summarize. Have the candidate present a 5- to 15-minute overview of his or her findings and then move to a Q&A session. A panel interview by itself, if well-organized, minimizes emotions, since these are held in check by the other interviewers. With the addition of a take-home problem, you also test true competency and interest. Some ideas for take-home cases include real business problems, a review of the financials, a marketing issue, a technical or design problem, or an operating plan review.

Try this technique if you want to reduce the emotions in your company's hiring decisions. The response we've had from candidates and clients alike has been very positive. One of the few problems we've observed has been lack of organization. Someone needs to orchestrate the process or anarchy prevails. Assign this to the hiring manager and give each interviewer a narrow range of questions to ask.

■ PULLING IT ALL TOGETHER—A REAL-LIFE EXAMPLE

It has been many years now, but I remember this situation as if it were only yesterday. A very large man came into my office for a sales manager position. My reaction to his size was not only extremely negative, but I became physically ill as near panic set in.

I had been working on this assignment for six weeks and had no other candidates for the position. To make matters worse, the day before I had talked to my client about the many strengths of this enormous person who now sat across from me. I had even gone out on a limb by setting up a client interview based solely on a phone interview. For added emphasis, I had strongly suggested to my client that he'd probably hire this person.

Luckily, these emotional responses are short-lived once we recognize these fears as unfounded. It took about five minutes for me to regain some control. I then remembered the phone interview. During that 20-minute conversation, I had asked this candidate to describe his most significant accomplishments at his prior two jobs. We also talked about his management style and team-building skills. Remembering these positive impressions relaxed me even further, and I conducted the next 30 minutes of the interview asking probing questions about management, team leadership, and initiative. I even had my candidate draw a point-of-sale display and had him walk me through the four-month selling process for a multi-million dollar order. He turned out to be a great candidate—extremely competent, with strong interpersonal skills. He was also affable, bright, and energetic.

After about 30 minutes or so, I remembered I was supposed to measure first impression again. Talk about shock. Except for my initial five minute blowup, for the last 30 minutes I had been in detailed animated discussion with this candidate and completely ignored his physical appearance. On careful reevaluation, I discovered this candidate was neither as large as I first imagined, nor as unpresentable. In fact, he had grown about four inches and lost 40 pounds in this short time span. He was still a big guy, a football lineman kind of guy, but not that big. When I first met him, my emotions had exaggerated his "largeness." If I hadn't used these techniques of emotional control, a great candidate could have gotten away. There are superior candidates out there who may not fit your personality or physical templates too well. If you can suspend your emotional reaction for at least 30 minutes, you'll find some stars hidden behind your own emotional blinders. By the way, our friend got the job and did very well.

In most companies, a $10,000–$20,000 investment decision takes a formal justification requiring at least a few hours. A $100,000 investment requires some level of sophisticated financial analysis taking at least 10 to 20 hours, if not more. Yet the decision to hire a $50,000 employee, the equivalent of a $250,000 investment,* is often just given a few hours! Hiring requires and deserves the same kind of sophisticated analysis. It starts by breaking the emotional link between yourself and the candidate and substituting the job as the dominant selection criterion. Use the performance-first hiring formula. Measure performance first, then determine whether the candidate's personality helps or hurts that performance. Just switching the order in which you measure the three trait groups will work wonders.

In this chapter, we have given you some practical techniques to break the powerful emotional response of personality and first impression. We all have our own examples of how our emotions got the better of us. The more obvious illustrations are those candidates we've hired who fell short of expectations. If they're still with you, you're reminded every day of your own hiring tendencies and failure modes. Study these real examples of your own great hiring decisions as well as your failures. Some of the failures, however, you know nothing about: These are the good ones who got away. Look for patterns. Determine if the hiring errors were due to premature emotional reactions or lack of job knowledge. Maybe you didn't cover all the critical job needs, assuming competence, but not validating it. Fatal flaws are often ignored. Start developing a personal profile of yourself to better understand how you make hiring decisions.

From these clues and what we've presented here, you'll be able to tailor a hiring program that works for you. Remember to move away from using a candidate's interviewing skills as the basis for the hiring decision criteria. Job competency is based on measuring past performance, not presentation. This is what hiring with your head is all about.

---

* A $50,000 salary plus direct overhead and actual benefits is about $80,000 per year. If the employee stays on average of three years, the total amount is about $250,000.

REPROGRAM YOURSELF TO CONTROL
EMOTIONS AND INCREASE HIRING ACCURACY

✔ Wait 30 minutes before you make any hiring decision.

✔ Most hiring errors are made because we make emotional decisions based on first impressions and then look for facts to justify those decisions.

✔ Break the emotional link between you and the candidate and substitute the performance needs of the job as the dominant selection criteria.

✔ Recognition is the key to controlling our emotions. If you feel relaxed or uncomfortable about the candidate early in the interview, you need to take some immediate countermeasures.

✔ Fight with yourself to focus on the candidate's ability to do the job, not get the job.

✔ Use the Performance First! Hiring Formula. First measure performance, then determine if you like the person.

✔ At the end of the interview, write down your evaluation. If your assessment had more to do with personality than competency, redo the interview.

✔ Image isn't everything. In fact it's nothing when it comes to hiring. Know your biases and seek diversity.

✔ Keep track of your emotional triggers. They'll reveal your interviewing style. Knowing what they are will allow you to control them better. Combine the intuitive hiring decision with enough fact-finding to minimize errors.

✔ Conduct 20-minute phone interviews before you see candidates. This will minimize the impact of first impressions when you meet the candidates face to face.

✔ Delay the buying decision until the end of the interview. This way all data has equal relevance.

✔ Delay the start of the interview. Take a tour. An informal dialogue about relevant business issues can counteract the impact of any initial emotional response to a candidate.

(continued)

✔ Measure your first impression again after 30 minutes, when you're more objective.

✔ Change your frame of reference. Be easier on those you don't like and tougher on those you do.

✔ Listen 4 times more than you talk and don't judge the answers during the answer.

✔ Treat candidates as experts. Assume they know more than you, and you'll automatically listen more.

✔ Talk about real work in a give-and-take manner.

✔ Use take-home minicases letting candidates present their summaries at a subsequent interview.

✔ Use panel interviews. Emotions are minimized and you have a better chance to assess responses since you don't always have to think of what to ask next.

The Performance-Based Interview

Q: When you choose men and women to promote, to be a leader of the company, what qualities do you look for?

A: *You clearly want somebody who can articulate a vision. They have to have enormous energy and the incredible ability to energize others. If you can't energize others, you can't be a leader.*

Jack Welch, CEO General Electric, *Business Week*, May 29, 1995

■ PREPARATION IS THE KEY

Half of the problem with interviewing has to do with avoiding dumb mistakes. The other half has to do with determining whether the candidate can do the work. If you understand the job and can control the urge to decide too soon, the candidate assessment part is straightforward. Preparation is the key. Don't wait until the candidate is in the lobby.

If you've got an upcoming interview, read the resume again. Even if you've already conducted a phone interview, it's good to examine this again. If you haven't conducted a phone interview, it's even more important. Somebody has already made the decision for you to talk to or meet this candidate. Figure out why. Circle the strengths and put big plus marks next to them. Asterisks and minus signs also help. During the interview, you'll ask for specific examples to validate strengths and clarify concerns. Don't forget that lots of work has already gone into the effort to arrange this first interview. It can all be lost in the first few moments if you don't carry the momentum.

Reread the performance-based job description, especially the SMART objectives. These performance objectives cover every aspect of the job—major objectives, interim objectives, problems that need to solved, changes to be made, team issues, management and organizational issues, and technical needs. These five or six deliverables form the foundation for the interview. They'll help you guide the questioning and determine the comparability of the candidate's past performance.

When you finally get into the interview, the candidate will know how prepared you are. Top prospects want to work for professionals with high standards of performance—people who know the job, who aren't overselling or too emotional, and who know how to listen. Floundering interviewers turn off the best candidates. Always assume you'll be meeting a first-rate candidate. This will help get you into the right frame of mind.

I lost a great candidate once, because the interviewer, the VP Operations, was unprepared and began talking too much, asking a bunch of meaningless questions, and selling too soon. Right after the interview, I got a call from the candidate. She was pulling herself out of contention. She was impressive personality and experience-wise, and felt that the hiring manager made a quick assessment on a few trivial facts and didn't really know the job. She told me his understanding of the requirements was vague and superficial, and she didn't want to work for someone who could make an important decision so quickly. This is a good warning.

The interview process we're proposing, along with the preparation needed to pull it off, increases objectivity and validates competency. In addition, it gains candidate interest. All three are critical if you want to improve your hiring effectiveness. It takes a few more hours to do it right up front. You'll more than make up for it by not interviewing unqualified candidates, not hiring unqualified people, and adding more stars to the team.

■ A FEW WELL-CHOSEN QUESTIONS: THE EIGHT-QUESTION PERFORMANCE-BASED INTERVIEW

It doesn't take a lot of questions to conduct a complete assessment. If you know what to ask, a good first interview takes about 1 to $1^1/_4$ hours. Figure 4.1 is a copy of the basic performance-based interview. Use this same structured format for every candidate. Don't waver. Interviewers tend to go off on tangents. This is a sure way to invalidate the process. You'll be able to compare candidate responses much more accurately if you ask them all the same questions.

This interview brings all the components of the POWER Staffing system together. Each of the categories has a specific objective:

➤ *The Opening* helps calm nerves on both sides of the desk, sets the stage for the performance-based interview, begins the recruiting process by creating excitement about the job, and establishes your control of the process. This should take about 5 to 10 minutes.

➤ *Assessing Past Performance.* Two questions get at the core traits of success—energy and team leadership. By combining them with good fact-finding skills when you ask for each past job, you can determine the trend over time of these essential traits. The questioning is simple enough to help control the interviewer's emotional biases early on. Spend about 20 to 25 minutes on these.

➤ *Determining Job Competency.* Two questions should be asked for each SMART objective. You won't get through them all in the first interview, but after completing one or two, you'll have a strong sense of job-specific competency. The comparability of past performance as it directly

Candidate: _____ Position: _____ Date: _____

Interviewer: _____

The Critical SMART Objectives:

1.

2.

3.

4.

5.

Opening (Spend two minutes presenting the overview of the position and about five on the answer. Spend a total of 6–8 minutes.)

1. *(State job title, importance and provide quick overview of company, then ask. . . .) Tell me how your background has prepared you for this type of position.*

Assessing Past Performance (Ask for the previous two to three positions. Combine with fact-finding for 20–30 minutes.)

2. *Impact. Give me a quick overview of your (current/prior) position and describe the biggest impact (change) you made (or when you took the initiative or describe some exceptional work).*

3. *Team Leadership. Describe your organization (draw org. chart) and tell me about how you built and improved this group (or tell me about some team project and your role).*

Determining Job Competency (Ask for 2–3 of the listed SMART objectives. Combine with fact-finding for 20–30 minutes.)

4. *Anchor. (Describe objective.) Tell me about a similar past accomplishment.*

5. *Visualization. How would you organize or manage this task?*

Unlocking Character/Values (Combine with fact-finding for 5–10 minutes. It can be saved until the second interview.)

6. *Tell me about a time you were totally committed to a task.*

Revealing Personality and Cultural Fit (This can be saved until later. Combine with fact-finding for 5–10 minutes.)

7. *What three or four adjectives best describe your personality? Give me actual examples of where these have aided you in the performance of your job and where they have hurt.*

The Close (This is important to ask. Spend about 5–10 minutes on this.)

8. *Initial Recruiting Question. Although we're seeing some other fine candidates, I personally think you have a very strong background. We'll get back to you in a few days, but what are your thoughts now about this position?*

Figure 4.1. The eight-question performance-based interview.

relates to job needs is the key to a good assessment. It's what this section is about. You should spend about 20 to 25 minutes on this area in the first interview.

➤ *Unlocking Character and Personality.* By this point in the interview, you'll have already discovered a lot about this, but these two questions will help reinforce your assessment. Character and personality are observable through past performance and that's the approach we continue. You can save this for a later interview or another interviewer, but spend about 15 to 20 minutes when you get to this part.

➤ *The Close* starts the recruiting process and helps improve communications. All of this is essential if the candidate is one you like. If not, interviewees still leave feeling good about themselves, you, and the company. It takes about 5 to 10 minutes.

■ "JUST THE FACTS, MA'AM"—FACT-FINDING: THE MOST IMPORTANT INTERVIEWING TECHNIQUE

The interviewing approach we recommend is more a methodology than a list of clever questions. The questions themselves are less important than the quality of the information obtained. Our approach is to get lots of information about the candidate's top five or six major accomplishments. This is all that's necessary to make an accurate hiring decision.

One of my candidates told me her greatest accomplishment was in never making a hiring mistake. She told me she clearly understood the work that needed to get done, she didn't initially care whether she liked or disliked the candidate, and she spent the first interview only getting examples, facts, and figures to verify a candidate's past performance. This is the way interviewing and hiring needs to be done.

To reinforce the point, I turned the tables on her and asked her how many people she hired, their positions, their names, how they performed after starting, the impact they made, and specifics regarding her role in their personal development. She got a laugh from this, but it was from my investigative (and somewhat skeptical) approach that it was clear to me that her hiring accomplishments were real and worthy of note.

Interviewing is not a casual conversation. It takes work. The difference between good answers and bad hiring decisions lies with fact-finding. The eight questions in the template are simple to use, but they need to be combined with fact-finding to make them most effective. Fact-finding will also naturally minimize exaggeration. There is a tendency on the part of candidates to overstate or mislead, either through outright fraud or generalizations. Good fact-finding skills can clear this cloud. The key is to start early, don't accept generalities, and remain skeptical.

Unearth facts, figures, dates, figures, names, and other specifics by fact-finding.

Fact-finding peels away the onion to get at the truth. By asking for specific examples to support any generalization, you force the candidate to justify a response. Ask . . . why? . . . when? . . . with whom? . . . how long? . . . and how? Get enough information for you to really understand the applicant's involvement in the task. Find out critical decision points, what went wrong, the resources available and how they were allocated, the strategies, the tactics, and who made the decisions.

Turn generalities into specifics by getting examples of everything.

While this inquisitorial approach to interviewing is somewhat challenging for both parties, you can soften it with a low-key approach. Don't get frustrated and contentious if the candidate doesn't immediately open up. Work at it. If you start early enough in the interview, candidates tend to provide more data unprompted. Don't accept generalities. Make the candidates prove their contentions. This will minimize exaggeration and make each response more revealing and meaningful.

Most interviewers ask lots of general questions, getting broad, but shallow answers. It's better to go narrow and deep. Focus on only a few of the candidate's most relevant past accomplishments and learn as much as you can about them. Collectively, these will become valuable predictors of future performance. Learn to take good notes. Basic interviewing skills include good note taking, the ability to listen, and strong fact-finding skills.

When you take notes, use a separate sheet of paper and write down a quick title for the topic or the accomplishment. Put a date next to it, and then the duration of the task. Get additional names and other quantifying data. Things like amounts and percentages help. As you paint a quantified word picture of the accomplishment, the follow-on questions quickly become automatic. Be inquisitive. Always convert generalities to specifics by using this basic question to start the fact-finding process: *"Can you give me a specific example describing what you mean?"* This should be the most important question in your interviewing tool kit. Use it to get behind any generality or broad statement. If someone claims to have great technical skills or to be creative or a real team player, ask for examples. If they say they are problem solvers, ask for an example of a problem. Use this technique often. It will be the key to real understanding. While certain candidates generalize to cloud reality, others do so as a result of upbringing. Some cultures minimize the role of the individual and children are taught at an early age not to talk about themselves. Fact-finding will help clarify this. Take notes like the one shown here and the fact-finding questions will be automatic:

Order-entry Project (12/94–2/96)

Used SAP module, 18000 orders/mo, growing 30%/yr, lead on project w/4 others, fill rate up from 87% to 96%+, redsn forms, screens, and set-up training. Coord specs for EDI and tracking. Supv: Carol Wilkes.

Fact-finding can be the bridge that improves communications and understanding. I recently met an articulate and professional woman seeking an HR management position. She said that her greatest accomplishment was to establish a framework and direction for the department. After asking for a clarifying example, it turned out she based this conclusion on updating the policy and procedures manual for her company. This was an important, but not glorious, task that took about three months of part-time work. A financial manager who stated he was a great manager was somewhat sheepish when asked to name the five best people he had ever hired and to describe why. He could only come up with one example from the previous five years. I was about to exclude a soft-spoken bearded engineering manager who seemed to lack assertiveness when he started to tell me about a crash program he had led to commercial success. He described the late nights and motivational talks to his engineering team. I can still hear his enthusiasm and energy. In the words of Sgt. Joe Friday on the early TV show *Dragnet,* "just the facts, ma'am." That's all you need, too.

➤ Fact-Finding Checklist

Use this checklist to gain additional information about each major accomplishment. Refer to it when you think you've run out of things to ask. Keep notes. After a few interviews, you'll be a great fact-finder.

FACT-FINDING CHECKLIST
Information Needed to
Validate Each Major Accomplishment

- ☐ Overview of the accomplishment.
- ☐ Candidate's actual title, size of organization, and title of supervisor.
- ☐ The bottom line or business impact of the accomplishment.
- ☐ When it took place—the year and duration in years and months (even actual dates are okay).
- ☐ Detailed description of the candidate's actual role.
- ☐ The candidate's leadership role—how did he or she develop the program and implement it?

(continued)

FACT-FINDING CHECKLIST (continued)

☐ The biggest challenges or most difficult aspects of the task. What constraints needed to be overcome?

☐ The reason the candidate considered this the most significant work in this job.

☐ The key steps or major deliverables involved in accomplishing the task.

☐ The people challenges with some specific examples.

☐ Details about the team—names and titles. Have the candidate rank each team member's performance and the role the candidate played in changing and developing these people.

☐ Examples of when the candidate had to change the opinion of others and deal with conflict.

☐ How the candidate grew or changed as a result of this effort.

☐ Whether the objective was met and completed on time, and if this was difficult.

☐ Why or how the candidate was chosen for this role.

☐ How the candidate would rank the overall success of the task and why.

☐ What others (supervisors, peers, subordinates) would say about the candidate's performance in this task.

☐ The aspects of the accomplishment the candidate enjoyed or disliked and why.

☐ The candidate's real contribution or value-added to this task.

■ THE OPENING—CONTROLLING THE JITTERS ON BOTH SIDES OF THE DESK

Remember there's lots of posturing and nervousness by both parties in the first 30 minutes of any interview. If you conducted a phone interview or used one of the other techniques described in

Chapter 3, you've already established some rapport. Some people suggest a warm-up, or get-acquainted period, for a few minutes before the interview. I think this is unnecessary, although some casual conversation is appropriate. My approach is get right into the interview. Accept that some candidates will be nervous and don't judge their early responses too harshly. Work with them to get better or more examples. Once you establish this kind of a give-and-take, even nervous candidates open up.

A manufacturing engineer I met a few years ago demonstrates this point. This fellow was so nervous, I was afraid he would fall out of his chair. It took about 10 minutes for him to calm down, but the changeover took place when he told me the specifics of an automation project. I had asked him to draw a sketch of a high-speed assembly device he was working on. Once he got into it, he was a changed person. Getting him to stop talking was the new challenge. I told the hiring manager to conduct the interview on the factory floor and talk about specific projects and problems right away. In his element—which wasn't interviewing—all traces of nervousness disappeared.

Accept that nobody likes to interview and that a nervous candidate is just a nervous candidate. Don't assume this response is related to performance. If you still have a problem after about a half hour, move on to the next person on the list.

The most common opening request, "Tell me about yourself," is too big and broad. You give up too much, too soon, to the candidate. There are better approaches that establish the framework we need for both an effective performance-based interview and applicant control. Here's the format of the opening question we suggest:

> *As you know we're looking for a [position]. Let me give you a quick overview of the importance of this position. [Give two-minute overview of position and company.] Tell me how your background has prepared you for this type of important position.*

While this is a "tell me about yourself" type of question, it narrows the focus down by requesting only relevant background information. Further, it establishes a recruiting opening by describing the importance of the job. When you make the job compelling this way, applicants tell you more about themselves. They sell you, rather than you having to sell them. This establishes the framework for good recruiting. Don't spend more than a few minutes on this pitch, one or two are all that's necessary to set the tone. Remember to listen four times more than you talk. A good interview is a fact-finding mission, not a sales pitch:

> *We're looking for a product manager. This person will lead the implementation effort on much of our new product introduction program. This is a critical initiative for next year with new products representing 10% of sales. We need someone who can coordinate the efforts of engineering, marketing, manufacturing, and sales to bring this new line out on time and within budget. Give me a quick overview of how your background has prepared you for this type of position.*

This question is a great warm-up. Don't forget the fact-finding. You might not want to start this too soon, but you want to establish a communication style that allows you to get enough information to validate the candidate's initial responses. A lot of this will depend on the candidate's style of presenting information. Work with the candidate on this. I openly tell candidates that I'm more concerned with specific examples about a few major accomplishments than lots of broad generalities. Quiet candidates open up more when constantly asked for more examples, and louder candidates stop generalizing and start to focus.

■ FIRST FIND OUT WHETHER YOU HAVE A PROMISING CANDIDATE—DISCOVER THE CORE TRAITS OF UNIVERSAL SUCCESS

Here's a new formula for success. Follow it yourself and look for it in others. It will take you as far as you want to go.

$$\text{Performance} = \text{Talent} \times \text{Energy}^2 + \text{Team Leadership Skills}$$

In this formula, personal energy is the most important component. We've all met people with great talent, but little energy. Sadly, they never live up to their expectations. Others of average talent, but with enormous energy, often achieve success beyond all expectations. This is why the focus on personal energy is so important. Team leadership is also significant. It allows a person to tap into the personal energy of others. As Jack Welch said, *"If you can't energize others, you can't be a leader."*

In more than 25 years of dealing with some of the best people in the country, I've come to a startling conclusion. The best candidates, regardless of their occupation, have a few common traits. For one thing, they are all highly energized. No matter what their individual talents may be, they work very hard, and most seem to enjoy doing it. The best of this energized group also have the ability to lead and energize others. This is team leadership—the ability to manage, motivate, and persuade other people to accomplish an important task, whether the person is a direct supervisor or not.

While energy and team leadership are both essential for long-term success, you can't even get started on this path without the energy part. This is by far the most important. Some call this quality initiative, or self-motivation, work ethic, drive, ambition, commitment, or anything else related to going the extra mile. Without it, even the most talented fail. With it, people with only average talent can become extraordinarily successful. These people consistently exceed expectations. They do more than they're required to do, year in and year out. Look for this pattern early in the interview. Assertive or socially confident people are not necessarily highly motivated, although many interviews falsely assume they are. Quiet people can be just as energetic as outgoing people. And outgoing people might not be energetic at all, once on the job.

Personal energy can even overcome weak team skills, although these people can sometimes be extremely difficult to work with or for. We all want good team skills—the ability to manage, motivate, and persuade others. Surprisingly, we rarely ask about these skills during the interview. The focus is all too often on individual contributor skills. Minimizing this can cause lots of trouble later on. Lack of team skills is the fatal flaw often ignored during the interview even though superior team and management skills can sometimes more than compensate for apparent weaknesses elsewhere.

High initiative and strong team skills are a winning combination. You won't find many successful people without both qualities. It doesn't matter if they're in accounting or sales, in a creative or technical position, the president or a clerk. It also isn't important if the person has 20 years of experience or is just starting out. Those who continually succeed have the core traits of personal energy and team leadership. In my mind, they're the foundation of performance and potential. I've minimized my failures and maximized my successes by setting my performance standards for all jobs to include these core traits. I also start measuring them right at the beginning of the interview.

➤ Assess Past Performance—The Impact and Team Leadership Questioning Pattern

We've developed two questions that quickly get at these traits. We call them the impact and team leadership questioning pattern. As always, combine this questioning pattern with fact-finding and good note taking. With this technique you'll quickly gain real insight into a candidate's core success traits.

In the first question find out about energy and talent by asking about the impact the person made in each previous job. While the question always reveals important information, it becomes powerful when asked for the past three or four positions.

Impact Question

Give me a quick overview of your current [prior] position and describe the biggest impact or change you made.

You can judge the scope, scale, and impact of the candidate's past performance by getting detailed information about a candidate's most important work over an extended period. Supplement these questions by getting lots of examples and fact-finding. You might want to change the first question slightly for previous positions by asking about the changes made, getting examples of initiative, or have candidates describe their most significant accomplishment, instead of impact.

The key here is to get at the candidate's personal role in implementing changes and making an impact. Don't accept generalities such as "created a new market," "turned the department around," or "developed a new procedure." Also, don't feel stupid by asking clarifying questions. You'll feel a lot more stupid after you've hired a candidate who snowed or intimidated you in the interview. Many interviewers are afraid to ask follow-up questions because they don't want the candidate to think they're confused. This is where good fact-finding comes into the picture. Probe deeply until you completely understand the true nature of the accomplishment and the applicant's role.

The focus of the impact question is on energy, not talent. Talent comes along for the ride. People tend to apply more energy on work they like, so it's important to keep track of what the work is. If it's totally unrelated or in conflict with the job demands, you might have a problem.

In the leadership question, team and management skills are revealed by leadership on the job. By the way, a person doesn't have to be in a leadership position to exhibit leadership traits. Again, ask this same question for the previous few jobs. This will help you identify a pattern of change and growth over an extended time frame. We have a few options for this question depending on whether the candidate is a manager or team member.

Team Leadership Question for Team Members

Please draw an organization chart and tell me about a team project and describe your role.

Team Leadership Question for Managers

Please draw an organization chart and tell me how you built and developed this team and describe the group's biggest accomplishment.

People who aren't yet managers, but will be soon, evidence strong team skills. The ability to motivate, work with, and persuade others is an important and recognizable talent. If the person is not a manager, or if you go back to a previous job when the candidate wasn't a manager, use the nonmanager version of this question. Ask for examples of team projects and be sure to explore the candidate's specific role. Get specific. Look for a pattern of implementing change, doing more than required, motivating and persuading others, and helping to define team objectives.

Get names, specific results, determine key obstacles, and find out how the candidate handled conflict and differences. This fact-finding helps paint a word picture of actual past performance. Spend 5 to 10 minutes or more on each question. Don't give up until you are satisfied. This fact-finding is important. It is hard work and you won't want to do it if you really like the candidate. You'll be trying to find reasons to hire, not exclude. For candidates you don't like, you won't want to spend the time. You must. This is tough mental exercise, but this is how good hiring decisions really happen. They're not random events.

One of my clients told me she uses this technique when she hires software developers. These are the people who design and write computer programs. She has them clearly define their contribution on each of their last few major projects. She wants to know what their impact has been and the specific role they played. She looks for a continuing and larger contribution in each successive position.

This approach even works for entry-level people. One of the young men in our neighborhood told me of his job-hunting experience. The hiring manager asked the recent college grad to describe his most significant leadership role or team project. This young man went on to describe his summer job organizing construction teams to clean up new homes prior to the formal inspection. He discussed the organizational and scheduling aspects as well as the standards of performance he established for these unskilled workers. He described how, when things got really hectic, he had to work overtime for an extended period while persuading others to do likewise. This is a remarkable performance for one with apparently little experience. It certainly demonstrates the core traits of talent, energy, and team skills.

Management and team skills allow people to leverage their own energy and competence. This is the heart of leadership and it is something you can easily observe with the team leadership question. If the candidate is a manager, use the second version of this question. Have applicants draw an organization chart and then describe how they've developed this group. Get names, dates, and specific changes that have been made. Have them rank the quality of their staff, and have them walk you through the changes made to improve the team's performance. Find out which workers they hired and fired and why.

Go back over the past few jobs doing the same thing. If the candidate has developed a pattern of only building average teams, he's only an average manager. Figure 4.2 shows the format for an organization chart candidates can use to fill in the names of the supervisor and subordinate staff as well as the title, rank, and performance of the person now in the position. Get a quick overview of each major function. The organization chart is important. Just filling it out will help you better understand the candidate's role, scope of responsibility, and management capability. The key in each case is to get facts, stories, and examples in enough depth for you to make a valid assessment of the candidate's true competency.

An East Coast distributor used this technique to hire an international manufacturing manager a few days after attending one of our seminars. The head of operations told me he truly understood the significance of the candidate's management skills when she described in detail how she had developed an individual improvement program for each of her staff members. She was animated and involved during the exchange, presenting herself as she really was. She described the strengths and weaknesses of each person and how the worker changed as a result of the program. The hiring manager felt this interviewing approach allows

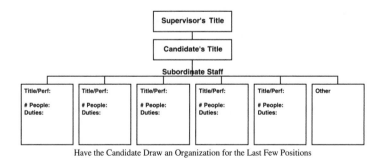

Have the Candidate Draw an Organization for the Last Few Positions

Figure 4.2. An organization chart for use by candidates.

the candidate to move away from the staged presentation of most interviews into a relaxed, more natural style of communicating.

Careful notes are important as you do this fact-finding. Look at the size, scope, and scale of the current and previous jobs. Drawing the organization chart is important to gain a visual sense of the reporting relationships and helps clarify communications. Big-sounding jobs often can look less significant when shown on paper with only a few direct reports. A director of accounting and planning job can be equivalent to a VP/Finance and look very big when it covers responsibility for 5 countries, 7 direct reports, and a staff of 100. Be tenacious. Combine the impact and leadership questioning pattern with thorough fact-finding and good probing.

➤ Develop a Trend Line to Measure Long-Term Impact

The trend line is also important. By going back 5 to 10 years, you'll be able to observe the trend of these important traits over an extended period. This approach works for managers and non-managers alike, and entry-level or seasoned personnel. Students can demonstrate these traits early on, even in non-work-related situations. You just have to look for them. Figure 4.3 shows a stylized version of the track record for a woman we worked with in a senior level marketing role. She had left the workforce about five years earlier to work back in her home community, but even there she left her mark. She was working with her state government to establish special tax opportunities for local industry. In each position she held, she made an increasingly bigger impact. The trend line approach summarizes it graphically.

The trend line isn't always this obvious, but getting major objectives this way will help determine if the candidate's performance is on an upward trend, has flattened out, or is declining. One of my business associates recently asked me to interview a few candidates for his warehouse manager's position. All of the candidates were strong and held similar positions, but only one was on a upward growth path and I recommended him, even though he was a little quieter. The other two had achieved significant success early in their careers, but for the past 10 years had settled into comfortable situations. While both of them could do

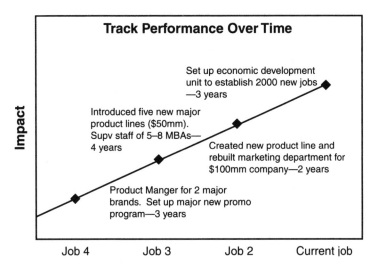

Figure 4.3. Track personal growth by developing a performance trend line.

the current job and professed a desire to grow, neither had taken any action to invest in themselves. The other candidate was taking night classes, learning and using personal computers, and was developing his staff. No matter what a candidate tells you, look for these signs of upward growth, even if they're not obvious in the candidate's titles.

The best candidates don't mind this inquisitive approach. These people like to talk about their accomplishments. They also feel more positive about managers requesting this information. It tells the candidate that the manager has high standards, is thorough, and has probably built a team of other strong people. Good people want to work for this kind of manager. They also feel positive about the situation and the person conducting the interview. If every interviewer is this thorough, this approach demonstrates the professionalism of the whole company. Weaker candidates get put off and squirmy with this inquisitive style. Since they have less to show for their efforts, their answers are usually short, shallow, and general. Don't settle for anything less than high-energy, team skills, and a hearty dose of talent or the ability to learn. This is the stuff stars are made from, but you sometimes have to look deep to find the sparkle, or to determine its real source.

■ NEXT, FIND OUT WHETHER THE CANDIDATE CAN DO THE WORK— DETERMINE JOB COMPETENCY

In the first half hour of the interview, you assessed the candidate's core success traits. The process allowed you to determine whether the candidate had the generic qualities of a superior employee. The iterative and fact-finding questioning approach had the added benefit of helping you remain objective. With this foundation, it's important to determine whether the candidate can meet the specific needs of the job. This assessment takes place in the second half of the interview.

➤ Anchor and Visualize Each SMART Objective

The Anchor and Visualize questioning pattern is used to validate job-specific competency. For each SMART objective, you'll obtain an example of a comparable past accomplishment. Next, for a few of the more important performance objectives, you'll ask candidates how they would accomplish the objective on the job.

This questioning pattern first allows the interviewer to accurately compare a candidate's past performance to the real needs of the job. Next, it determines how effective candidates can apply their capabilities to the new job needs. To accomplish this, you need to ask two questions for each SMART objective.

Anchor Every SMART Objective

We would like to accomplish [objective] during the next year. Tell me about your most significant related accomplishment.

Use the anchor question to obtain an example of a relevant past achievement. Combine this with the fact-finding techniques discussed earlier to paint a word picture of what the applicant actually accomplished. Use this anchoring technique for all the SMART objectives. Regardless of the quality of these accomplishments, try to keep an open mind until you've anchored them all.

With the anchor question, we're looking for a comparable, though not necessarily identical, accomplishment. Get details such as staff size, comparable scope and complexity of the assignment, and similar company environments. Try to stay in a fact-finding mode as you obtain anchors for all the other performance objectives. Remember, they were created to be broad, covering all aspects of the job. Frequently, we hire someone who is great at one or two things but doesn't have a full complement of abilities to handle the whole job.

By anchoring every objective, you'll get a better picture of the candidate's ability to handle every critical facet of the job. This is also true for candidates who seem initially weak. Often other skills discovered later in the interview can more than compensate for an apparent weakness. If you exclude too soon, you could inadvertently miss a great candidate. The apparent weakness might not even be a real weakness. It could just be the result of an incomplete response.

I interviewed a financial manager who had tremendous technical skills. He was personable, smart, and well educated. One of the major performance objectives of the position, but not number one, was to work with other functions in setting up company-wide performance reporting systems. He struggled with this anchor. His answers were more general and shorter—two classic signs of lack of experience or interest. Even fact-finding didn't help. His best examples were superficial. The candidate's greatest successes were all individual projects. While he was a likable person, it wasn't clear he could work with manufacturing and operations people to meet the company's needs, and we moved on to another candidate for the job.

This is not the typical reaction. More often a strong person, who's smart and personable, gets the nod even if they're one-dimensional. When you anchor all the SMART objectives, you eliminate this possibility. You still might hire someone without all the requisite skills, but you do it knowingly. You then have a chance to institute developmental programs to compensate for these deficiencies.

Here's the second part of this questioning pattern. It requires candidates to apply their skills and experiences to the specific needs of the job at hand.

Visualize the Most Important SMART Objectives

As we've discussed, [objective] is an important aspect of this position. If you were to get the job, what additional information would you need to know and how would you go about accomplishing this objective?

With the visualization question, we get into a give-and-take discussion with candidates. We want them to tell us how they would accomplish the objective initially discussed in the anchor question. For me, this is the most important part of the interviewing process. This visualization methodology determines a candidate's ability to understand, organize, and anticipate the needs of a new task.

The best candidates (for any position and any level) understand how to mentally organize the work before starting it. It's a sign of success. They can anticipate the needs and challenges of the job before even beginning. In the past 25 years, I haven't met one top-notch person without this ability. These candidates ask for more information or describe specific steps on how to begin. They recognize the need to proceed efficiently from Point A to Point B and are not afraid to discuss what they don't know.

You don't need to visualize all the SMART objectives, just using the top two or three will provide you with the insight you need. Also, you don't need to ask this right after the anchor; any time later in the interview is fine. This form of questioning is more of a two-way discussion, insted of a Q&A session.

I introduced Chapter 2 with one of Stephen Covey's "Seven Habits," from his all-time business bestseller, *Seven Habits of Highly Effective People* (New York: Simon & Schuster, 1989): "Begin with the end in mind." It was used there to stress the need to understand the performance, or SMART, objectives of the job before interviewing candidates. It's an equally important trait to look for in candidates. During the interview, you directly test for it with the visualization question.

Here are some skills and traits you'll observe in a good visualization session:

➤ Job-specific problem solving.
➤ Verbal communications.

➤ Reasoning and thinking skills.

➤ Adaptability and flexibility.

➤ Self-confidence.

➤ Insight and job knowledge.

➤ Creativity.

➤ Organizational skills.

➤ Logic and intellect.

The visualization process is less like an interview and more like a working session. This is how and what you would talk about after hiring the candidate. Sometime during the employee's first week, you'll sit down with the new employee to discuss the objectives of the position. You'll normally get into a discussion on how to handle these tasks. You'll outline strategies and tactics, talk about schedules and resources, allocate staff, and reprioritize. This is also your first chance to understand the candidate's true competency. Why wait? You can do the same thing with the visualization question before the candidate ever starts. This is an efficient way to transition the new employee into the job. Candidates know what is expected of them before they start, and you have a better sense of how they'll function in the new environment.

One of my clients used the visualization technique with great success to hire someone to head up a new business unit. My client told me they spent the whole second half of the first interview laying out the plan on a flip chart. Together, he and the candidate developed the strategies, tactics, an organization chart, and even prepared a preliminary budget. Both the candidate and my client believed this was one of the most revealing and insightful interview sessions either has ever had. A few months later, my client called to tell me how happy he was with the new employee. He indicated that the approach to problem solving and understanding that the candidate used on the job was the same quality as that shown during the interview. You don't have to go to this extreme to get similar results for yourself. Discuss a problem that has just come up, or an issue that needs to be resolved after the person comes on board. The key is that it be job related.

➤ The Greatest Predictor of Success—Use the Anchor and Visualize Approach Together

Some caveats are appropriate as you begin using this approach. Combining the anchor and visualization questions is what makes them so powerful. There are some great communicators who can visualize, but who have never actually done anything comparable. Consultants or staff people fall into this category. They're often bright, persuasive, and self-confident. This is a great combo, but an incomplete mix. They can tell you how to do the task, but they have never done anything similar.

We placed a very bright MBA in an industry job. He had just finished a two-year tour with one of the top consulting firms, his case load had been impressive, and he had conducted high-level cost studies for two Fortune 100 manufacturing companies. He struggled in this new position, though. In his new role as a planning manager, he had to do a lot of detailed, gritty analysis, wading through accounting detail. While important work, the lack of much conceptual planning combined with the monthly routine did him in. He was great at talking about and studying the problem, but not as effective at getting out among the functional departments and doing the real work. By combining the anchor and visualize questions, you'll overcome this classic hiring problem.

Some interviewing experts don't like the situational nature of the visualization question. They insist that past performance is the only accurate predictor of future performance. These experts contend visualization questioning is too hypothetical. I agree—if the questions are unrelated to the job. When combined with an anchor and a valid, job-specific problem, though, it's a solid technique. I have met many apparently strong candidates who can effectively anchor performance objectives, but still fall short once on the job. No two jobs are identical. Some people have difficulty adapting their skills and experiences to new situations. Their thinking is more structured, less adaptable, often too analytical or rigid. The visualization question quickly tests for this. Candidates are required to demonstrate their ability to apply their knowledge in solving realistic job-specific problems. Combining the anchor with the visualization question eliminates these potential concerns.

If you are concerned about the confidentiality of company plans, it's best to disguise the performance objectives with something ambiguous. For example, rather than describing your new Internet strategy in detail, be vague. One of our software clients watered-down a specific game strategy to describe a broad, all inclusive "edu-tainment" project. Just make sure the projects require the same kinds of personal attributes for success.

People sometimes express concern that they are telegraphing the answers to the candidate by openly describing the required performance objectives. I have not had this problem. While we're describing desired outcomes, we're not describing the desired process. The candidate needs to do this by describing comparable accomplishments. Also, we demand proof of competency. The anchor, visualizing, and fact-finding process we use validates the candidate's ability to do the work.

This approach works for all levels and different types of positions. If you are looking for a technical skill, some kind of test to demonstrate competency would be equivalent to an anchor. In a jewelry manufacturing company we've worked with, candidates are given pieces of jewelry to examine and are asked to describe their quality level. The company looks for people in the manufacturing area who have an eye for detail and this is the way they test for this ability.

One of our engineering candidates for a consumer products company was asked to examine a detailed design drawing for adequacy. He was then asked how he would have changed the design to function better. This was a combination of the anchor and visualize approach. At a retail pet supply store, entry-level sales personnel (generally, recent high school grads) are asked how they would handle some typical customer complaints. Then they're asked to describe similar interpersonal conflicts they've ever experienced. With this dual approach, the anchor and visualize pattern can be used to increase hiring accuracy for any type of position.

If there are lots of objectives, you'll never be able to complete all your questioning during the first interview. I suggest you anchor the top two or three SMART objectives and conduct one visualization exercise. Leave the remaining for a subsequent interview or another interviewer. You can assign the assessment of specific SMART objectives to the person most impacted by it. For example, have the manufacturing manager interview a cost manager who's required to improve the factory reporting system. Make sure that the interviewers know they have to provide a written assessment of the candidate's ability or inability to do this work. Knowing the write-up is a requirement helps minimize the initial emotional reaction of the interviewer to the applicant. This is important since these other interviewers won't have conducted a phone interview.

■ UNLOCK CHARACTER—A KEY TO LONG-TERM SUCCESS

Character and personality are always revealed through performance. Sometimes you just have to probe deeply to discover it. To get at these important traits more quickly, it's sometimes worthwhile to pursue them more directly.

My favorite character question has to do with commitment, and it quickly gets at the heart of character.

Tell me about a time you were totally committed to a task.

The ability to persevere under difficult conditions is an essential trait of top performers. It is the character component of energy. It is easier to work hard under ideal conditions than in difficult situations. Real character is better observed in less than ideal circumstances. Use fact-finding techniques to understand the extent of the applicant's commitment to the task and the underlying environment. Determine the challenges faced and the results achieved. Also examine the response and determine whether the commitment is to an individual, to the team, or to the company. Find out why the candidate felt strongly about the commitment.

Throughout the performance-based interview, we focus on energy, self-motivation, and the ability to achieve results comparable to the job needs. Use this commitment question to validate all the applicant's previous accomplishments. Examine the response to determine the scope and complexity of the jobs the candidate has held. Look for a pattern of commitment in all the examples of significant accomplishments. While this approach doesn't cover every aspect of character, it covers the most important.

A controller candidate told me about his role in helping to rebuild his manufacturing plant, which was partially destroyed by the 1994 Northridge, California, earthquake. To get the plant up and running required two weeks of around-the-clock work and another few months of extended hours. He said this was the most satisfying experience he had ever had. The camaraderie and team spirit kept him and the others going through some very difficult times. While he was a strong financial type, it was this team orientation and sense of commitment that made him exceptional.

You also might use the character question if you're unsure about a candidate or have a candidate you think might be weak. Often the response will eliminate a marginal candidate or revive one you thought lost. You should use this question in the later part of the interview when candidates are more likely to be candid with you. You have to stay open-minded, though. If you've already made a decision, the answer will have little value. Although it's very difficult to override your own internal decision once made, always use this question on commitment to validate your judgment. The answer can sometimes be powerful enough to overcome even the most strongly held beliefs.

■ REVEAL PERSONALITY AND CULTURAL FIT— GETTING A HANDLE ON A CLOUD

By the time you measure personality and cultural fit—at the end of the interview—you should already know the answer. By the time the interview ends, you'll have explored in depth five or six accomplishments. Personality, interpersonal skills, and management style will come out of this assessment. Personality in an absolute sense is unimportant. How candidates have used their personality and style in achieving results is what's really important. You'll have discovered this with the impact and leadership and anchor and visualize questioning patterns, and the fact-finding techniques we've suggested. Use this question to confirm your insight and add a few more specifics.

What three or four adjectives best describe your personality?
Give me actual examples of when these traits have aided you
in the performance of your job and when they have hurt.

A candidate who knows himself will be able to quickly list off a few critical traits and provide some detailed examples. Many of them should have been previously discussed. If they seem inconsistent with your own evaluation, do some probing to uncover the differences. Raise the caution flag if the candidate seems evasive or if you notice extremes of behavior. Also look for flexibility. If the person appears overly dominant, ask for examples of coaching, patience, and team skills. For the overly analytical person, probe for examples of team skills and the ability to persuade others. People who are the supportive type often have difficulty making tough decisions. Explore for this. The outgoing salesperson is often weak on details. Don't reach this conclusion without getting some examples of analytical work. Good candidates are sometimes excluded because they don't seem to fit the required personality profile. You'll get at flexibility in personality by looking for the candidate's apparently missing parts.

Also, look for growth. I often ask candidates to describe how their personality has changed over the years. This gets at maturity. A formerly arrogant MBA from one of the nation's top B-schools, told me how he became more sensitive to others after working with a tight team on an extended crash project. Of course, I got the details of the project to confirm his makeover. I'm always the skeptic in the face of a smooth-talking professional.

Look for candor. It might be time to raise the caution flag if the candidate can't openly describe some failures. The second part of the question is revealing: *"Give me examples of when your personality has hurt your performance."* Don't ignore this part. Continue probing. Be concerned if you get a runaround, or a vague response. Good answers here are also a sign of character.

Last year, a sales manager told me he was sometimes too rough on his team, particularly when they were short of quota. He told me his New York personality sometimes got the best of him. He knew this was a weakness, but he said he hadn't lost any good people as a result. His solution was to work more closely with his team members in developing monthly objectives, so that they were both equally committed to the results. Previously, he didn't get into the details as much, so he didn't understand their specific strengths and weaknesses. Getting this close to the process was unnatural for him, since he was more the entrepreneur, but it was helping him become a better and less confrontational manager. As a result, he became more proactive than reactive. I'm sure the hard-driving personality is still there, but by adapting to a more analytical style this person was able to compensate for a potentially fatal flaw.

You can't really separate personality from performance. Personality is naturally revealed with the fact-finding and probing techniques discussed earlier. You might want to add more emphasis to personality if this is a major area of concern. You can even make it a SMART objective. For example, one of my clients was looking for a property manager with good interpersonal skills. It turned out that the real problem was with a very demanding owner who required 100% attention to his every whim. We created a SMART objective that stated, "Set up a quick response, support program to deal with a very aggressive and demanding property owner." The candidate had to have the personality to deal with these kinds of people, but it was more than just having good interpersonal skills.

The ability to handle and resolve conflict with other departments or with difficult people is the most common issue that requires real attention on personality. During the interview, get some examples of how the candidate handled similar interpersonal problems. This gets at a specific area of personality. Personality is important, but by measuring it through performance and again at the end of the interview, you'll be in a better position to understand its importance in getting the job done.

■ THE CLOSE—USE RECRUITING TO END ROUND ONE

You can use this classic ending to the first interview for all candidates, but it's essential for those who are likely to make the initial cut. This starts the formal recruiting process.

Although we're seeing some other fine candidates, I personally think you have a very fine background. We'll get back to you in a few days, but what are your thoughts now about this position?

Three essential things occur with this close.

First, you create supply. Good jobs are more attractive when other good people are being considered. Jobs are not only less desirable when no when else is being considered, you also lose control of the interview, since the candidate now knows he is the only one in the loop. Create competition. Never tell the applicant you have no other candidates. This is a surefire way to pay more than you need to, or lose the only candidate you have.

I remember an engineering VP telling a manufacturing manager candidate that she was the only good candidate he had seen. When we tried to close the candidate, she demanded, and got, another 15%. Everyone else on the interviewing committee knew what to say, but we forgot to give this one person the guidelines. Subsequently, the plant manager, the hiring manager, tried to take this unnecessary salary increase out of the engineering budget.

Second, with this closing question you create demand by expressing sincere interest in the candidate. A compliment goes a long way. Candidates think more about why they want a job when told they are well liked and qualified. They think about why they're not going to get it when the ending is left neutral or flat. By itself, *"We'll get back to you in a few days,"* is the classic kiss of death, so never use it, particularly for those you like.

Third, the reason for asking the candidate for a response to the job is to gauge true interest level. The supply-and-demand prefaces are used as setups to obtain this in an unbiased fashion. Get candidates to openly discuss their thoughts, feelings, and concerns. Suggest they call you back with other questions after they've thought the situation over. It's important to establish this open dialogue as soon as possible with all the potential finalists. As discussed in Chapter 8, this is the key to smoother negotiations and closing.

If a candidate you like is not interested, it's important to understand her concerns. Most often, good candidates don't see all the merits of a job right away. They need more strategic information or just have to digest what they've heard. Don't push it. Make sure you take the time to explore their issues, but don't attempt to resolve them at this time. Your objective is only to keep the lines of discussion open. Tell the candidate you'd like to get back to her in a few days for further discussion. Suggest that at that time you'll be able to give her a different perspective on the job, but first you want to finish interviewing all the candidates. Also indicate that if the candidate does want to come back for a second interview, there will be another series of interviews. State that it really won't be until after the complete assessment that the candidate will truly understand the scope and importance of the position. Your objective with reluctant candidates is get them to stay open-minded and come back for another series of interviews.

■ THE TELEPHONE INTERVIEW SETS THE STAGE FOR THE CANDIDATE AND THE INTERVIEWER

We always suggest you conduct a phone interview before you meet the candidate. Figure 4.4 shows a template for this interview. It is essentially a shortened version of the performance-based interview. The phone interview will help minimize the visual aspects of the first impression before you physically meet in a one-on-one session. On the phone, ask the candidate to describe his most significant accomplishments at his previous few jobs. Get some specific details about each. This is the impact question. Next ask him to describe the biggest team he's ever managed. Have him describe his organization chart and ask for specific job titles of his subordinate staff. Find out how the candidate built and developed this team and what it accomplished. This is the team leadership question. Just ask about a team project if the person is not a manager.

Finally, anchor at least one of the most important SMART objectives. Make sure to use a little bit of fact-finding to validate all the responses. If the candidate passes this screen, invite him in for a personal interview. I always ask candidates to be prepared to discuss their most important team and individual accomplishments, sometimes even suggesting a written summary as an addendum to the resume. A half-page for each accomplishment is enough. This helps the candidate respond to your questions. In addition, the effort put into writing the accomplishments provides some insight into interest and writing skills. This performance-based phone interview by itself will help minimize the impact of first impressions when you first

Candidate: _____ Position: _____ Date: _____

Interviewer: _____

The Critical SMART Objectives:
1.

2.

3.

4.

5.

Opening (Spend about one minute presenting the overview of the position and about three on the answer. A total of 4 minutes.)

1. (State job title and importance, and provide quick overview of company, then ask . . .) Can you give me a quick overview of your related experience and your current situation?

Assess Past Performance (Ask these two questions with fact-finding for the most recent job. Ask in only general terms for the prior position. A total of 10 minutes.)

2. Impact. Give me a quick overview of your (current/prior) position and describe the biggest impact (change) you made (or when you took the initiative or describe some exceptional work).

3. Team Leadership. Describe your organization (draw org. chart) and tell me about how you built and improved this group (or tell me about some team project and your role).

Determining Job Competency (Ask this question for the most important SMART objective listed. Combine with fact-finding for about 4 minutes. Use the same questions for the other objectives if you want to extend the interview.)

4. Anchor. One of the most important objectives of this position is (describe objective). Can you describe your most comparable past accomplishment?

The Close (Spend about 2 minutes on this. If you decide to invite the candidate in for an interview ask for written write-ups of the candidate's most significant individual and team or management accomplishments.)

5. You seem to have a very strong background. Although we're considering some other fine candidates, I'd like to invite you in for an interview. Is this situation something you'd like to consider? Why?

Figure 4.4. The 20-minute performance-based telephone interview.

meet. The accomplishment write-up is an added touch that speeds the assessment process along.

■ PERFORMANCE-BASED QUESTIONING AND TEAM-STYLE INTERVIEWS

These same performance-based questioning and fact-finding techniques can be applied in a panel or team interview. Sometimes it is a good idea to have more than one person interview a candidate at the same time. Since there is less one-on-one involvement with multiple interviewers, this is an easy way to reduce the emotional aspect of the assessment. Use the panel session for the second or third round; it can be too intimidating for the candidate at the first interview. The panel interview is also a good way for subordinates or weaker interviewers to get involved in the assessment.

If you decide to use a team-style interview, spend the most time on the impact and leadership and anchor and visualize questions, but let one or two people lead the questioning. This is important. These people will ask the major questions while the other interviewers do the fact-finding. You'll never probe deeply enough if everyone is asking top-level questions. You'll gain more insight in a panel interview, since you're not always pressured thinking about what to ask next. It also allows you to reflect on the answer, rather than judging its value on the spot. The panel session is an important interviewing tool. It saves time, increases insight, and reduces the artificial emotional reaction to the candidate. (See Chapter 6 for more information on conducting panel interviews.)

■ WHAT NOT TO ASK—THE INAPPROPRIATE AND ILLEGAL QUESTIONS

At the beginning of a seminar this past year, one of the attendees complained that one of the causes of hiring problems was the inability to ask personal questions. Another person affirmed this and in rapid-fire sequence asked what questions she wasn't allowed to ask. My response to both was that you don't ever need to ask a personal, compromising, or illegal question to conduct a great assessment. I further went on to say if a question doesn't pertain to job performance don't ever ask it. You won't gain any more insight. In my mind, performance is all that matters.

While this is a good general rule to follow, knowing what's illegal and what's not can keep you out of trouble. The following guidelines cover most of the basic issues, but contact your HR or legal adviser for more details.

Don't Ever Ask About . . .

➤ A candidate's age or anything related that can determine it, such as "When were you in the Army?"

➤ Race, nationality, or related issues, or anything that can determine it. Something like "Where do you live?" is an inappropriate question.

➤ Clubs, social groups, or religion. Avoid questions like "How do you spend your spare time?" or similar questions that pry at a candidate's personal life. It's okay if the candidate volunteers the information, but don't solicit it.

➤ Anything about the candidate's arrest record. Being arrested is not the same as being convicted for a crime, so avoid this line of questioning. You can ask about a candidate's felony convictions and the details.

➤ Children or family issues, now or in the future. Don't even attempt to bring this up. If the candidate begins talking about his or her family, it's okay to respond, but don't pry.

This is a sampling of illegal areas for questions. There are others, but they're all in the same family. Avoid all personal questions. There are plenty of performance-based questions to ask that will give you valuable insight into a candidate's ability to perform the work. Personal questions won't give you a clue, and asking them could compromise your whole hiring program.

Don't be afraid to ask questions that relate to the needs of the job. You're certainly allowed to ask about the candidate's academic background, if it's job related; just don't ask for the graduation date. If travel or extended hours are important, ask the candidate directly if she can travel or work unusual hours; don't go around this by asking about the family. You can inquire about professional groups and certifications. If these relate to specific job qualifications, they're appropriate.

➤ Complying with the Americans with Disabilities Act

The Americans with Disabilities Act (ADA) prohibits discriminating against an applicant with a disability who is otherwise able to perform the essential requirements of the job. The employer might need to make some modifications to the workplace to address some of the candidate's needs, if the person is otherwise capable, but there is no need to lower the performance standards of the job as defined by the SMART objectives (this topic was introduced in Chapter 2). You may ask candidates with a disability how they would meet the performance needs of the job, given the disability. For example, you can ask a person who uses a wheelchair how he would conduct an operational audit of a manufacturing plant, if this is a critical part of the job. Make sure these performance objectives are essential and then don't generalize the physical requirements. This is a mistake I often observe. If the performance objective requires the employee to work with PCs, don't require the person to lift one. This has nothing to do with job performance.

■ THE PERFORMANCE-BASED INTERVIEW TIES ALL THE PIECES OF THE PUZZLE TOGETHER

Good interviewing skills are only one part of an effective hiring process. You need to know the work, control your emotions, have enough good candidates to interview, and be a great recruiter. All these factors are integrated into the eight-question performance-based interview. The SMART objectives define the work in a compelling manner. This reinforces the recruiting aspect of the closing question. The structured questions when combined with careful fact-finding increase objectivity. Peeling away the onion, taking notes, and listening are all essential to an accurate assessment. Practice these skills on all candidates. This is the only way you'll become proficient. The process itself will impact sourcing. You may find some great candidates you would have eliminated and some weak candidates you initially thought were stars. This is the what the learning process is all about.

At some point along the way, you'll recognize that the questions are not the important part of the interview. Objectivity, probing, fact-finding, and skepticism combined with a thorough knowledge of the performance needs of the job are all it really takes. You'll know your reprogramming is complete when you reach this stage.

CONDUCTING A PERFORMANCE-BASED INTERVIEW

✔ Review the SMART objectives. These set the standards and guide the selection process. They're also the compelling vision of the job required for good recruiting.

✔ Read and annotate the resume. Know the candidate's strengths and weaknesses before the interview.

✔ Conduct a 20-minute preliminary phone interview before meeting the candidate. This will eliminate unqualified applicants sooner and minimize emotions for those you meet.

✔ Ask candidates to submit a short addendum to their resume describing one team and one individual accomplishment. This quickly establishes the performance-based nature of the interview.

✔ Be a fact-finder. Turn generalities into specifics. Get examples and quantify everything. Ask for facts, figures, dates, names, and measurements. This will reduce exaggeration and validate responses. It will also quickly minimize candidate nervousness.

✔ Be skeptical. Interviewing is a fact-finding mission, not a popularity contest. As long as you know what you're looking for,

(continued)

don't give up until you find it. As long as the job is great, great candidates won't mind.

✔ Get examples of impact and team or management projects for each past job. This lets you measure and compare the core success traits of energy (motivation, initiative) and team leadership over an extended period.

✔ Anchor and visualize each SMART objective to determine job-specific competency. This directly measures the candidate's ability to apply past performance and talent to meet future objectives.

✔ Get examples of commitment to gain insight into character.

✔ Find out how personality has hindered performance to better understand personality. You'll also see growth, candor, and character development.

✔ Maintain applicant control. This is important as you recruit. At the end, state your sincere interest, create competition, and then ask the candidate to state his or her interest.

Ch*a*p*t*er

Work-Type Profiling: Matching Abilities with Needs

I cannot commend to a business any artificial plan for making people produce. You must lead them through their own self-interest. It is this alone that will keep them keyed to the full capacity of their ability.

—Charles H. Steinway

■ GREAT MANAGEMENT STARTS BY TAPPING INTO THE ENERGY AND MOTIVATION OF OTHERS

People work harder and achieve better results when they're doing work that gives them a great deal of personal satisfaction. Conversely, applying extra energy over the long term is difficult if a person doesn't find it enjoyable. To maximize the quality of every hiring decision, it is important to match the critical performance aspects of the job with a candidate's ability and true interests. This way you tap into self-motivation and drive. This is what effective management is all about.

130

We've developed a new technique that directly addresses this important issue, called work-type profiling. With this new assessment technique, we're able to directly match a candidate's interests and competencies with the performance objectives of the job. If you've ever hired a great person for the wrong job, you already know the importance of work-types. These are the people who are bright, capable, and often energetic, doing only parts of the job. While they're praised now and then for these areas of performance, the missed deadlines and marginal work elsewhere are constant reminders of a bad hiring decision.

You can tap into personal motivation through the work-type profiling and matching process. This improves the quality of the fit and prevents the classic mismatching of a great candidate with the wrong job. I still run into this problem if I don't remain diligent. Certain traits excite me more than others, even if the job requires ones I'm less excited about. We also have a tendency to believe that people who are superior in one area are competent at everything. This is true if the competencies are similar, but potentially disastrous, if not. Just recently, we lost a marketing executive who was great at strategy, but weak at management and organization. Strategy development was the number one SMART objective and we got plenty of examples to back it up. During the interview, we accepted generalities for the management tasks, which were number three or four on the list of performance objectives. The problem was that when number one and two were under control, management competency then became the number one issue. If we had conducted a thorough work-type profile, it would have been obvious that the candidate was ill-suited for the job.

■ THERE ARE ONLY FOUR TYPES OF JOBS IN THE WHOLE WORLD

Over the past 20 years, I've been involved with hundreds of different jobs. These have run the gamut from the technical to the creative, and from entry level to management. From this experience, I learned that work can be divided into four distinct and fundamentally different work-types. These are an adaptation of the more familiar "technical, manager, leader" or "process, tactics, strategy" categorizations found in many management texts. Work-types combine these and address the dynamics and flow of work a little more precisely. For these reasons, the following four types are better suited for our purposes:

1. *The Creator or Strategist.* This is where all work begins, and the people who do best here are those with a future perspective. Those with vision. It's the idea phase, the world of concepts and future plans. People in these jobs do everything from developing new products to coming up with ideas for new business opportunities. We call people who are at home in this phase the visionaries, consultants, strategists, or creators. While their jobs may differ in content, they all see things before everyone else.

2. *The Entrepreneur or Builder.* This is where the idea becomes reality. On a small scale, it could be the salesperson closing the deal or someone starting up a new business or ramping up for a major project. These are the risk-takers. They tend to be more dominant and more individual. They're great at persuading and pushing, often in the face of insurmountable odds. People who like this intense world of rapid change are entrepreneurs, developers, deal-makers, builders, or turnaround specialists.

3. *The Improver or Organizer.* This is where the business is run on a day-to-day basis. It's the world of tactics, plans, and implementation. People doing this are the managers, improvers, planners, and organizers who make the organization work better. Their focus is on upgrading and improving the processes and people that deliver the goods and services of a company. While change is gradual, the activity is broad, addressing people, systems, resources, and all the interrelated activity. These people make companies run better.

4. *The Producer or Technician.* This is where the work really gets done and is represented by the people who sustain the business. Their focus is at the process or at the transaction level. The key is the application of a skill or technical proficiency in producing a product or service. Process control, quality, technical competence, and detail drive their work. These people run equipment, design products, administer processes, and analyze results. In a broad sense, we label them producers, technicians, analysts, or administrators.

➤ The Ebb and Flow of Work-Types and Life Cycles

The four work-types represent a distinct flow of activity from the idea phase to start-up, then into a managed growth phase, and ultimately into a sustaining mode. The cycle then begins again. This is the normal life cycle of a product or a business, as shown in Figure 5.1.

In a thriving business, these activities go on concurrently. Even if the top line of the business is represented as a point on this life cycle, below the surface, change can take all these forms. New products or projects are being started; older ones are being updated or discarded. Some jobs and functions require all of these skills, others just one. We have taken this simple concept and applied it to the hiring process to improve the quality of the assessment. Most people tend to hire in their own image. We intuitively match traits within ourselves as we assess candidates. Frequently, these traits fall within these four work-type profiles. Entrepreneurs hire other entrepreneurs, even if the job requires management skills. Managers hire other managers even if the job requires detailed analytical skills. This is why we often hire people who are good in a few aspects of the job, but not across the board. Sometimes these mismatches are the catalysts for catastrophic failure.

Work-type profiling is a great technique to bridge the gap between the analytical fact-finding mode and the intuitive hiring decision. It allows interviewers to remove their own biases from

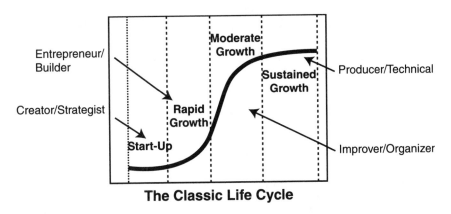

The Classic Life Cycle

Figure 5.1. The ebb and flow of work-types and life cycles.

the evaluation. This is a critical stage. Only then can the job really become the dominant focus of the selection process.[1]

■ DEFINE THE JOB USING WORK-TYPES TO BRIDGE THE GAP BETWEEN THE JOB AND THE CANDIDATE

In every performance-based job description we've prepared, one or two work-types stand out. For technical jobs, it's usually the technical or creative work-type, although sometimes the organizer replaces one of these. For senior executives, it's typically the strategy need combined with the manager/organizer. For sales jobs, start-ups, or a major project launch, the entrepreneurial style dominates. Once we define the work-type profile, our objective is to find candidates whose accomplishments match these job requirements.

A well-written performance-based job description, combined with good listening and note taking are all you need to do a great job of work-type profiling. Table 5.1 brings this all together. The work-types are further defined with examples of some typical jobs. Use the key phrase section as you listen to the candidate's response. You'll then be able to assign the candidate's major accomplishments into these same work-types. This is how you'll match job needs with the candidate's abilities.

As you listen to the responses, you'll assign the accomplishments to work-types. Most people are strong in one or two work-types, rarely all of them. Flexibility across work-types is important for managers and team leaders. The words and phrases a candidate uses are as insightful as the accomplishments described. Look at the key phrase section above. These will help guide you to the right work-type category. For example, a candidate might describe a

---

[1] To learn more about this topic, read Ichak Adizes' *Corporate Lifecycles* (Prentice Hall, 1988) and Kathy Kolbe's *The Conative Connection* (Addison Wesley, 1990). We each came at this similar concept independently, but you'll notice the common theme of the work-related life cycles. *Work-types* is my own term, but it represents a commonsense way to categorize work into different activities. This is a big cause of hiring errors, and one easily prevented.

Table 5.1 Assigning Candidate Responses to Work-Type Profiles

Work-Type	Producer or Technical Process Oriented	Improver/ Organizer Manager	Entrepreneurial/ Builder Rapid Change	Creator/Strategist Visionary— Consultants
Definition Assign the SMART Objectives and the Candidate's major accomplishments into these categories.	High-quality, process and procedure oriented, maintains, sustains, supervises, or executes. Conservative and detail-oriented. Technically focused. These people work from the process outward. The process determines the result. Any field that has an important technical foundation (engineering, accounting, law) tends to breed this work-type. They're more analytical and detail oriented than intuitive. Generally they want a clear picture with details of where they're going before starting. Often an individual contributor at the technical level. Can be too structured in their thinking and inflexible.	Upgrades, organizes, changes and/or manages existing operations. Is a planner and team-oriented. This is the core of the "organizational man." These people have balanced egos, tend to be risk averse, they bring order out of chaos, they see issues from a pragmatic standpoint and know how to plan to meet an objective. They are better at cleaning up and running a business rather than starting something from scratch. Their focus is on the infrastructure—the people, systems, facilities, and resources.	Implements the big ideas or one-time projects, impatient and risk-oriented. These people like multiple projects, they're fast-paced, deal well with ambiguity and tend to be individualistic. They don't like details and follow-up is often weak. They'd much rather build the business than run it. Range from the individual salesperson hustling to make a deal, to the more sophisticated developer. These are the people who bring the ideas into reality and get them rolling, but they want to soon move on to something else. Often dominant.	Focused on long range or future development. Ideas and concepts oriented. These people are the consultants, visionaries, strategists, R&D leaders, the creative, and long range planners. They're into new products, research, the creative side of marketing and think about the future more than the present, sometimes too much. As a result, these people can be impractical.
Key Phrases Listen for these in the candidate's response.	Quality—Detail-oriented Technical or individual skills Craftsman—Design Evaluate—Analyze Probe—Produce—Repair Supervise—Sustain Maintain—Learning—Teach Control—Focus on process	Organize—Plan Pragmatic—Tactical Focus on existing operations Manage group/team Coordinate resources Upgrade—Improve—Change Persuade Compromise—Realistic	Sell—Close—Fast-paced Convince—Deal-making Build from scratch Develop—Promote Improvise—Make it happen Focus on implementing ideas/concepts Risk-oriented—Individualistic	Creative—Intuitive New ideas—Develop long range strategy Conceptual—Consultant Staff work Research—Theoretical Focus on future

(continued)

Table 5.1 *(continued)*

Work-Type	Producer or Technical Process Oriented	Improver/ Organizer Manager	Entrepreneurial/ Builder Rapid Change	Creator/Strategist Visionary— Consultants
Typical Jobs	Accountant— Administrator	Manager	Salesperson— Entrepreneur	Researcher— Consultant
	Lawyer—Engineer	Jobs requiring organization	New project manager	Long-Range Planner
	Doctor—Clerical	Planner	Turnaround artist	Business Adviser
	Supervisor— Auditor	Tactician	New venture— Dealmaker	R&D—Strategist
	Facilitator— Teacher	Product manager	Real estate developer	Creative marketer
	Machine operator—Repair person—Process control	Implementor	Jobs with risk or rapid change	Jobs with a long-range focus
		Director	Closer	Business development

major accomplishment as "upgraded the manufacturing performance reporting system." This sounds like an organizer-type task. Use the key word phrases to confirm the candidate's true role. Perhaps she did the long-range planning for the task, or liked getting it completed under some tight time constraints. This could change the project into a strategic or entrepreneurial job. Work-type profiling allows you to better understand the nature of work from a different perspective. This will be useful not only in hiring, but also in assigning projects to your current team members.

■ DETERMINE WHAT DRIVES JOB SUCCESS BY MATCHING SMART OBJECTIVES TO WORK-TYPE PROFILES

Table 5.2a lists some SMART objectives for a few typical jobs. We've categorized the first group into work-types. Review these and then try your hand at the second group in Table 5.2b. This will give you practice.

As defined in the second practice group, the machinist is a technically oriented and individual contributor position. For the best fit, you'll want to avoid candidates who are more

Table 5.2a SMART Objectives Categorized by Work-Type

Job Title	SMART Objectives	Work-Type
Engineer	• Design hydro-electric valves.	
	• Develop new ASICS circuit design tools.	Technical/Producer Creator/Strategist
Accounting Manager	• Improve the closing process.	
	• Review state sales tax system for compliance.	Improver/Organizer Technical/Producer
Brand Manager	• Develop marketing strategy for new category.	
	• Launch product rapidly to meet narrow market window.	Creator/Strategist Entrepreneur/Builder
Secretary	• Implement weekly mail merge to key accounts.	
	• Maintain and co-ordinate all travel programs.	Technical/Producer Technical/Producer
Sales VP	• Set-up sales training system.	
	• Develop the annual sales plan and strategy program.	Improver/Organizer Creator/Strategist
Materials Manager	• Implement the new MRPII system.	
	• Evaluate and upgrade the staff.	Improver/Organizer Improver/Organizer

management focused or who want to develop new methods. The CEO objectives are typical. These leadership roles usually require a forward-looking strategist and a strong manager able to build winning teams. This financial analyst requires good technical skills plus an ability to interpret the results. This requires some forward-thinking, strategy component. The VP/IS has to combine good technical skills with the vision to plan ahead (the strategist). The national accounts manager has to combine some detail fact-finding (the technical) with the actual process of getting the business (the entrepreneur).

Table 5.2b   SMART Objectives Categorized by Work-Type

Job Title	SMART Objectives	Fill in the Work-Type
Machinist	• Produce high-quality molding tools • Debug molds on first article inspection	
CEO	• Create a strategy to penetrate market • Build a professional team and organization	
Financial Analyst	• Prepare monthly operations analysis review • Interpret impact of price changes on market share	
VP Information System	• Evaluate all existing systems and processes • Develop long-range IS plan for growth	
National Accounts Manager	• Identify key potential accounts • Contact and close five new accounts	

Sometimes these requirements conflict and it's difficult to find candidates who meet all the criteria. The financial analyst is a good example. It's hard to find people who are both detail-oriented, yet can also interpret how these results will impact the business. The same is true for the national accounts manager. This person is expected to do both the detailed prospecting and the cold-calling and closing. If you are having trouble finding a good fit, it might be better to split the job up to take advantage of strengths in one area, compensating for weaknesses in another. Think about restructuring jobs this way especially if the most important performance objectives are in different work-type categories. Although there are people who can be strong at both, finding the ideal candidate might not be worth the extra time needed.

The key to all this is the ability to clearly define the work that needs to get done through the SMART objective process. The work-type profiling analysis is a natural subset of this. It allows the manager to better understand the nature of the work. Whether you are selecting candidates or assigning work, you can use work-type profiling to tap into personal energy and competence.

■ CASE STUDY: WHO WOULD YOU HIRE FOR THE CUSTOMER SERVICE DIRECTOR?

Table 5.3 will help you match job needs with candidate skills. The SMART Objectives are from the performance-based job description prepared in Chapter 3 for the Customer Service Director. Most jobs, even individual projects, typically require more than one work-type, but generally there are two key types. Of these two, one is usually more dominant than the other. Understanding these differences allows you to better understand the work as you match different candidates' skills and interests. To complete the work-type profile for a specific job, assign a "D" for the dominant category under the appropriate heading for each SMART objective. If the objective is too broad for just one, assign a "S" to the secondary work-type. Complete this for each SMART objective. Add up the score for the complete job by giving two points for each "D" and one point for each "S." The completed form for the Customer Service Director is shown as Table 5.3.

The customer service director position is a challenging one. The best candidate would be someone balanced across all the work-types, although the improver/organizer manager needs to dominate. A strong process and systems orientation is also important; the producer/technical work-type is secondary, but the pace of the rebuilding effort also demands some entrepreneurial/builder skills. There are some long-range planning and system integration aspects as well, which require the creator/strategist. It would be very difficult to find a person with all these characteristics, so some compromises will probably be necessary.

There are two ways to look at this assignment. Once the department is rebuilt, the position will clearly be an improver-producer. (We've combined the first term of each work-type to show the dominant-secondary relationship.) In the short term, the ob requires an improver-entrepreneur, to handle the big projects. You will need to make trade-offs regardless of your choice. Neither is ideal. My suggestion would be to think long term. Find

Table 5.3   Work-Type Profile Analysis for Customer Service Director

SMART Objectives	Work-Types*			
	P/T	I/O	E/B	C/S
Improve customer service from 93% to 99% and reduce customer complaints by 75% within 12 months.	S	D		
Rebuild the customer service department to support a 25% per year growth rate. This includes upgrading supervisors, a reduction in turnover, and a complete process reengineering of the group.	S	D	S	
Take a management lead on organizing a multifunction task force in developing companywide customer service improvements. This will support the 18-month IS conversion program now underway incorporating new technologies such as EDI, bar coding, and Internet catalog and ordering.	S	D		S
By June, conduct a complete process review of all aspects of the department identifying key staff issues, system problems, and bottlenecks. Coordinate with major customers addressing their needs and begin a corrective action plan immediately.	D	S		
Develop a series of interim solutions to reduce backorders, improve returned material replacements, and improve communications with the field support team. Present action plan within 90 days.		S	D	
Totals**	4	8	$2^{1}/_{2}$	$^{1}/_{2}$

*Categorize each SMART Objective into a dominant (D) and secondary (S) work-type.
**Assign 2 points for each "D" and 1 point for each "S" to determine total points.

someone who is a strong manager (the improver) plus the strong process and systems orientation (the producer). Make the short-term rebuilding effort a focused team project. This will raise its visibility and importance. People and teams can sometimes temporarily act as entrepreneurs if there's a lot at stake. In the long term, the pace, the risk, and intensity of these projects can wear most people down.

Thinking through a job this way allows the management team to get comfortable with the real job needs and with the person ultimately selected. This planning process alone will increase the likelihood that the person taking the job will be successful, since potential land mines have already been identified.

Now that the job is clearly defined, the next step is to develop the work-type profile for the candidates. Our ultimate objective is to find a candidate whose interests and competencies match the profile required. The impact/leadership and anchor/visualize questions (the four core performance questions) will get us started, and in most cases they are all you'll need to prepare a work-type profile for a candidate.

■ THREE REVEALING QUESTIONS: FINDING OUT WHAT CANDIDATES LIKE TO DO

We've determined a candidate's competency to do the work using the four core performance questions. While this is important, there is a chance that the candidate prefers to do something else. The key to hiring high performers is to find people who continually apply extra energy and initiative to their work. To tap into this energy source on a long-term basis, competencies and preferences must be in alignment. Three simple questions address this vital area:

➤ The Three Work Preference Questions

1. Think about a favorite work experience, something you felt was exciting, energizing, and personally fulfilling. Please describe it and tell me why it was personally satisfying.

2. You've indicated to me that you're a real problem solver. Can you give me three examples of the types of problem you like to solve?

3. This job requires a real self-starter. Can you please give me three examples of initiative in one of your more recent positions? This would be something you did over and above the requirements of the job.

These questions get directly at the issue of positive, sustainable, personal energy. The work described motivates and fulfills the candidate. If you can tap into it, the person will be unstoppable. They are free-choice questions. The candidate can choose any examples of accomplishments for the answers. Comparing these responses with the four core past performance questions allows us to match preferences and competencies. Many times, the accomplishments used as examples will be the same. That's great. It means competencies and preferences are similar. If they're not, and they represent different work-types, you have a potential problem. Probe a little harder. Find out what really drives the candidate to excel. If the job can be structured to take advantage of this and not compromise some other critical area, both you and the candidate win. The following sections examine each question in turn to emphasize the implications of various responses.

Work Preference Question 1

Think about a favorite work experience, something you felt was exciting, energizing, and personally fulfilling. Please describe it and tell me why it was personally satisfying.

The favorite work experience question can provide critical information. Use fact-finding to uncover the candidate's true role and the significance of the work. Conduct a work-type profile analysis and compare this result with the candidate's other major accomplishments. If the work-types are different, find out why. It could be a major concern.

We were interviewing a candidate recently for a manager position, and the applicant described several comparable accomplishments. His favorite work experience concerned us, though, since it was significantly different. This person described a research project during his early career that tapped into his individual and technical skills. Interestingly, the candidate became more animated and expressive when describing this task than when describing his other accomplishments. The technical undoubtedly was this person's dominant work-type, with the manager a distant second. While he was acceptable for the position, we wanted a candidate who was as equally motivated by the team and organizational effort, and we decided to move on to other candidates.

Sometimes the work-types are the same, but the accomplishments selected are different. Still probe to find out why. It could be something as simple as the candidate didn't want to be repetitive. It could also reveal something about the prior company, or even the supervisor. This is useful information to know as you assess best fit.

Work Preference Question 2

You've indicated to me that you're a real problem solver. Can you give me three examples of the types of problem you like to solve?

People will work long and hard on problems they like to solve, so this question is also very insightful. Sometime during the interview, everyone says they're problem solvers. What's important though is the scope, scale, and type of problem. As soon as this comes up, get specific examples of the problems people like to solve. Assign the problems to one of the work-types.

This is a great way to understand motivation. Managers should like to solve management problems. If they don't, be concerned. If someone really likes to solve complex systems issues and he gives three examples to support this, he might not be suited for a fast-paced project role. On the other hand, if a candidate for a creative marketing assignment describes overcoming a problem by coming up with the perfect ad, you've found your ideal match. Also compare the scale of the problems solved to the needs of the job. This is another good indicator of job fit.

Here are some typical problems I've recently run across. How would you categorize them into work-types?

Typical Problems Candidates Like to Solve	Work-Type
1. Finding out why one particular robotic assembly machine is always breaking down.	_____
2. Determining what drives different types of customers to respond to different marketing and ad campaigns.	_____
3. Resolving conflict with people.	_____

4. Determining the best way to achieve a
   team objective given limited time
   and resources.   _____

5. Overcoming a customer's reluctance to buy.   _____

6. Debugging a piece of computer software.   _____

Depending on your perspective, there could be more than one correct assessment. The assembly repair appears to be largely technical, but it could involve some creative design. The customer analysis problem requires some real creative analysis. Resolving conflict is more management and organizational. This is also true for the team objective in item 4. Overcoming buyer reluctance is the individual dealmaker or entrepreneurial work-type. Debugging the software requires detailed, analytical skills.

The next time one of your candidates says she's a problem solver, ask for some examples. You'll discover this is a straightforward way to better understand personal motivation.

Work Preference Question 3

Can you please give me three examples of initiative in one of your more recent positions? This would be something you did over and above the requirements of the job.

People rarely do more than they're required to do unless they really like doing it. This is even more valid if they keep on doing it over a long period of time. That's why the initiative question is such a good one. In some way, this is similar to one of our core questions. Instead of asking about impact for each previous job, you might want to ask candidates to describe some examples of when they took the initiative.

As in the previous problem-solving question, get three examples of initiative. Everybody can come up with one example of anything, but few people can quickly describe three unless they've really done it. This is especially true with initiative. If the third example of initiative is as credible as the first two, you found a high performer. These people constantly do more than required.

Following are three examples of initiative a controller candidate described to me many years ago:

1. Helped set up a new accounts payable system.
2. Upgraded the monthly financial statements.
3. Researched tax compliance.

This is one of the few interviews I ended early. The examples chosen were superficial, none took more than a few weeks to complete, and the candidate had been working at this job for over three years. I had to even pry the third one out of the candidate. In responding to the second one, the candidate was more general, less interested, and the answer was much shorter than the first one, less than a minute compared with about three. Furthermore, the job I needed to fill was a manager's role, not a staff accountant's. With one simple question, I learned all I needed to make an informed "no."

When the responses to these three questions overlap responses to the four core performance questions, it means preferences and competencies are the same. Sometimes the examples used are different, but the type of work is the same. The problem arises if the preferred work is different. This happened in the marketing executive example mentioned earlier in this chapter. The job required a strategic focus plus strong technical product management effort. The candidate described great examples for both. From his references, we got the sense that there was a preference for the long-range, strategy-oriented aspects of the job. While we brought the candidate back in for a panel interview, we didn't take it far enough. We accepted his assurances of the product management work, which he only described in general terms. He outlined his plans to address this, but we didn't push hard enough to get multiple examples of when he did it. He was a bright, articulate visionary who could do the management and team-building task, but he was not motivated to do it.

If we had asked these three preference questions we would have observed that they all had to do with long-range marketing and strategy development. It's important that competencies and preferences match the job needs. Whenever they don't, you'll probably wind up with a short-term success story.

■ INCREASE PERFORMANCE BY MATCHING JOB NEEDS WITH CANDIDATE WORK-TYPES

Following are the comments from two candidates for the customer service director position. Remember we're looking for someone who is first the improver/organizer manager and second, someone strong at the process level—the producer/technical work-type. At least initially, the job requires a major effort to rebuild the department, so we don't want to ignore this as we assess the candidates. Review the following responses to the four core performance questions and the three preference questions and determine who would be the better candidate.

Candidate A—Selected Responses

Major accomplishment included setting up a nationwide distribution system.

Took the initiative in upgrading the team, including lots of personal development.

Likes problems that involve systems, processes, and people.

Took the initiative in analyzing and specifying with the IS group the new order-entry system.

Favorite work experience was starting up the logistics department especially working with other department heads.

Candidate B—Selected Responses

Developed system and business strategy for new on-line order-entry and package tracking.

Favorite work experience was leading crash systems conversion effort for customer service.

Likes problems that involve quick decisions with limited information and time.

Took the initiative on developing a backup plan for meeting with problem accounts.

Took the initiative in organizing project teams to address each process bottleneck.

Table 5.4   Work-Type Profiles

Candidate A

	Work-Type			
Summary of Accomplishments	P/T	I/O	E/B	C/S
Set up a nationwide distribution system	1	1		1
Upgraded team		3		
Problems related to people processes and systems	1	2		
Specified new order-entry system with IS	2	1		
Joint project in setting up new logistics department	1	1		1
Totals	5	8		2

Note: Each objective is worth three points' spread among the work-types.

Candidate B

	Work-Type			
Summary of Accomplishments	P/T	I/O	E/B	C/S
Developed new systems and strategy	$1\frac{1}{2}$			$1\frac{1}{2}$
Crash effort on systems conversion	1		2	
Problems with quick decisions, limited time, and info			3	
Backup plan—addressing problem accounts		1	1	1
Organizing project teams		1	1	1
Totals	$2\frac{1}{2}$	2	7	$3\frac{1}{2}$

Note: Each objective is worth three points' spread among the work-types.

Both of these profiles are summarized in Table 5.4. We assigned a total of three points for each accomplishment and spread them among the four work-types, as appropriate.

In Table 5.5, the two candidate work-type profiles are compared with the job. This clearly shows that candidate A is a better fit.

Table 5.5   Comparing Job Needs with Candidate Fit

	Work-Type Profile			
	P/T	I/O	E/B	C/S
Job Profile: Customer				
Service Director	4	8	$2\frac{1}{2}$	1
Candidate A	5	8	0	2
Candidate B	$2\frac{1}{2}$	2	7	$3\frac{1}{2}$

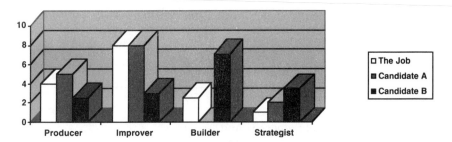

Figure 5.2. Work-type comparison for the customer service director position.

Candidate A didn't have a lot of direct customer service experience, but the scope and scale of the jobs were comparable. The systems involvement was also very close. At the work-type level, this person is more the improver and producer. This is a direct fit. The candidate is well-balanced as both a manager and individual contributor. Strong people skills are also evident. Candidate B is more the entrepreneur and strategist. While these are aspects of the customer service job, they are not the most important, at least in the long term. This candidate is also more an individual contributor than team player. Most of the work is of a personal nature and while Candidate B can work with groups, even lead them, the individual component is strongly evident. This candidate's success relies heavily on personal traits such as intelligence, insight, and quick decision making. Although this candidate has more direct customer service experience, the pace of the job, once the short-term problems are resolved, would likely be too slow. Given these two choices, I would select Candidate A for the Customer Service Director.

The work-type profile for these two candidates is compared graphically with the job in Figure 5.2.

■ FINDING THE BEST JOB FIT: MATCHES AND MISMATCHES

There are five different matching possibilities with work-type profiling, as shown in Table 5.6.

Table 5.6   Work-Type Matching Possibilities

Work-Type Match	Hiring Process Decision
1. Dominant and secondary match are identical.	Okay to proceed.
2. Dominant and secondary match are reversed.	Okay to proceed.
3. The dominant is a match, but the secondary is different.	Proceed, but get more examples of comparable work.
4. The secondary is a match, but the dominant is different.	Proceed with caution. Get lots of examples of comparable work to make sure the candidate can do the work required. Also make sure the candidate is aware that the job is not a perfect fit for her skills.
5. Neither dominant nor secondary is a match.	Stop the process. You're only fooling yourself.

This is not an exact science, and as long as the match is close, it's more important to compare the candidate's accomplishments with job needs. Points one and two fall within this category. Proceed with caution if there's only one match. Sometimes we get fooled here, especially if we are intuitive interviewers. Well-spoken candidates, especially the creative/strategy work-type, can often sound like any of the other types. These are the bright, insightful consultants who can tell you how to do something, but haven't ever done it themselves. Once on the job, all they do is plan and talk, rather than do.

A similar mismatch can happen with the great salesperson promoted to the sales manager position. If you want a sales manager, get examples of sales management accomplishments. Don't accept plans or ideas as substitutes, no matter how clever they sound. Many technical people want to get promoted into management. Not all succeed. With technical managers, you need to get examples of technical management. These include activities like meeting launch dates, controlling budgets, persuading other technical people to modify their work, and working closely with other functions. Good technical managers need to possess all these skills. Look hard for examples of them during the interview. Excellent people often fail because they were hired for the wrong job. As long as you're aware how it happens, you're unlikely to become prey to this classic hiring error.

■ AVOIDING FAILURE: MEASURING WORK-TYPE RESISTANCE

People tend to work hard at work they like to do. They sometimes work equally as hard at avoiding work they don't like. Few people like every aspect of their job, but this aversion can be serious if what a candidate doesn't like is a critical performance need. This was the problem with the marketing executive described earlier. He liked the strategy aspects of the job and did a great job with them, but avoided the detailed product management component. This resistance can lead to failure. Work-type resistance is a fairly common problem. Many of these people have great first impressions and have a series of significant accomplishments under their belts. But if these don't match the job needs, you're headed for a mismatch. Watch for these clues:

➤ Voids in the work-type profile may indicate resistance. In the interview for Customer Service Director example, Candidate A did not indicate a preference for any fast-paced project-type or entrepreneurial work. If this area is important, on a follow-up interview ask the candidate to give you examples of this type of work. Likewise, ask the great salesperson to give examples of an ability to handle complex order transactions, if this is critical to the job. Salespeople in the printing industry need to have a strong attention to detail to make sure press runs don't result in expensive scratch pads. Not all great salespeople can fill this need.

➤ The candidate tells you he doesn't like one aspect of his job. This great clue is sometimes ignored. Ask why the person doesn't like it, get examples, and look for patterns. Assign the disagreeable work to a work-type. If it's an important part of the job, you could prevent a costly error this way. You can also ask, "Tell me about a work experience that you didn't find particularly interesting," to force the issue. A candidate told me she didn't have the patience to deal with the myriad people problems her management job entailed. It turned out she was better suited for the entrepreneurial life. She was great at launching new products, and she ultimately landed a more appropriate individual contributor job in this field.

➤ The candidate's answers to one type of question seem shorter or shallower than others. I asked one candidate to describe his most significant management problem because I sensed he was more an individual contributor. While he professed otherwise, his response was more general, and the example chosen was superficial, compared with his individual accomplishments. I hated to interrupt this candidate when talking about work he enjoyed, but I had to wring a one-minute response out of him about work he wasn't interested in.

Few people are strong in all work-types. Applicants tend to cluster toward a few common pairs. Those on the building-the-business side (the builder/entrepreneur and creator/strategist) tend to be less comfortable on the operations side (the improver/organizer and the producer/technical work-types), and vice versa. This isn't completely true of all types—the academic is a combination of the technical and creator and the organizational leader is a combination of the improver and strategist—but it's a place to look for clues.

If actual examples of performance seem to be concentrated in only one or two work-types, use forced-choice questions to test for the other types. For example, just ask the candidate to give an example of his most significant accomplishment in the area that concerns you, whether it's technical, management, a fast-paced project, or some long-range or product development activity. This type of questioning will enable you to paint a profile of the candidate's competencies across all four work-types.

Use the information in this section to better understand personal motivation. Start with yourself and maybe some of your team members, to get some practice. Keep track of the type of work that you (and your team members) seem to work harder at. Where do you do superior work? What's your favorite work experience? What types of problems do you like to solve? Where have you taken the initiative lately? Keep track of shortcomings the same way. What don't you like to do? Where are you weaker? Assign all of this to specific work-types and look for patterns. You'll learn more about yourself this way as well as about the people whom you hire.

If you have a tendency to hire in your own image, you'll be able to prevent some problems. It's always better to match job needs than to mirror ourselves. With your staff, it will help to broaden your understanding of their strengths and weaknesses. If you want to increase their motivation, assign projects to them that tap into their specific strengths. Once you get comfortable with this approach, you'll be able to quickly recognize sources of strength and areas of resistance when you're meeting candidates.

■ BEYOND THE WORK-TYPE MATCH: COMPARABILITY OF JOBS

On a recent senior engineering management search, my client was concerned that the top candidate was more a technical expert than a manager. The job was evenly split between technical and management, with some solid long-range product development needs. The candidate was apparently great at the technical side and the long-range development, but lighter on the management side. Figure 5.3 shows his work-type profile.

The candidate actually brought a lot more capability to the job than hoped, but still appeared short on the management side.

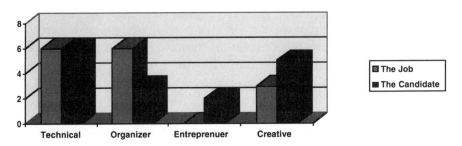

Figure 5.3. Using work-type analysis to measure comparability.

This was confirmed by the references who questioned his management skill. When we looked at comparability, the issue immediately became moot. The size and complexity of his previous management task was enormous when compared with the current role. In his previous position, the candidate was thrown in over his head and was judged too severely by some of the sales references we spoke with. The candidate had supervised over 80 engineers through 3 directors and 5 managers. In fact, he built most of the team, after inheriting the job during a rapid ramp-up. In the current job, the staff size was about half as much, with the growth rates comparable.

When everything was put together, the jobs were quite close. The staff size was somewhat smaller, the pace was the same, the products were slightly less complex allowing more forward-looking thinking, and the business issues and decision-making needs were similar. All in all, he was perfectly suited for the job. He's doing a great job now, one he might not have had if we hadn't gone beyond the work-type match.

Just because someone meets the work-type profile, it doesn't automatically mean she can do the work. You still have to have comparability. This means that the jobs have to be reasonably similar in terms of management scope, sophistication, scale, complexity, and standards of performance. This is usually pretty obvious. For example, you can meet a great organizer/improver who has only managed five people and the job requires managing a staff of 50. A lot of this information will come out in your fact-finding, but the following list will help you quickly sort through this comparability issue. (The Work-Type Profiling and Job Matching worksheet in the Appendix ties all of this information together for a quick analysis.)

➤ Have the candidate draw an organization chart and compare it with job needs according to total size, number of direct reports, types of people and functions managed, the pace of change, the standards of performance, and the level of sophistication of the systems and support functions.

➤ Use the ABC rule to evaluate interpersonal skills. The responses to the different accomplishment questions can be categorized into the following three interpersonal skills

categories—**A:** **A**lone or individual contributor; **B:** **B**e-
longing to a team; or **C:** in-**C**harge, or a management
role. This analysis will quickly reveal the candidate's preferred interpersonal role. Compare this with the needs of
the job. Don't put individual contributors into important
management roles if this is inconsistent with all of their
previous significant accomplishments. Be concerned if individual contributors have few team projects. The opposite is equally true. Don't put great team players into
individual roles, that are critical to job success. Get some
examples if there's an apparent void.

➤ Look at the complexity of the individual and group assignments including the scope of the assignment, technical
needs, decision-making differences, the expectations and
the results achieved, the pressure, and the available resources. On the surface, a candidate might have a comparable job title, but one job might be to maintain a functioning
group, while the other requires creating one from scratch.

➤ Understanding the company environment provides major
clues to fit. Compare your company culture and environment with the candidate's. Consider the sophistication of
the systems, the pace, the rate of growth of sales, the pressure, the demands of the job, the quality of the staff, the
quality of the reporting systems, and the expectations of
senior management.

➤ Consider the financial issues and business issues. Comparability can easily be measured in dollars. Are the budgets
comparable? Also consider sales growth, headcount, the
number of products, the number of facilities, receivable
and payable levels, debt levels, financing needs, and the
quality of the outside professional support, including CPA
and legal firms used.

There are lots of ways to compare fit. To me, the worst is to
hire people with the same type of experience in the same type of
job in the same industry. While this is easy to do and logically
comfortable, you'll continually underhire. People who are willing to do the same old things over and over again are just cruis-
ing along. These aren't the top performers. The best people want

new challenges and a chance to grow and develop. Work-type profiling is an alternative. It considers comparability from a new perspective based on the real content of the work, not just the titles. It also meets the top candidate's need for growth, while minimizing the hiring manager's risk.

■ WORK-TYPE PROFILING MATCHES JOB NEEDS WITH A CANDIDATE'S ABILITIES AND INTERESTS

Work-type profiling solves the most fundamental of all hiring problems—matching job needs with an applicant's abilities and interests. I've seen many great people get hired for the wrong jobs and for the wrong reasons. The intuitive interviewers evaluate competency based on a few important, but narrow traits. Sometimes they get lucky and these traits directly match job needs. Often they don't, and an otherwise capable person winds up in a job ill-suited for her ability. The technical interviewer misses the mark on the other side. These people want direct comparability at every level of the job. This approach overvalues experience for the sake of potential and drives the best away. Work-type profiling bridges this gap and provides a common ground for both approaches.

Work-type profiling is an advanced technique that can help you make more informed and better reasoned hiring decisions. You can quickly identify sources of strength and potential mismatches, and can appraise internal candidates the same way to increase fairness. The hiring decision needs the combination of technical fact-finding plus intuitive decision making. Rarely are two jobs ever the same. This is why the hiring decision must be intuitive. The best candidates never want to do the same job over again anyway. A good hiring decision has to account for both these factors, while making sure the candidate can do the work. Work-type profiling requires the intuitive decision maker to collect lots of facts to make an informed decision. This reduces risk and appeals to the fact-finder need. Work-type profiling is an intuitive technique we've converted into a technical process. That's why it works.

USING WORK-TYPE PROFILING TO IMPROVE JOB FIT

✔ There are only four different types of jobs and all work falls within these work-type profiles. They are:

1. The **Creator/Strategist** is the forward-looking visionary or consultant coming up with new ideas, products, and strategies.

2. The **Entrepreneur/Builder** brings ideas into reality and usually is an impatient fast-paced person willing to take risks and earn the rewards.

3. The **Improver/Organizer** is the manager who brings people, systems, and resources together to improve, upgrade, and change the way things are done.

4. The **Producer/Technical** is the person who sustains the business, gets into the details, designs and makes the products, delivers the goods and services, and maintains the quality.

✔ People apply more energy toward work they like to do. The work-type profile analysis allows the hiring manager to quickly identify these areas.

✔ You can increase hiring accuracy preparing a work-type profile of the SMART objectives of the job and matching this to a specific candidate's work-type profile.

✔ The words and examples candidates use to describe their work can be easily categorized into work-types.

✔ By anchoring each SMART objective, you can determine a candidate's competency within a narrow range of work-types.

✔ Get examples of each work-type to paint a complete profile of the candidate's competency across all of the job factors. Balance and flexibility across all work-types is an indicator of upward potential.

✔ Ask candidates the three questions that elicit their favorite work experience, examples of initiative, and problems they like to solve. This gives you a good idea of preferences and underlying motivation.

(continued)

✔ Be concerned if preferences and competencies don't match. You might have a candidate who can't deliver on all job needs.

✔ Always get three examples to validate an answer. The third is the most difficult to recall, but if it's substantive, you have a winner.

✔ Watch for clues for resistance at the work-type level, especially if it's a critical job need. Raise the caution flag if the answers to some questions are shorter and generalized or lack details. Watch out for philosophical statements that sound good, but have no substance.

✔ Use the ABC (Alone, Belonging, in-Charge) comparison to determine fit based on preferred interpersonal style.

✔ You need to investigate job comparability even if the work-types are a strong match. Look at things like staff size, company size and growth rates, sophistication of the systems, performance measurement issues, decision-making needs, and complexity of the job.

✔ Work-type profiling requires enough fact-finding to support the intuitive hiring decision.

Chapter 6

Reference Checking, Follow-Up Interviews, and Other Evaluation Techniques

Far more crucial than what we know or do not know is what we do not want to know.

—Eric Hoffer

■ STAY OBJECTIVE—THE FIRST INTERVIEW REPRESENTS LESS THAN HALF OF THE TOTAL ASSESSMENT

Additional interviews, reference checks, and testing are all valuable if used objectively. They rarely are. Once a candidate is on the short list, which is sometimes so short it isn't even a list, most managers use the added time to look for information to confirm a "yes" decision. By this time, we have so much time invested in the candidate that a "no" possibility is only passively being considered. Once someone passes muster on the first interview, there's better than a 50% chance an offer will be made. Positive data is magnified, and negative data is rationalized away, ignored, minimized, or most times never even obtained. This is a major cause of bad hiring decisions. Objectivity must prevail throughout the evaluation process. Negative information must still be sought as aggressively as positive data.

Other useful tools are available to assess candidate competency. They're very effective when used in conjunction with the performance-based interviewing process. Alone, the performance-based interview can consistently achieve a 70 to 80% accuracy rate. When combined with some of the other tools suggested in this chapter, accuracy can increase to 80 or 90%. Good hiring takes work, but not as much as the afteraffects of bad hiring.

If you're serious about a candidate, you need to conduct reference checks. Here's a basic rule. Even if it's not 100% true, you should still follow it.

The Basic Rule about References

Strong candidates have strong references, who will openly tell you about them. The lack of good references is a sign of a potential problem.

There are very few exceptions to this rule. Here's one. Some strong candidates want to leave their job search confidential. If they've been with their current organization for a long time, it's sometimes hard to find a colleague willing to vouch for the candidate's accomplishments. Even in this case, there's probably someone who has left who can tell you about the candidate. Since I started doing this in 1978, I've never had a problem getting a reference from a good candidate. Once a candidate is serious about a job, a reference check is in order. Candidates who will go out of their way to find a few for you are serious about the position. I become nervous if a candidate can't give me a few people to call. Good candidates are proud of their accomplishments and *want* you to call their references.

At one of our seminars, a buttoned-down HR VP vehemently disagreed with my contention about references. She told me she would only give the bare minimum of information about a employee who has left her firm. She obviously feared potential legal reprisals. I then asked her about one of her co-workers whom we both knew very well and asked if she would give me an open reference about her. She said, "Of course, but that's different, I know her." And that's why there are no exceptions to the basic rule. Good people know other good people who will tell you openly about them. Weaker people come up with excuses about why they can't give them to you.

■ HOW TO DO REFERENCE CHECKING

You can ask the reference any performance-based question you want. Don't ask any personal questions ever, especially those that involve family, age, or racial issues. Although the laws differ by state, the reference only has to give minimal data. This minimal information guideline was established to protect employers from lawsuits from their former employees if they gave negative or less than stellar references. Many companies are now stating that employees can give open references if they clearly state that the reference is personal.

The hiring manager should personally check at least one or two references. It doesn't matter when you conduct the reference. Sometime after you've established intent and before the last round of interviews is best. Don't quickly delegate this important task. The HR department or the recruiter has a vested interest in placing the candidate, so they won't be as inquisitive as they should be. Plan on at least 20 minutes for each reference. This gives you time to do some fact-finding. The key to good interviewing and good reference checking is to ask lots of questions and get examples. Use peers, subordinates, and supervisors as references. Subordinates are sometimes the best references, so don't ignore these.

Although not getting a reference is a sign of a weak candidate, getting flowery, glowing comments is not the sign of a good candidate. References, even from strong candidates, need to be validated. This is done in two ways. First, by determining the quality of reference. Second, by getting the reference to give specific examples to validate the hyperbole and generalities.

➤ Qualifying the Reference

The Reference Check checklist shown here is divided into two distinct parts: Qualifying the Reference, and, Qualifying the Candidate. The quality of the reference is as important as what the reference tells you about the candidate.

REFERENCE CHECKLIST
Part 1—Qualifying the Reference

☐ First determine the relationship to the candidate. Find out the titles of both the reference and the candidate, how long the working relationship lasted, and their most recent contact.

☐ Obtain the reference's current title, company, and the scope of the job compared with the job when the reference knew the candidate.

☐ Determine the reference's scope of responsibility. Just ask about the size of his or her organization and the number and types of people on the staff.

☐ Determine what the company environment was like—pace, standards of performance, quality of the people, and the quality of the processes and systems.

☐ Ask the reference how he or she measured performance.

Under "Qualifying the Reference," start by understanding the relationship between the candidate and the reference. Get position titles for both, duration of contact, and the current relationship, its basis, and extent. Also ask how large a department the reference has supervised and how many people like the candidate the reference ever supervised. If the reference was a peer or a subordinate ask similar questions, but find out the reference's track record. This allows you to substantiate the significance of the reference. Also ask the reference about the environment of the company where they worked together. Determine whether it was intense or casual. Find out how sophisticated it was in your area of concern. Ask about systems and methods.

This information will allow you to place the reference's subsequent comments in context. Use your own techniques if you don't care for these, but don't just accept a reference's comments without some validation. If the reference is personal, ignore it. If you decide to use it for some strange reason, you then must get great examples of exceptional, above-the-call-of-duty activities. From non-work-related references, you must determine why the candidate is special and how this relates to on-the-job performance. Volunteer work of some sort would apply here. This is especially useful for candidates starting their careers.

Ask how tough the reference is in giving ratings. Find out the basis of the company's rating system. This not only provides additional insight into the quality of the reference, but also helps to validate the reference's comments. The reference might value traits differently than you do, so this could be important. Some of the more common value systems include teamwork, interpersonal skills, results independent of methods, intelligence, commitment, character, and loyalty. You can get lots of different answers about accomplishment depending on the rating system used.

➤ Qualifying the Candidate

It is unlikely you will get all the information shown on the checklist for qualifying the candidate, but this list will help guide your thinking when you're on the phone. The key to good reference checking is to get details and examples to back up general statements about the candidate's competency. For example, if the reference states that the candidate was really committed, ask the reference to give you an example that best demonstrates this trait. Do this just a few times and the reference will realize you're serious. Most reference checkers aren't. They just want to check boxes. By separating yourself from the pack this way, you will encourage the reference to be more open and frank with you.

REFERENCE CHECKLIST
Part 2—Qualifying the Candidate

- ☐ Please give me a summary of (candidate)'s strengths and weaknesses.
- ☐ Get examples of accomplishments to support major strengths and weaknesses.
- ☐ How did the weaknesses affect job performance?
- ☐ Can you give me some examples of where the candidate took the initiative?
- ☐ How would you rank this person as a manager?
- ☐ What was his/her biggest management accomplishment?
- ☐ How strong was this person in building/developing teams?
- ☐ How would you rank this person's overall technical competence in [job specific] area? Get specific examples.
- ☐ Is technical competence a real strength? Why?
- ☐ Get example of best work for top one or two SMART objectives.
- ☐ Team and interpersonal—get examples of group projects.
- ☐ Determine timeliness—get examples when under pressure.
- ☐ How strong are his/her verbal and written communications? How were these measured?
- ☐ Find out ability to handle pressure, criticism. Get examples.
- ☐ How strong a decision maker is this candidate? Can you give me some examples and how they were made?
- ☐ Can you give me an example of commitment?
- ☐ What single area could the candidate change to be more effective?

(continued)

> **REFERENCE CHECKLIST** *(continued)*
>
> ☐ Would you rehire the candidate? Why or why not?
>
> ☐ How would you rank this person's character and personal values system? How did this affect performance?
>
> ☐ How would you compare this candidate to others you know who are at the same level? Why is the candidate stronger (or weaker)?
>
> ☐ How would you rank overall performance on scale of zero to ten? What would it take to move up one point?

Start the second part of the reference check by asking for an overall summary of strengths and weaknesses. From this, you can "cherry pick" your way through the balance of the reference items. The key is to ask for a specific example demonstrating the skill or behavior the reference mentioned. For example, if initiative was mentioned as a key strength, follow up by asking for a specific accomplishment demonstrating initiative. Do this for weaknesses also. Don't form judgments about the candidate based on generalities from a reference. Get proof with good examples. This is the most important aspect of good reference checking.

Ask the reference to compare the candidate with others at the same level. Find the size of the group, and where the candidate ranks. *"How would you rank this person among other people you know at this level?"* is a good opener. Ask how many are in the group and what percentile the candidate falls within (e.g., the top 10%, top 25%, or top 50%). Then find out the basis for this ranking—team skills, energy, technical competence. Ask what would it take for the candidate to move into the top 10% or 5%. This will get at weaknesses. Also ask where this person excelled, and again get an example for proof.

There are other ways to get at weaknesses. Ask the reference to describe the single thing the candidate could do or change to be more effective. Then find out how this inadequacy affected performance. Also, at the end of the interview, you could ask the reference to summarize the candidate's overall performance on a scale of zero to ten. Usually you'll get a number anywhere from 6 to 9. Find out the basis, or meaningfulness of this score, and then ask what would it take for the candidate to move up one point.

Asking whether the reference would rehire the candidate and for what type of position can also be revealing. Probe this to confirm previous statements.

Use the reference to confirm the information obtained during your interview of the candidate. Throughout the interview, you obtained numerous examples of the candidate's greatest accomplishments. Ask the reference to validate this information. Get examples of core success traits and see whether the traits and examples are the same as the candidate described. If different, find out why. From the reference, get the candidate's actual involvement in the major accomplishments. Compare this with what the candidate has stated. It's easier to correlate information if you focus on the most exceptional work the candidate has done in each job.

Conduct the reference check with an open mind. If you really want to hire the candidate, you might unintentionally avoid asking the tough questions. Many years ago, a senior executive at a large health care company told me he was asked to provide a reference for a candidate we both knew. The candidate was solid, but not a star, more an individual contributor than a manager. During the reference the senior executive intimated that the candidate in question was a superb analyst, but only an average manager. He said that once he mentioned this, the HR person conducting the reference ignored the management side and tried only to reinforce the strengths.

You can get any answer you want conducting a reference check this way. If you don't have an open mind and are not willing to change your opinion, it's a waste of time even to contact the reference. It's hard and always embarrassing to admit you've made a mistake in judgment and eliminate a candidate at the last moment. It's a much bigger mistake to go forward.

Reference checking allows you to validate the candidate's true role in each major accomplishment. Concerns about style can also be addressed. Weaknesses can be validated with other references and with the candidate and through outside testing. As the hiring manager, you'll also get some great tips on how to better manage or motivate the candidate if hired. You can prevent more hiring mistakes with a good reference check than by any other method. But we've seen hiring managers ignore negative data because they were too sold on the candidate. This is another important reason to stay objective until the whole evaluation process is completed.

■ THE SECOND ROUND—HANDLING SUBSEQUENT INTERVIEWS AND ADDITIONAL INTERVIEWERS

You'll never have enough information to make a foolproof hiring decision. Use a second interview to confirm core issues and address new important issues. Make use of additional interviewers the same way. Tell them what you want them to look for. By itself, this will make their interviews more meaningful. Courtesy interviews can wind up being popularity contests. Little real investigating goes on. Following are some points to get maximum benefit from these subsequent interviews.

➤ The Complete List of Things You Need to Know before Making a Hiring Decision

The following checklist represents all the information you need to make a well-considered hiring decision. Check everything you don't know yet, and assign this to the second round of interviews, for yourself and the other interviewers.

☐ Level of drive, energy, initiative, and self-motivation.

☐ Trend of growth based on examples of major accomplishments in last two to three positions.

☐ Job (work-type) alignment and fit.

☐ Technical competency and ability to apply.

☐ Ability to meet all the SMART performance objectives—anchor and visualize each one.

☐ Managerial, team, and organizational comparability with job needs.

☐ Experience, education, and environment compared with job needs.

☐ Problem-solving and analytical skills using real problems as tests.

☐   Thinking—technical, tactical, and strategic—using visualization of SMART objectives.

☐   Goals—get examples of major past goals already achieved.

☐   Commitment and responsibility.

☐   Character, values, and integrity.

☐   Individual, management, and team skills.

☐   Personality and cultural fit.

☐   Confidence and positive attitude.

➤ Conducting the Second Interview

Before the second round, make sure you have written down everything you don't yet know about the candidate. The preceding checklist will help you sort this out. Even without specific questions, the basic interview guideline to follow is to ask the candidate to give you an example of an accomplishment that best demonstrates the desired skill, behavior, or trait. Then validate the response with good fact-finding.

The questioning techniques already introduced combined with fact-finding are suitable for any stage in the interviewing process. In fact, this is often all you'll need to conduct additional interviews. Anchoring and visualizing all the SMART objectives is best done over two or more sessions. It takes lots of time to do this accurately and this should be the foundation of all subsequent interviews. Format the second interview around some of the SMART objectives you haven't yet evaluated. It's also a good idea to assign these performance objectives to other interviewers. If your boss is involved in the interview make sure she anchors and visualizes at least the most important SMART objective. Give all other interviewers a copy of the Fact-Finding Worksheet found in the Appendix and list the SMART objectives you want them to explore. This will dramatically increase their objectivity, especially if you ask to see their notes.

Have peers anchor and visualize the SMART objective most relevant to their work. For example, we had an engineering manager ask a potential marketing manager about the development of product requirements documents[1] as the main focus of his interview. This tightened the focus of the interview.

Candidates don't mind this line of questioning, even though you may seem to be asking similar questions over again. Anchoring SMART objectives and fact-finding always result in new lines of questioning, because the trail followed is always different. As a result, you'll continue to get enlightening answers and gain additional insights. By controlling the breadth of the interview this way, you can obtain useful and more objective information from each interviewer. Request written summaries from each person involved. E-mail is great for this.

Spend time in the second interview on management, team, and organizational skills. The team leadership question, one of the four core questions, addresses this directly. Make sure you consider this for at least the past few jobs. The focus of much of the first interview is on individual contributor traits, so use later interviews to restore some balance here. Also use additional interviews to probe into some of the important work-type matching issues. Later interviews are a useful means to ensure a strong match between job needs and abilities and interests.

The POWER Staffing Comprehensive Interview in the Appendix summarizes all the questions presented in the book. This is a useful refresher. Use questions from this form in subsequent interviews. It includes the eight basic questions, all the work-type questions, and some additional questions on character and personality. In addition, the following few questions are specifically geared toward obtaining added insight about the candidate's background traits.

➤ All-Purpose Performance-Based Question

[State trait or desired skill or characteristic] is important to success in this position. Can you tell me about a time when you had to use this trait to achieve a major objective? Please give me a specific example.

---

[1] These documents describe in detail the marketing needs of a specific product. The layout of a keyboard would be an example for a new hand-held computer.

Use fact-finding to validate the example given by getting dates, the names of the people involved, the importance of the task, and the impact on the company and the candidate.

➤ The Two-Step Questioning Pattern to Better Understand Motivation and Values

Step 1. *What two or three things are you looking for in a new job?*

Step 2. *Why are having [A] and [B] important to you?*

The first question is the set-up. The second question gets at underlying motivation and values. Also look for the source of motivation or goal setting.

The following question gets at how values were formed. The preface is important, and it's a good question only if you've established a strong bond with the candidate. You'll get a superficial response if you haven't. Avoid it then.

➤ Value Formation Question

Values are usually formed through an early youthful experience, sometimes difficult or uncomfortable. Do you have any experiences like this that helped shape your values and character?

This question is not required in every interview. I only suggest it when the person you're hiring is critical to your success or the success of the project or business. If you try it, don't speak after asking it. Let the candidate open up. This underlying source of motivation and character can sometimes reveal the true measure of a person. Only attempt the question when a lot of trust has been established between the candidate and the interviewer. Be sensitive to this. This bond can often overcome other problems later on with the offer (like compensation). If you get a superficial response, it usually means the candidate was unwilling to reveal his innermost feelings. Try to answer this question yourself first, before trying it on others. This will give you a sense of how revealing it is. Make sure only the hiring manager or a senior level HR person asks this question.

I am leery of interviews by subordinates. They can have hidden agendas, and there are too many variables to control. One way around this is to include subordinates in a panel interview, which eliminates most of these problems.

■ THE PANEL INTERVIEW—A GREAT WAY TO LEARN MORE AND NATURALLY CONTROL EMOTIONS

In the late 1980s a potential client asked me about panel interviews. "They're intimidating, cold, a poor recruiting tool, and unwieldy," was my instant reply. The CEO looked at me and said, "That's too bad, because that's all we use here, and if you want the CFO search [which at the time would have been our biggest assignment], you'll have to use them." Without hesitation, I indicated that I'd be willing to try them. You should, too. They're a great tool. I was totally wrong.

As long as they're organized well, panel interviews provide a much truer picture of a candidate than the one-on-one interview. Here's why:

➤ There's less emotion because it's easier to avoid getting personal in a panel session.

➤ You have a chance to think more about the candidate's responses. You're more an observer than a participant. This increases the validity of the assessment. In most one-on-one interviews, you're often thinking about what you're going to ask next, rather than listening to the candidate's answer.

➤ You don't judge answers during the response, because others are asking for clarifying information. More in-depth responses are possible this way.

➤ The interviewer's body language isn't as meaningful. Even if one of the interviewers doesn't like an answer, the physical clues (slumped shoulders or glazed eyes) aren't so obvious to the candidate.

➤ It's a great way for subordinates to meet the candidate without the typical awkwardness. Since it's less of a personality-based interview, their hidden agendas tend to stay hidden.

➤ Strong candidates don't mind it, if it's not too soon in the process. They don't have to put on an artificial show to be friendly, they can just be themselves. You see more of the true personality in a panel interview.

➤ It saves time. Three or four people can get to know a candidate in one or two hours, rather than a whole day.

➤ It allows weaker interviewers to participate. This is especially important if the weaker interviewer is the hiring manager. In the preceding example, the CEO didn't consider himself to be a good interviewer, so the panel was arranged with him in mind. He felt he always talked too much, since he didn't know what questions to ask, and the panel interview eliminated this problem.

The panel should include no more than three or four people to avoid being both intimidating and unwieldy. Make sure all interviewers have read the SMART objectives for the job before convening. Have one or two people lead by asking the major performance-based questions. Make the thrust of the interview a discussion of major accomplishments. Get lots of examples and have everyone on the panel use the fact-finding checklist in the Appendix for follow-up questions. It's okay to ask the candidate to come prepared to discuss a few of her most relevant major accomplishments. This will improve the information exchange. Consider individual contributor, team, and management projects. At the end of the interview, get the group together to summarize their findings. This process itself offers good checks and balances. Strengths and weaknesses are tempered, resulting in a much more objective assessment. Personality naturally takes a second position behind performance when evaluated in a panel session.

One of my manufacturing clients excluded a great candidate for an operations management position, because he was too chatty during the first interview. My client got put off by this superficial banter, most likely caused by initial nervousness. Our client was a typical entrepreneur—bright, fast-paced, prone to make instantaneous decisions, and strong-willed. These are not the traits of good interviewers. The candidate was top-notch, though. He was a perfect match for the entrepreneur to build the solid infrastructure that could maintain his fast-growing import and distribution company.

We didn't want to let this one die, so we arranged a panel interview with one of my associates leading the session. There were about four people in the room, but we orchestrated the questioning. It lasted about 90 minutes and covered everything, focusing largely on comparable past accomplishments dealing with rapidly changing environments. The candidate passed this much more grueling session with flying colors. After a subsequent three-hour one-on-one interview with the entrepreneur, the candidate was offered the position and accepted. During this interview, they created the operations plan and budget for the next 12 months. My client recently thanked us for intervening and indicated that job performance is as expected: top-notch.

The only potential problems with panel interviews are that they can be intimidating to the candidate and that they need to be well-coordinated. Review everyone's role beforehand and you won't have a bunch of people asking miscellaneous questions. This will solve the organizational issue. (Use one of the standard interview forms in the Appendix to assign questions and roles.) You'll ease the candidate's fears if you describe the format of the session a few days beforehand. Put the candidate in the middle, not at the end of the table. This way the candidate will feel like one of the team. One of the leaders should ask all the leading questions, with the rest of the panel members following up with fact-finding questions. Don't make it seem like an interrogation. Stay low-key by requesting information in a neutral tone of voice.

■ THE TAKE-HOME CASE STUDY: DON'T JUST TALK ABOUT THE JOB, HAVE THE CANDIDATE DO IT!

You'll see instant results with a panel interview—more agreement and fewer hiring errors. The process can be even stronger if you give the candidate a take-home problem to present in the panel session. This is another useful tool you'll want to try out.

The take-home project is something the candidate does outside the interview that's discussed at a subsequent meeting. Topics run the gamut from reviewing reports, and evaluating new products to assessing tactical or strategic plans, solving problems, or providing advice on a miniproject. The take-home project is effective because the candidate must do real work, not just talk about it.

The take-home case study approach has several tangible benefits. For one, it reveals true motivation and desire. Candidates won't spend time preparing if they're not truly interested in the job. It does a better job of revealing competency through direct observation, as opposed to opinion, gut feel, or second-hand information. Also, the spontaneity of the session allows true character and personality to come out.

A few years ago, a CEO called me about three months after we had placed a Controller at his company. He wanted to tell me how pleased he was with the candidate. He said that the candidate's performance, sense of humor, and interpersonal skills were exactly as demonstrated in the panel interview. This had not been his initial assessment. After the first interview, the CEO thought the candidate was not confident enough for the job and had some quirky mannerisms, and he was unsure of the candidate's technical competence. He thought the two other contenders were far stronger.

I knew all three candidates very well and was sure that this person was the best of the three, although he was nervous in the interview. I suggested the CEO conduct a panel interview coupled with a take-home problem. Each candidate was asked to assess a potential acquisition. After reviewing the financial reports, the candidates were told to make a 15-minute presentation about the merits of the opportunity. This would be followed by a 45-minute open discussion. During the panel session, this candidate wowed everyone. He explored the financial impact on taxes and earnings. He raised serious questions about costing and financing. He was confident, funny, and insightful. In this element, which was much more natural for the candidate than the interview, he had a chance to show his true capability. This is the real test, since it measures substance, not showmanship.

Many times, first-rate candidates don't get a fair chance, because they're eliminated too soon in the process. In this case, I personally intervened to bring a dead situation back to life, but this is rare. You can avoid discounting superior candidates by waiting until the second interview to measure personality and fit. Use the first interview just to measure performance. Then, intervention, divine or otherwise, won't be as necessary.

One of our clients in catalog distribution went a bit overboard with this advice. After reading the preceding information on panel interviews, the management team took it to an extreme. The day after the first interview, our candidate for the marketing manager position was asked to come in for a panel interview with a few people. The candidate was not 100% sold on the job, so this type of panel session was premature. After arriving, she was told that there would be six people in the panel and she had to present her solution to three marketing-type problems. She was given 25 minutes before the panel was to convene to evaluate these problems, which weren't all that relevant to the job.

Although the candidate handled it well, the problems could have been avoided. If you're going to use take-home projects, give the candidate a few days to prepare, and then only if the candidate has expressed a desire to be considered as a finalist. Also make sure the issues explored are relevant and job specific. If you have more than three or four people in the session, it can be both intimidating and unwieldy.

Here are some specific ideas for the take-home project. You don't need to have a panel session to review these, but if you do, you get the benefit of both assessment techniques:

Some Take-Home Project Ideas

➤ Review reports, financial statements, studies, or plans.

➤ Give the candidate a SMART objective to study. Have the candidate first describe a significant anchor. Then have the candidate tell you how he would accomplish the task (visualize). Use a flip chart and get into a serious give-and-take discussion. This is what and how you'd discuss the task after the candidate starts. Why wait?

➤ Give a loan officer a credit application to assess.

➤ Have an engineer assess a design, and then present some alternative solutions or approaches.

➤ Describe a problem in a process (e.g., order entry, logistics, manufacturing, or accounting), and have the candidate describe how she would come up with a solution. Also have her give you examples of similar past accomplishments.

➤ Have a salesperson explain how he would attempt to penetrate a big account.

➤ Have a product manager describe how to develop and launch a new product.

The types of issues are endless. The key is to make them job specific. Situational questions that don't directly relate to the job and what needs to get done are a waste of time and will give misleading results. The take-home project is actually an expanded anchor and visualize exercise. It reveals true job competency by applying the candidate's knowledge in solving job-specific problems. In addition, the amount of time spent on the assignment directly reflects real interest.

■ BACKGROUND VERIFICATION: CHEAP INSURANCE YOU MUST HAVE

Many reliable firms conduct background checks. Most check degrees, employment, credit, driving, and criminal records for a relatively inexpensive amount, $50 to $200 per candidate. This is cheap insurance. Do it for every finalist. It will level the playing field. While most resumes describe the basic truth, many camouflage sand traps. Of late, I've become a real cynic about resume content. This sad story makes the point. A few years ago, we were looking for candidates for a material control manager position. In a search through our main database, consisting of everyone we had met personally since 1980, we found some strong candidates and we called them personally to determine interest. Three were interested and sent in their current resumes. They must have forgotten we had earlier versions. One was identical, other than being updated for the current period. Another falsely added a master's degree in an earlier time period. The other eliminated a job from the earlier resume to minimize turnover. The latter two candidates were eliminated from contention without further contact. This is disturbing and I believe reveals a trend in the validity of resumes. Caution is advised. Remember that resumes are marketing tools only. A clever layout is okay, fraud is not. Spend the money and wait the two days it takes to conduct a background check to separate fact from fiction.

On your applications, you can state you'll be conducting a background check and ask the candidate to validate the truthfulness of the information, affirmed by his/her signature. This will minimize fraud. You can also use the background check as part of the close to test both interest and truthfulness. Before the second or third interview, tell the candidate you'll be conducting a rigorous background check. Ask the candidate to reconfirm that everything on the resume and application is 100% consistent with the facts. If the candidate says yes and agrees to come in for another interview, he's demonstrating sincere interest and honesty. You can learn a great deal about the candidate by using this conditional approach to move forward.

■ TESTING TO CONFIRM, NOT PREDICT, COMPETENCY

I've been interviewing candidates since 1978, and I'm still not sure about the validity of testing. Some tests are better than others. This section provides a review of the tests we have used and explored over the years. Tests can be divided into two broad categories—those that test competency and those that test personality. Competency tests measure ability in some way, whether intelligence or specific job-related skills. Personality tests measure traits and behaviors.

Any test that accurately measures a specific job-related skill is a useful indicator of subsequent performance. Some of these include demonstrating software knowledge, equipment usage, PC skills, solving job-specific problems, and showing manual dexterity. If the job is narrowly confined to this specific area, the test should weigh more heavily in the hiring decision. For other jobs, the application or use of these skills ultimately determines success, and in these cases the testing may give the wrong conclusions. But it's not because the testing is invalid. The real problem is that the true job is ill-defined. That's why the most important component of good hiring is the performance-based job description and SMART objectives.

Despite these drawbacks, some tests are useful tools if used to confirm a strong performance-based interview. Raise the caution flag if the results of the test don't confirm the information obtained during the one-on-one interview.

Randy Kirner, the former VP Human Resources at Wyle Electronics, the nationwide distributor of electronic supplies, uses a few different tests depending on the position. For warehouse personnel, the company uses a test that measures honesty, trustworthiness, and work-ethic. While Kirner recognizes that the tests don't predict performance, they do reveal areas where the line managers need to conduct follow-up personal interviewing. Guiding the interview this way is the appropriate use of this type of testing.

For sales reps, Wyle uses the Gallup organization to benchmark their sales team. By carefully studying the traits of their best and the worst salespeople, the company was able to develop a trait model of the ideal candidate. After the first interview, the best candidates are measured against this model. If the results of the personal interview were satisfactory, but not confirmed by the test results, the candidates are reevaluated to make sure something wasn't missed. This helps confirm the interviewer's initial assessment. According to Gallup, the test itself is only 61% accurate in predicting subsequent success (which is typical of most of these instruments[2]), but when combined with a strong, follow-up interview, it becomes a useful tool to confirm the hiring decision.

Following is a rundown of the most common tests and some tips and how to get the most out of them.

---

[2] Gallup's figure.

➤ Ability to Learn

The most commonly used intelligence tests used by businesses are the Wonderlic Personnel Test and the Thurston Test of Mental Agility. There is a strong correlation between ability to learn and on-the-job competence, but it's far from 100%. We use this type of test to confirm our judgment, not predict performance.

I recently read about a candidate for a police officer position who was denied the opportunity because he scored too well on the Wonderlic. The community leaders felt he would have been bored by police work, since his score exceeded their norms. My suggestion would have been to get examples of work the candidate had done that best duplicated the routine nature of police work. If the work was similar, then I would discount the high Wonderlic score as meaningless. On the other hand, if the past work required a higher degree of intellect than police work, then the high Wonderlic would confirm this tendency. This is how this type of test should be used.

Many years ago, I was working with a top-notch candidate for an HR manager's job. She seemed great, but scored low on the Wonderlic. The score was totally inconsistent with her track record of success, based on our personal interviews and her reference checks. Checking further, we found out that English was her third language! She grew up in Italy, lived in Quebec as a young adult, and went to school in the United States. Surprisingly, she had no noticeable accent. In this case, the test was flawed. The woman was ideally suited for the job. If we had relied on the test for guidance, which used a number of idiomatic expressions, we would have eliminated a top-notch candidate from consideration.

The problem with these tests is that they're often used as predictors of performance, but they weren't developed with this in mind. They do not substitute for a good performance-based interview. They only tell you where to look when the results are inconsistent with your expectations.

➤ Measuring Personality

Personality-style tests measure traits and behaviors. While there is some correlation between these traits and subsequent performance, it's not all that high, between 55 and 70%. For a psychologist, this is great. At the high end, it's worthy of a Nobel prize. For a line manager, it's fairly useless. That's why psychologists praise these instruments (this is their term), yet they are of little use in the field.

One problem is that these tests measure preferences, not competencies. This is an important distinction. If you prefer to be at a party than to read a book of poetry, you will be classified in a certain way. You might be competent at neither. In fact, the party goer might be able to offer more insight to Robert Frost, and the poetry reader might be a more effective leader of others. Another problem is that most of these tests present an "either-or" choice. You might like to read poetry and go to parties, but the test only lets you select one. This forced-choice distinction doesn't give a true reading of personality balance.

For these reasons, personality tests should only be used to confirm, not predict, performance. If the test indicates an inconsistency with the performance-based interview, further investigation is mandatory. Use panel interviews, take-home tests, and additional reference checks. The only valid means to determine competency is past performance. If a specific test raises concerns, use examples of past performance to address the issue.

One of our candidates for a marketing position did well on the creative portion of a personality-style test, but quite low on detail orientation. Our client was concerned. On further investigation, we discovered the problem was in the format of the test and its interpretation, not the candidate. This test forced the candidate to indicate a preference for the creative over the analytical work, since this is what she preferred. The job required solid database marketing skills to supplement the creative aspects of the job, and our client was correct in raising this issue. To address the concern, we gave the candidate the Wonderlic Personnel Test for intelligence and she did well on the math component. In addition, we conducted a number of references to confirm her analytical abilities by getting specific examples of some of her analytical projects. Finally, the client had her interpret some of their database reports and present her findings at a panel interview. With this added insight, it was clear she had the ability to handle the analytical aspects of the job. In this case, the personality testing was used correctly—only to raise the concern, not to predict performance.

The following tests are useful tools if used to confirm past performance.

The Comprehensive Personality Profile, (also from Wonderlic)

We often use this test. It addresses the typical personality traits and indicates best fit for some classic jobs. It also adds test-taking honesty to the list of traits. This is unusual. It's also inexpensive, about $30 each, with self, computer-based scoring. The results for this test vary a lot, so reliability is a question. Since we use it as a confirmation tool, this is not a problem, but it can add confusion. The automatic write-ups at first seem to provide a lot of insight, but the advice is too broad and covers a lot of different profiles. Despite this flaw, the test provides good tips for both test taker and the hiring manager, and for this alone, it's worth looking at.

Predictive Index (PI), the DISC Instrument, and the Myers-Briggs Test

These tests are based on the early work of Hippocrates regarding the four temperaments. In the first part of the 20th century, Carl Jung developed this concept into a theory of human nature based on the four personality types. This led to the Myers-Briggs test. The DISC and Predictive Index instruments arose out of the style and behavior analysis work conducted shortly thereafter by Dr. Bill Marston. Both of these tests are quantitative describing the degree to which a person is **D**ominant, **I**nfluencing, **S**teady, or **C**ompliant. Figure 6.1 provides a quick overview of the four types.

The primary style is determined by a person's tendency to be active or passive (the horizontal axis of the graph), combined with their thinking or feeling orientation (the vertical axis). Plot yourself to get a quick sense of your primary style. Through word choices, the tests quantify how strong you are in each of the four styles. Although these tests are valuable in team building and improving communications within a group, I'm less convinced of their ability to predict job competency. Nevertheless, if the tests results are inconsistent with past performance, we always con-

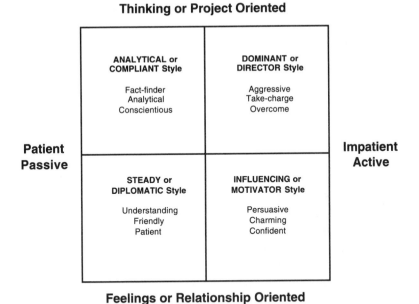

Thinking or Project Oriented

ANALYTICAL or COMPLIANT Style Fact-finder Analytical Conscientious	**DOMINANT or DIRECTOR Style** Aggressive Take-charge Overcome
STEADY or DIPLOMATIC Style Understanding Friendly Patient	**INFLUENCING or MOTIVATOR Style** Persuasive Charming Confident

Patient Passive (left)   **Impatient Active** (right)

Feelings or Relationship Oriented

Figure 6.1. The four basic personality styles.

duct more reference checking or have another round of interviewing. As a checkpoint used this way, the tests are great.

The Myers-Briggs is based on similar behavioral theory, but the output is more qualitative than quantitative. You wind up with 16 different personality types by classifying people as **I**ntroverted or **E**xtroverted, **S**ensing or i**N**tuitive, **F**eeling or **T**hinking, and **J**udging or **P**erceiving. By mixing and matching the four fundamental behavioral traits, you can wind up at one extreme being an ENTJ, the natural leader, or at the other end of the spectrum as one of nature's observers, the ISFP. This is a useful tool to understand people better, but it doesn't add much to the hiring process. I've met many supposed ENTJ leaders who are incompetent, and some great leaders who are introverted and quiet.

There's a classic logic argument, *asserting the consequent,* which addresses this situation. The phrase means that specific truths are incorrectly generalized for all conditions. For example, assume that a test revealed that seven out of ten leaders are extroverted. From this, some would conclude that you need to be extroverted to be a leader and that all extroverts are leaders. Both generalizations are untrue, but the underlying details get lost somehow. This is why these personality style tests are flawed. In my opinion, you should look for the leader first: She'll either be introverted or extroverted.

The Calipers Test

This is a much more extensive and more expensive psychological test (about $150 each) put out by the Princeton, New Jersey, Caliper Corporation. The test is much longer and includes a module to better assess fit with a specific job. My experience with this test is limited, but the results seem more professional and more insightful than some of the competing tests. By comparing personality profiles to a specific job, the conclusions drawn are more reasonable. The variety and number of questions asked provide a more accurate personality profile over a range of different circumstances. This gets away from the quick 10-minute tests that can be more easily faked. The validity of the test is also well founded. Since you have to send the results back to get the candidate assessment, the company is better able to track their results. In addition, they follow up after a period of time to compare test recommendations with candidate performance.

The company also provides personal guidance to help you interpret the test results. This is extremely valuable and worth the added cost. Dr. Herb Greenberg, the CEO of the Caliper Corporation, believes that this test, like all other psychological tests, is a useful tool to validate but not replace the interview. I recommend using this test for your one or two finalists. It's a more advanced form of the behavioral styles analysis and does a better job of matching the candidate with the job. The personal feedback also gives you a chance to discuss potential problems and other areas of concern.

The Enneagram

I discovered this in Don Riso's book *Personality Types* (Boston: Houghton Mifflin, 1987). It has the same behavioral underpinnings as the tests noted earlier, but the Enneagram adds the dynamics of personality change to reveal healthy and unhealthy personality types. These correspond to different styles ranging from leaders and thinkers to artists and helpers. You can find a number of Enneagram tests on the Internet. I like this concept a lot, but it's still not a good predictor of subsequent performance. Have candidates take the test and then compare their profile with the job needs. If you have conducted a good performance-based interview, the results from the test will be similar to your own assessment. If not, check out the candidate in more depth, as well as your assessment skills.

After a while, you'll discover that your assessments and the test results usually yield similar results. When they don't, it's time to conduct some more in-depth probing to better understand why the two results differ so much. It could indicate a problem with the test or provide a clue to a flaw in the candidate—possibly a fatal flaw. These typically include extremes in behavior—too smart, too aggressive, too warm, too intense. The Enneagram is good for sorting out some of this.

While all these testing instruments offer insight into personality, none are substitutes for a detailed performance-based interview. Personality and character are clearly revealed in a person's past performance. By getting the best examples of compatible past performance in the interview, we have ensured a correct personality and behavioral fit. Testing can only confirm this. If it doesn't, it means either the testing was bad, our interviewing wasn't as exhaustive as it should have been, or we didn't clearly understand the needs of the job. Any one of these is possible. That's why you need to reassess the candidate if the testing indicates something is amiss.

Many managers use a test to replace a good interview. It can't. Tests are great tools when we use them to validate all our assumptions and interviewing techniques. In this way, they force us to conduct a in-depth performance-based interview.

■ PUTTING IT ALL TOGETHER

Although the one-on-one performance-based interview represents the heart of the hiring decision, it needs to be supplemented with other tools. If you use the POWER Staffing

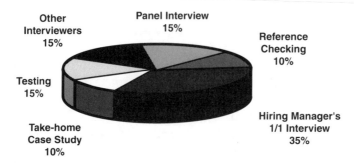

These techniques are not substitutes for a performance-
based interview. They're complements to it.

Figure 6.2.   Candidate assessment techniques.

techniques described throughout this book, you'll be about 70 to
75% accurate, maybe even as high as 80%. You'll get close to 90%
if you add the other techniques described in this chapter. The
percentages shown on the pie chart in Figure 6.2 indicate the relative importance of each assessment technique.

The quality of the input of others and of the references cor-
relates directly with the quality of the job spec. If all members
of the interviewing team know the performance objectives, the
assessment approach we recommend will work smoothly. It
falls apart if the interviewing team is unclear about the job.
Then there's a tendency to substitute emotions, stereotypes,
personal biases, testing, and more reference checking to compensate for a weak performance-based interview. Problems
arise if the supplementary techniques overshadow the interview
itself. In this case, it's time to reassess your complete assessment approach.

My philosophy is that you should try anything and everything helps. Just conducting your one-on-one interviews with
the candidate at different times of the day in different situations may be helpful. I know one CEO who conducts three interviews: one in the office, one during a meal, and one in a
social gathering. He gains something from the change in set-
tings. Personality and style are revealed in natural fashion this
way. I learn a great deal about my candidates during casual
phone conversations to schedule meetings and negotiate offers,

even when talking with a spouse or children. Don't base the hiring decision on one interview by one person. Use all the techniques in this chapter to increase the accuracy of the assessment.

LEARNING EVERYTHING YOU NEED TO KNOW TO MAKE AN ACCURATE HIRING DECISION

✔ The one-on-one interview cannot provide all the information you need to make an objective hiring decision. Use reference checks, panel interviews, take-home projects, and tests to better understand competencies, motivation, and preferences.

✔ Always conduct reference checks and don't accept any excuses from candidates that they don't have any. Good candidates always have strong references who will talk openly about them.

✔ Make sure references give lots of examples to prove every positive statement.

✔ Validate the competency of the reference by first getting her to discuss the job and scope, and then the relationship to the candidate.

✔ Get at weaknesses by asking the reference how the candidate can improve in the technical, team, managerial, and decision-making areas.

✔ Use second interviews and other interviewers to gain more facts about past performance. Get additional examples to support the critical SMART objectives. Forget courtesy interviews. Have other interviewers get useful examples of past performance as it relates to their specific function and need.

✔ Use panel interviews for every candidate on the short list. They minimize emotions, allow you to think rather than judge, save time, and encourage participation by subordinates and weaker interviewers. Candidates like them since they're more performance and less personality dependent.

✔ Use take-home case studies to test job-specific competency and candidate motivation. The typical interview relies too

(continued)

(continued)

much on spontaneous responses. The take-home project taps into reasoning, judgment, and motivation. The quality of the take-home case is a better indicator of ability, since it demonstrates real work, not just the talk about it.

✔ Background verification is a cheap insurance plan. Resumes are prone to misrepresentation. The background check will uncover most it.

✔ Personality testing is fine, but use it to confirm, not predict, performance. These tests sometimes indicate areas for additional performance-based interviewing questions or reference checking.

Chapter 7

The Ten-Factor
Candidate Assessment

There is something rarer than ability. It is the ability to recognize ability.

—Elbert Hubbard, American Author

■ BALANCE IS THE KEY

Do not base a hiring decision on a few narrow traits. It should cover all job needs and all job-related performance factors including self-motivation, technical competence, job fit, leadership, management, cultural fit, and character. An accurate measurement of these factors requires information from the initial interview, subsequent interviews, test results, and reference checks.

Hiring is not at the top of the list of fun things to do. There is a natural tendency to want to short-circuit the process. In the rush to decide, managers often emphasize one piece of data or the input of one influential person. Even if the data collection has been thorough, information is sometimes arbitrarily overvalued. Don't compromise your decision at the last minute. Too much time and energy has been spent in conducting a complete evaluation. The best hiring decisions balance strengths and weaknesses across all the important job-related needs. Overvaluing one or two factors at the expense of a few others magnifies the opportunity for error.

I learned the value of balance a number of years ago during a search for a director of quality for a chemical manufacturing company. The final candidate had a low-key personality, and I was concerned about her ability to lead change. While otherwise qualified, she just didn't seem dominant enough for me during the interview process. We didn't have a lot of candidates, so we reluctantly sent her to meet the client.

A phone interview with the CEO and HR Vice-President the next day set me straight. Their first interview was a combined three hours. They got detailed examples of complex quality improvements the candidate had instituted, team-building efforts she had managed, and projects she had led when working with government agencies in developing industry standards. Her values and character were explored at subsequent meetings, as well as technical competency, motivation, and critical thinking skills. This was a superbly well-rounded candidate with tremendous upside potential. She is still with the company, now a senior vice-president. This was our first search, of many, with this company, and this person established the ongoing standard of quality for top candidates. Without the company's thoroughness in seeking balance, this person probably would not have been hired. We can all learn from this lesson in hiring techniques.

It doesn't take any extra time to complete the assessment across all the critical factors. Once you become familiar with the concepts, the evaluation will naturally occur during the interview. The eight-question interview, especially the four core performance-based questions, will be enough to uncover most of the information you need to make a well-reasoned hiring decision. You just have to know how to interpret the answers. The rush to judgment is what causes most of the problems.

Many years ago, a VP Finance at one of the entertainment companies let a top-notch candidate slip away. He was an intuitive interviewer and liked applicants who were smart, socially confident, and assertive. We sent in a great candidate who had all three traits in spades and more, yet tended to be a little tongue-tied early in the interview. I knew this and suggested to our client that he wait at least 30 minutes before making any judgment. The VP ignored my advice, and within 15 minutes had eliminated this very promising young man from consideration. This candidate subsequently took a job at a competing entertainment company, and now, 10 years later, is one of their senior executives.

You can't afford to lose top-notch people for the wrong reasons. To prevent it from happening, you need to keep an open mind and carefully measure all the critical factors before reaching any conclusions. If you're getting input from others on some of these factors, make sure they also conduct a thorough interview. Your interviewing and assessment skills are as important as the quality of the candidate in getting to the right answer.

■ THE TEN-FACTOR CANDIDATE ASSESSMENT— WHAT YOU NEED TO KNOW TO MAKE AN ACCURATE DECISION

To ensure this balance, use the template shown in Table 7.1 when assessing a candidate. The Ten-Factor Performance-Based Assessment identifies the areas we've determined to be most critical to overall success. The columns provide brief guidelines for evaluating each category. Rank each trait factor on a scale of 1 to 5, based on the description shown. This provides an easy means to rank the candidate by trait group. Don't make a hiring decision if you haven't measured all 10 factors accurately. Take notes during the interview. If a candidate is particularly strong or weak in one category, make sure you indicate why in your notes. These notes will help you make the necessary trade-offs later on when you begin comparing candidates. Major strengths may offset what initially appears to be a deal-breaking weakness. Likewise, major strengths don't appear as important in the face of a critical void. Try not to make the final decision until each factor has been considered. When there is a rush to hire, people always tend to make premature decisions without all the facts.

➤ Energy, Drive, and Initiative

Don't ever compromise on this one. It's the universal trait of success. The best people in any job have lots of energy and initiative.

Table 7.1 The Ten-Factor Performance-Based Assessment

Trait/Factor	Scale—Weak (1) to Strong (5)					Score
	1	2	3	4	5	
1. Energy, Drive, Initiative	Little energy shown in any previous job. Passive work performance.	Generally consistent performance, but never exceeds expectations.	Consistent level of performance with spotty periods of high levels of energy.	Generally highly motivated, but some periods of average performance.	Consistent self-starter. Many examples of exceeding expectations in all jobs.	
2. Trend of Performance over Time	Growth trend spotty and inconsistent with the basic needs of the position.	Trend of growth down, but meets the basic needs of the position.	Trend of growth flattened, but still consistent with needs of position.	Trend of growth strongly upward although candidate might not be quite there.	Upward pattern of growth and increasing track record of performance.	
3 Comparability of Past Accomplishments (Anchor SMART Objectives)	No job needs are directly met. The gap is too wide to overcome.	Only one or two SMART objectives are met, but too many voids to address quickly.	Meets key SMART objectives with some voids that can be addressed.	Meets majority of SMART objectives with only little compromise needed.	Favorable comparison of past accomplishments with all SMART objectives.	
4. Experience, Education, and Industry Background	Weak fit on all standard measures: not enough experience or education.	Adequate experience, education. A stretch to meet minimum standards.	Solid education and experience, consistent with needs of position.	Direct education and experience exceeds current job needs.	Very strong comparable experience with good industry and educational fit.	
5. Problem Solving and Thinking Skills (Visualize SMART Objectives)	Structured thinking. Inability to adapt knowledge to new situations.	Some ability to upgrade and modify existing methods and processes.	Able to understand basic issues and come up with some alternative solutions.	Has ability to understand most issues and develop new solutions.	Has ability to understand all issues and develop and communicate solutions.	
6. Overall Talent, Technical Competency, and Potential	Little direct technical competence and inability to learn within reasonable time.	Some technical ability and talent, but might take too long to come up to standard.	Technically competent. Reasonable ability to learn. Narrow focus on job only.	Technically strong, smart, ability to learn quickly. Broader focus. Sees related issues.	Very talented, learns quickly, strategic, tactical, and technical focus. Very broad perspective.	
7. Management and Organizational Ability	Little relevant management experience or unable to organize similar projects.	Some management ability, but insufficient to make contribution anytime soon.	Reasonable management experience. Will have to grow to become more effective.	Solid manager and organizer. Exceeds the needs of the position.	Has strong ability to manage and organize groups of similar size and type of staff.	

Table 7.1 *(continued)*

Trait/Factor	Scale—Weak (1) to Strong (5)					Score
	1	2	3	4	5	
8. Team Leader ship—Persuade/Motivate Others	Little evidence of persuading or leading others. Tends to be more individualistic.	Some evidence of team skills, but inconclusive. Generally more individualistic.	Solid team leadership skills or potential, but not completely apparent.	Seems to have very strong team leadership, but not completely tested.	Strong track record. Has the ability to motivate and develop others. Positive Attitude.	
9. Character—Values, Commitment, Goals	Questionable values and integrity. Self-serving. Misleading.	Reasonably solid values and ethics, but questions remain regarding candor.	Appropriate values and ethics. No significant problems and no unusual strengths.	A committed person. Good character, values, and attitude.	High integrity, committed person with strong values and ethics. Frank and candid.	
10. Personality and Cultural Fit	Fatal flaw or some imbalance or poor attitude and fit with existing team.	Adequate fit, but could cause some degree of conflict or might have negative impact.	All around solid person. Will fit with group without causing much conflict.	Generally positive attitude. Personality will help in performance of job.	Balanced ego, positive attitude, flexible, can work with others. Personality strength.	
Total Point Score	Rank each trait on a 0–5 scale. Reinterview the candidate if insufficient information is available for any category. Multiple total score by two (× 2) to compare with 100.					

The key to personal success is to do more than required. Look for this in every past job. Get examples of initiative and extra effort. People who have lots of energy show it in lots of ways. Don't assume that an extroverted personality means lots of energy. Have the candidate prove it with lots of examples including specific facts, dates, and quantities. You'll be able to eliminate a number of candidates who are socially assertive, but not necessarily leaders on the job. Likewise, don't stereotype calm or quiet candidates; they can often be more energetic on the job than outgoing people, but you still need to get proof.

One of the most frequent mistakes made by interviewers is to assume that a low-key person lacks energy and enthusiasm. You need to be patient to bring these people out, but once you find their area of interest, you'll often find a star. These are the great surprises—the people who exceed expectations. Don't forget that the anxiety of the interview can put a damper on even the most confident. The process of fact-finding and getting examples will help overcome this temporary condition and allow you to find the core of all great success—personal energy, commitment, and initiative.

Don't ignore those just starting their careers from this examination. Look for special projects, extra effort, and major accomplishments even in recent grads. This could be in the form of schoolwork, extracurricular activities, or part-time jobs. Highly motivated people always do more than required, and this trait is evident early in a career. The work might not be comparable to your needs, but that's secondary.

My son spent the last semester of his senior college year putting together a CD for his singing group under a concert deadline. This took many 12- to 14-hour days for about eight weeks, and while his grades suffered, he got some great experience. He and his partners in what I first considered an ill-advised project went the extra mile in dealing with vendors, printers, publicists, and a recording studio 150 miles away. All this, while rehearsing for the major year-end concert. Both were successes. Extra effort, wherever applied, is an important characteristic of all successful people. Look for it in every person you hire.

If there are no big projects to focus on, go for the smaller successes. In this case always ask for three—three examples of initiative, three examples of exceeding expectations, or three examples of where the candidate did more than required. Everyone can come up with one or two. Few can come up with three good ones. And these are the ones you want to hire. You know you have a problem if the second or third example is pretty lame.

During an interview to hire a secretary, I asked the candidate to describe three things she did on her previous job that she started on her own. She promptly told me about learning and writing a number of complex Word macros, setting up an open-invoice tracking system on Excel, and reorganizing large mailings with an outside production company. This is the stuff of heroes, and she's still doing it for us today.

Rank the candidate at five if you observe a pattern of consistent and high energy in every job. Average people do just what's expected of them. A two or three is appropriate for this group.

➤ Trend of Performance over Time

Using the impact/leadership questioning pattern, we get detailed examples of major accomplishments and organizational changes for the past 5 to 10 years. From this, it is easy to see how the candidate has grown and impacted the organization. The ideal candidate is one who has had comparable jobs and who is still showing signs of upward growth. Rank this person a five.

A comparable job doesn't need to be an identical job. Look at staff size, complexity of the issues, standards of performance, rate of company growth, and level of sophistication. Combine these factors and look for an upward growth pattern.

On a recent engineering management search in the telecommunications industry, we had a close match with staff size, growth rates, the product development process, and the level of systems support and sophistication. The candidate was pretty far off on the technology side, though. He compensated for this by demonstrating an ability to learn new technology very quickly and to hire great people. By taking a balanced look at strengths and weaknesses, we looked at engineering managers who demonstrated an upward trend of management growth, independent from the technology. This allowed us to find a great candidate who otherwise might have been overlooked. He scored a strong four on this upward growth factor.

If the growth pattern had been flat for this candidate, we would have required him to be stronger on the technology side. Give a two or three if the trend is flat and the comparability is a little weak. You need to use your judgment on this because there are so many factors to consider. A pattern of upward growth is always more important than experience. These are the people who get promoted, so look for this in the people you hire.

I recently met a VP Finance candidate who had a strong work ethic, was highly energetic, and always seemed to be taking on new projects. I ranked him a five in Energy, but only a three in the Trend of Performance category. While he was self-motivated, he had been at the same management level for the past 10 years, an indication that he had plateaued careerwise. I still recommended that the company consider him for the position, since his skills were consistent with the needs of the job, but I didn't expect him to ever take on a significantly bigger job.

➤ Comparability of Past Accomplishments

Anchoring SMART objectives allows the interviewer to compare a candidate's past accomplishments with the required performance objectives of the open position. Except in one area, this same candidate for the VP Finance position ranked very high in this comparability of past accomplishments category. He fell short on an important strategic objective of the job. His accomplishments, while great, were technical or tactical in nature.

The company needed someone to guide their long-range planning process and bring business level advice to a relatively young management team. The candidate was adequate in this area, but did not bring the leadership qualities the company needed. He was so strong in all the other areas—systems, performance reporting, internal controls, and financing—that I still ranked him a four, downgrading him slightly for one deficiency. The CEO ranked him a three since he felt the lack of the strategic focus was a critical void. He weighed this one SMART objective higher than all the others combined. We quickly resolved our difference of opinion since it was based on the real performance needs of the job, not some artificial criterion. This is why understanding the performance objectives is so important to an accurate assessment.

Also be concerned about mismatching. Work-type profiling can really help here. While personal energy is a prerequisite for success, it's even better when the candidate applies natural energy to real job needs. For example, a highly energetic designer might be ineffective as a manager. Work-type profiling ensures that a candidate's accomplishments match the needs of the job as determined by the SMART objectives. Mismatching at this level is one of the most common hiring mistakes.

This can happen when you hire a bright consultant-type for a technical or management position. These people sound great, but often flounder when they have to do the work, not just talk about it. Equally common is hiring a great technical person for a management position. When you want to hire a manager look for management accomplishments, not technical ones. And just because entrepreneurs exude energy, don't assume they can apply it equally to all tasks. Work-type profiling is a technique to break down the job and analyze best fit. A mismatch can often be confirmed by some of the more traditional measures such as the lack of comparable anchors.

Make sure you have a copy of all the SMART objectives with you during the interview. Get anchoring accomplishments for each one. Give a five if the candidate has a comparable accomplishment for each one, a four if all but one matches, and so on. The accomplishments don't have to be identical to match up. Look at the scope and complexity of the task against the needs of the job. In a recent assignment, I categorized a logistics position in a food packaging plant as being similar to a materials manager in office products. Both positions had about 12 people in the department, the systems issues were similar, and the needed changes required the same organizational and team skills.

Rank the candidate very low on the category if there are only one or two reasonable matches out of a total of five or six SMART objectives. Also rank the candidate low if the work-types don't match too well. This happens most often when you need a strong manager. Be careful if the candidate applies most energy to technical or creative areas, or seems to like the deal-making aspects of business. There's a tendency to compromise on this point. If management skills are important, make sure you hire someone who has a track record of proactive management accomplishments.

➤ Experience, Education, and Industry Background

Assess this Experience, Education, and Industry Background category in conjunction with the Past Accomplishments category. Strong experience and education can sometimes offset a weaker accomplishments rating.

Examine experience in the context of the environment. By this, we mean the pace, style, and standards of performance of the companies where the experience was earned. This background is very important. If the candidate's previous company had lower standards and the pace was much slower, ten years of seemingly relevant experience doesn't mean much. Likewise, 2 years of experience can be worth 10 if the candidate performed at stellar levels in a world-class company going through rapid change.

Experience and accomplishments have to be measured in context with this underlying environment. As you gain information about the candidate's accomplishment, always spend a few minutes to explore this environmental area. Ask about the candidate's supervisor, the standards imposed, the quality of the systems and support structure, and the pace of the work activity. This information will provide you with important clues to address this important issue.

Give the highest ranking to those with accomplishments and experiences that are comparable to the job needs, and that took place in more challenging environments. I'd still give very strong rankings to those that have done well in these more challenging environments, even if the jobs don't seem as big. Assign lower rankings to those candidates who seem to have comparable experience, but in less stellar organizations. Of course, don't ignore candidates from these organizations if they've been able to rebuild and upgrade them. You need to consider the experience and accomplishments in combination with the environment. Together, these factors tell you a lot about the real competence and quality of the candidate.

Give some credit to direct industry experience and education. Add a point or two to the score if these add significantly to the candidate's ability or improve the job fit. Subtract a point or two if they detract from the experience and the environment.

➤ Problem-Solving and Thinking Skills

Somebody asked me how smart a person needs to be to be effective on the job. My response was just smart enough, but any less and you're in trouble. A strong candidate needs to understand the work, solve job-related problems, and anticipate what needs to get done. Collecting and processing information to make appropriate decisions is part of it. So is the ability to apply previous knowledge and experiences in solving new problems. This is what the visualization question is intended to assess. You'll be directly testing for problem-solving and thinking skills when you have the candidate visualize the SMART objective. Their responses, discussions, and even questions will give you direct insight into this important area. Intelligence tests get at this issue indirectly and are less reliable.

How the candidate organizes a job-specific future objective or evaluates a current problem requires insight and understanding.

The quality of the questions asked are a strong indicator of insight, knowledge, and their practical application. From the give-and-take of the visualization questioning, you observe the intellect at work. This overcomes the traditional problem with most interviewing questions in that you only talk about work, not really do it. With the visualization approach, and good give-and-take, the planning aspects of the work are actually being conducted. From this, you'll gain an understanding of the candidate's thinking and reasoning skills, adaptability, communication skills, logic, decision making, knowledge, and problem-solving ability. With this added insight, you'll know whether the candidate is smart enough.

The quality of the candidate's questions form a part of the visualization component. Ask the candidate what kinds of questions she would ask to get the information needed to start on one of the performance objectives. Lots of pertinent questions, but limited experience, is a sign of a high potential person. Raise the caution flag if the candidate's experience is strong, but the questioning is weak. These people have difficulty adapting to new situations. Don't give more than a three to a candidate who is poor at visualizing. When selecting candidates, you often must make a trade-off between experience and potential. My favorite mix includes lots of potential, just enough comparable experience, and a track record of being able to learn quickly. Ask candidates to describe their greatest accomplishment with the least amount of experience. You'll get at all three with this answer.

On an assignment a few years ago for a marketing director for a direct mail company, I asked each of the candidates to describe how they would re-layout the company's catalog. About a third of the candidates knew exactly what to do. They spent a few minutes reviewing the catalog, asked me some insightful questions, described what additional information they needed, and then suggested a number of courses of action based on different alternatives. This group deserved a five in this category. Another third of the candidates asked some good questions, but didn't take them anywhere. Their ideas about what to do were vague and too general. This was worth a three. The remaining third didn't even ask relevant questions. They seemed to be clueless as to what to do. This group barely ranked a one.

The catalog re-layout was a real task for the position, and within five minutes it was very apparent who was going to be able to get it right and who wasn't. This is the power of the visualization question. Use it with the most important SMART objectives to get a well-rounded picture of the candidate's problem solving and thinking skills across all dimensions of the job. You'll get misleading results with indirect approaches. I know one senior financial executive in the food industry who asks all his candidates how they would market and produce a lightbulb. While this might get at good creative and strategic thinking, it has little relevance to financial analysis work. The job-related visualization questions provide a great alternative.

Sometimes we hire very bright, capable people for the wrong job. A clue to this is revealed in the way a person thinks. Different jobs require different types of intelligence.[1] During my executive search work I've observed three broad categories of intellect. Interestingly, being good at one doesn't imply being good at another. Review these to see where your candidate fits based on the needs of the job.

Technical Intelligence

This has to do with analysis, processing of detailed information, and systematic thinking. Those ranking high in math do well in this area. Have the candidate give you examples of this type of problem solving to assess competency here. For a visualization question, ask the candidate to describe the process he'd use to solve an analytical problem. Ask someone in financial analysis to describe the process for finding out why costs have increased in a certain area. In manufacturing, find out why a certain process has gone awry. Match needs with competency and rank the candidate high in this area if the job demands this type of analytical thinking.

Tactical Intelligence

This is oriented toward marshaling resources, getting team results, coming up with practical and pragmatic solutions, and being focused on the bottom line. These organization skills are found in

---

[1] The book, *Emotional Intelligence,* by Daniel Goldman (New York: Bantam Books, 1995), addresses this issue to some degree, by describing a variety of different types of intelligence.

some of the best managers, or those with a more practical attitude. These people have the ability to adapt to the situation at hand. Get the candidate to give you examples of where trade-offs had to be made, or even have her prioritize the list of SMART objectives. To get at this trait for a copy center manager, we asked candidates to describe how they would prioritize and schedule five different types of copy orders. Look for a commonsense approach to thinking and decision making. It takes the real world into account, recognizing the need to balance competing objectives.

Strategic or Creative Intelligence

Thinking about or planning the future or being able to understand long-range consequences of current actions is one aspect of this type of thinking. This also covers creativity, conceptualizing ideas, seeing the big picture, coming up with new products, or new approaches or anything that's out-of-the-box. Get examples of related accomplishments to validate competency. To test this I had a functional VP describe the strategic impact on the company of her department's new role. She did okay, but it was clear she had a more functional than business perspective, and I ranked her a three. The key is to get examples of creativity or of this strategic thinking. This is an important skill for all VP level positions. Be careful. Some candidates possess this skill, but it could backfire if that's all they have. We often hire bright people like this and are later disappointed when they don't deliver on other aspects of the job. Don't be overwhelmed by a bright, creative mind if it's one-dimensional.

Superior thinking and problem-solving ability requires a combination of skills. Rank the candidate a five for a clear understanding of the work requirements, insightful questions, and strong responses. Drop the candidate down a point or two if there are too many questions, too few, or if they are widely scattered. Too many is a sign of good reasoning, but lack of experience. Too few is a sign of structured thinking. Widely scattered is a sign of floundering. Listen carefully and take notes. The candidate's responses to the visualization questions will help validate your assessment. Look for crisp responses. Assign a one or a two when a candidate doesn't even know how to begin a project, or what to look for in solving problems.

➤ Overall Talent, Technical Competency, and Potential

This broad category encompasses a lot of related but separate competencies. How you'll rank a candidate will depend on the needs of the job. The score should represent the candidate's ability to grow and develop and take on bigger roles. High potential people have the ability to handle the current job, and eventually larger challenges. To get a four or five in this category, candidates have to have a broader focus than demanded by the job. I look at three areas to gauge this:

1. Thinking skills.
2. Breadth of business understanding.
3. Application of technical skills.

The first category addresses the same technical, tactical, and strategic thinking area described in the problem-solving section. That category is more job specific. Since these same skills are also one aspect of potential, it's important to reconsider them in combination with some other traits when evaluating potential. I'll rank someone high in potential when they demonstrate a strong ability in each of these three broad areas. These are the skills that will allow a person to move to another level and they need to demonstrate competency in each, over and above the immediate needs of the job.

I remember an impressive financial analyst I met about 10 years ago. He was technically competent, and even though he was only a few years out of school he was already managing small groups. In addition, he really understood the strategic impact of all the financial advice he was providing. He was an insightful problem solver, and also recognized the role that finance could play in helping other functions operate more effectively together. I lost track of him until just this past year and was not surprised to discover that he is now the president of a mid-size and fast-growing medical products company. He demonstrated all the traits of high potential thinking and competency long before they were to come into play. At our luncheon meeting, I could tell he still had the capacity to continue his rise up the corporate ladder.

The second area of potential has to do with breadth of understanding and business perspective. Candidates who see the broader needs of the business beyond their own functional requirements add strength to an organization. Effective product managers understand the competing needs of engineering, sales, marketing, and manufacturing. That's why many of these people move into general management. I recently interviewed a candidate for a manufacturing position, who was also very strong in systems and cost accounting. While she didn't have all the direct experience needed to handle the manufacturing job right away, I was comfortable recommending her and ranking her a five in potential, because she added more to the job in other important ways.

CPAs get the bad rap that they're too focused on the internal process accounting issues and don't appreciate the needs of the other functions. It's frequently true, but you need to test it out with the visualization questions, rather than stereotype all CPAs this way. MBAs in finance and accounting tend to be weaker technically, but broader in focus. As a result, they are better able to balance all the business needs. Whether MBA, CPA, or whatever, look for this broader perspective when evaluating potential, since this is a prerequisite for upper management.

The third area has to do with the application of technical competency. Unless you have a technically intensive job, I'd be more concerned about the ability to learn these technical skills than looking for someone who already has them. Minimal technical knowledge plus the capacity to learn is often a better trade-off. If you do have a technical job, I'd be more interested in the application of the skills in problem solving and accomplishing real work than in the quality and quantity of these skills. For example, if you need products designed that rely on a technological base, it's better to get examples from the candidate of comparable products they've designed and under what circumstances. The technical skills, while important, are secondary to the organizational and business conditions.

I've seen lots of technical people miss the mark here by focusing too much on technical issues and not enough on their practical application. A number of years ago, we had a search for a CFO of a Fortune 500 company. The CEO insisted that the candidate must have hands-on experience as a cost accountant and be good at it. This was his number one priority. I asked how would this skill be used on the job. The CEO said it was needed to set up a multiplant performance reporting system, evaluate each manufacturing plant's performance, and hire good plant controllers. As he wrote these down, he recognized it wasn't the cost accounting skill that was important, but its application in preparing and evaluating reports, and in hiring people with the skill. This then became the job requirement.

Look at the prioritized list of SMART objectives for clues to see if you're overvaluing technical competency at the expense of potential. This is a bad trade-off. If the technical performance objectives are not at the top of the list, you can soften up a bit on this requirement. By focusing on the outcome of the skills or knowledge, instead of on the skill or knowledge itself, you get a much more realistic assessment of the candidate's competency.

When ranking talent and potential for management positions, be more concerned with broader thinking skills and business understanding. Give a five to those strong in both. Give a four for strength in one, without the other. A three goes to those who are solid in both, but not superior in either. For technically intense positions, your ranking should reflect the candidate's technical strength, but you need to consider all three categories based in real job needs. A great technical person still needs to have breadth of understanding to move up. Be cautious about a great technologist who doesn't have a practical side, or doesn't understand some of the related business or management issues. These will become determents to upward growth. Under this condition, a score of three or less is appropriate.

➤ Management and Organization

Most interviewers focus on individual competency instead of managerial skills. This approach is a major cause of hiring error. If the management and organizational aspects of the job are important, spend as much time as necessary to validate the candidate's competency. Rank candidates high if their management track record compares favorably with the needs of the job. This means they have managed, built, and developed groups of similar size and have achieved similar results. Be careful not to measure individual contributor skills as you assess this factor. This is a common mistake.

Use projects to get at organizational skills, even if the candidate doesn't have a big staff. I recently met a candidate for an operations position requiring a person to organize a number of small teams over many facilities. The job required strong communications, coordination, and planning skills. At first, I didn't think the candidate possessed the necessary management skills to handle the job since he seemed too technical.

To better understand his organization skills, I asked him to describe the most complex project team he had led. He told me about a eight-month crash project to get a complex piece of automation equipment debugged, installed, and operational. He took over when the project was eight months behind schedule. The successful completion of the task required the coordinated efforts of a dozen engineering and manufacturing personnel, while balancing the competing needs of his own company, the customer, and two other major vendors. Budgets were tight, tempers were on edge, and the credibility of his company was on the line. He won an award for his efforts and the appropriate kudos. There was no doubt he could handle what now appeared to be my client's pretty tame management need.

Early in the interview, have the candidate draw an organization chart for the last few positions. Assign names, titles, and direct and indirect staff size. This provides a size and scope of responsibility comparison for your current job needs. Have the candidate rank the performance of each key staff member. Look for a pattern of building, managing, and developing strong teams. Ask the candidate to describe her most significant management accomplishment. Compare the insight, enthusiasm, and detail provided in this response with the individual contributor accomplishments. Even the length of the answer is important. These differences can reveal a candidate's preferences for individual contributor or management projects.

Rank the candidate high if she's a proactive manager with a track record of managing similar sized groups, handling similar work, and completing comparable projects. To earn a five, the candidate would need to have these abilities, plus demonstrated performance building top teams wherever she went. I give a three for solid, basic comparable management experience. These people can adequately run the department, but not grow it into anything special.

Be concerned about candidates who have lots of turnover within the group, complain about their staff, and seem to talk less or in more general terms about management successes. This is a one. A person would get a two for solid management skills that are, however, too light for the current job. You still might want to consider this person if there are some offsetting strengths, especially team leadership and strong organizational skills. Get references from subordinates to validate any of your conclusions. They have the best perspective on someone's management skills.

For nonmanagers, look more at team projects to get at this trait. Give high rankings to those who have taken on extra duties in getting team results. Make sure you check out the results in detail, the steps taken to achieve them, and any challenges the candidate had to face along the way. People who become strong managers have the ability to persuade and motivate others, possess very strong organizational skills, and go the extra mile for the good of the group. These people are ready to be managers when the circumstances warrant it.

➤ Team Leadership—The Ability to Persuade and Motivate Others

Team leadership is a component of both management and the interpersonal skills part of personality. It is important enough to consider separately. In sum, it represents the ability to tap into and harness the energy of others. Getting people to do something they don't want to do, or to get a group of people to move in the same direction, without threats or coercion, is a wonderful skill.

Team leadership has two dimensions, one organized around the subordinate team, and the other having to do with coworkers in different departments. Whenever a person has some degree of power over another, the team leadership component gets clouded. Motivating a subordinate is easier than motivating someone who doesn't work for you. In this case, I look for managers who have a track record of developing their staff. They can point to a number of people whom they have personally helped become successful. They are proactive with respect to this staff development issue and take great pride in it. As a result, they have the ability to inspire their own staff to exceed expectations. When you ask about these achievements, get names and examples of people they have helped. Find out whether it was a formal program or ad hoc. Give high rankings to those who consistently go out of their way to hire superior people and then take a sincere interest in upgrading the skills of each team member.

Team leadership is also important in dealing with people outside a person's own department. The ability to persuade and motivate people who don't work for you is a critical component of leadership. Examine this area for managers and nonmanagers alike. Get examples of major team projects and use fact-finding to uncover the candidate's true role. Ask for examples of dealing with conflict and persuading others to change their position; determine how compromises were made. Inquire about dealing with difficult people in other functions and find out how this was handled. People who rank high in this aspect of team leadership are often selected to lead groups, always do more than they're required to do within the group, and understand how to develop win/win situations. They are sensitive to the needs of others and can describe numerous examples of similar team leadership roles.

People who are extroverted have an easier time with this team leadership trait, but don't jump to quick conclusions. Not all extroverted people are strong at team leadership. Those who are too individualistic or have overblown egos create more problems than solutions. Introverted people can be great team leaders, too, you just have to work more to get them to open up.

Another aspect of team leadership is attitude and confidence. Don't be fooled. Social confidence in the interview is not the same as real confidence in getting the work done. Confidence and a positive attitude of a "can do" optimism go hand in hand. Together, they can inspire individuals and teams. It's a core trait of strong leadership. A positive attitude is an essential trait of all continuing success. In Martin Seligman's fine book, *Learned Optimism* (New York: Pocket Books, 1992), the author describes the importance of a positive attitude and how to measure and develop it.

Having a positive attitude doesn't ensure success, but not having it is certainly a step toward failure. You can get some direct sense of positive attitude and confidence by examining the candidate's greatest challenges and even failures. The ability to bounce back from defeat or handle lots of conflict and pressure is a strong indicator of a positive attitude. Get examples of what the candidate did when things went wrong at both the individual and team level. Find out how the candidate handled adversity whether personal or as a leader of a group. Getting others through tough times combines this positive attitude with team leadership. I heard Paul Westphal, the former NBA and college basketball coach, say that the strongest trees weather the strongest storms. It's good interviewing advice. Find candidates who have weathered tough storms.

Rank managers a four or a five if they can develop and inspire their own team as well as take on team leadership roles with peers, supervisors, and even higher-level managers. Also look at team projects with customers, vendors, and outside professional service providers. This will give you insight into the range and degree of team leadership skills the candidate possesses. Being able to tap into the energy of others is a useful gift, especially if the other person is at a higher management level, has superior credentials, or is more influential. For nonmanagers, use team projects to get at this external ability to influence, persuade, and motivate others. A positive attitude and self-confidence are important aspects of this skill.

Rank the candidate a three if you're concerned about attitude, don't get as many examples as you'd like, or sense that this isn't one of the candidate's obvious strengths. Weak communications skills, a bad attitude, not a lot of personal confidence, and faulty logic are clues to weakness in this category. Rank the candidate a one or a two if you observe these clues. These rankings should be adjusted to reflect the degree of leadership required on the job. This trait is more important for companies going through significant change, less if you just want someone to maintain the status quo.

➤ Character—Values, Commitment, and Goals

Character is a deep-rooted trait that summarizes a person's integrity, honesty, responsibility, openness, fairness in dealing with others, and personal values. Save this whole topic until the end of the first interview, or wait for the second interview. Not only is it more relevant then, but candidates will also be more comfortable and more open with their responses. On-the-job performance reflects the person's character, so you'll learn a great deal about character during your performance-based questioning.

Ask candidates the basis of their personal value system and how they developed it. Be sure to listen carefully. If you've built an open relationship with the candidate, this answer can be very revealing. At one presentation, I asked a similar question of a volunteer. His response was heartwarming. He told the group he was once an addict and had lost everything. As a result of rebuilding his life, he learned the value of relationships and personal commitment, which were far more important to him now than material possessions. The relationship between him and the rest of the group changed instantly as a result of this revelation. This is what can happen when true character is revealed.

It's important to know why someone wants to change jobs and what aspects of work the person finds important. Just ask. This will help determine both fit and satisfaction. If the basic needs of the job are incompatible with the candidate's motivational needs, you'll only create problems later on. Understanding a person's value system allows you to predict how the candidate will react under various work-related circumstances. If work is a secondary priority in the person's life, you could be in trouble if you need to rely on him for an upcoming crash project, even if he agrees to do it.

Having goals is an important part of character and personal motivation, but the typical questions can be misleading. Everyone has goals, many of them lofty, but most people rarely achieve them. A better approach is to first ask the candidate to describe one or two major goals already accomplished. Look for a pattern of goal setting and achievement. Once you establish this sequence, then ask about future goals. If they're consistent with the pattern, you've got a winner. It's easy to talk about future goals, but it means little if nothing has ever been attained. Compare the size of the goals already reached with any future goals and with the needs of the job. Ask if the goals are in writing. This helps validate the candidate's real, versus stated, philosophy. Goals always require a series of steps before they're completed. Ask about this progress.

Every one of my candidates wants to be promoted to the next level. I ask them how they are improving themselves to get ready. A few are doing something proactively by continuing their education, volunteering for new work, or taking the initiative on expanding the role of the job without any expectations of reward. Goals are meaningful when there is a pattern of constant personal growth, self-motivation, self-sacrifice, and a track record of goal setting and achievement.

Commitment is a critical component of character that complements energy and potential. Ask the candidate to give you an example of when he or she was totally committed to a task. Some high-energy people are great starters, but poor finishers. Look for a pattern of meeting deadlines. Get related examples. Find out when the candidate missed an important target. Determine the recovery response. A one-time commitment while important, just sets the stage. It's the consistent pattern that counts. Determine the source of the commitment and the failure. Was it an internal factor like a personal commitment to another person or a desire to achieve a long sought-after goal? Was the failure due to lack of resources, insufficient knowledge, or weak personal commitment? This is an important topic with many possible outcomes. You might not come up with the complete answer, but you'll always learn more about the candidate if you look hard.

A reference check for an engineering manager seemed to indicate an inability to achieve commitments on product delivery. It turned out to be true for reasons other than lack of personal commitment and desire. This was the first senior management assignment for the engineer, and while he worked 12- to 14-hour days, this still wasn't enough to get the job done. Initially, he was over his head. Once new resources became available, his growth as a manager began to change. His personal commitment was always there. Now he was learning how to make commitments for his department, a different and much more challenging skill.

When assessing character, look for frank and open responses, especially regarding the failures. Does the candidate take responsibility for both the successes and the bombs, or is it all one-sided? Also be concerned if the answers become vague, too short, or too general. This is a sign of misleading or avoidance. Rank the candidate a five in character when you observe the combination of sincerity with a sense of commitment, strong values, and a pattern of goal setting and achievement. Look for honesty, actions, and decisions based on right and wrong, and an ability to openly express a point of view.

Rank the person a three if you have no strong sense about character and values, either strong or weak. If something disturbs you about the candidate, like the feeling of being misled, a fraudulent resume, or an answer that doesn't ring true, rank the candidate a one or two. We immediately eliminate a candidate in this case.

➤ Personality and Cultural Fit

Personality is revealed in the individual's accomplishments. So without any specific questioning or personality tests, you'll still get a good sense of how the candidate will work with you and your group just by asking about major accomplishments. Look for flexibility and a pattern of accomplishments in different situations, as a team member, leader of the team, and as an individual contributor. Be concerned if every accomplishment relies on the same strengths. I met a VP/Controller candidate who relied on his strong analytical and negotiating skills in each major accomplishment. He sounded good during the first half hour of the interview describing significant financing roles and describing how he identified all the operating problems of a major company. Soon the real pattern emerged. He was weak in building and developing teams. He was excluded as candidate since his individual contributor style wouldn't work well either in managing others, or in dealing with the senior management of the company.

You can discover a preferred relationship pattern by categorizing the person's accomplishments according to the ABC scale—**A**lone, **B**elong to team, or in-**C**harge of the team. This type of analysis becomes even more valuable when the candidate is free to pick the accomplishment. Ask the candidate to describe a favorite work experience or to give you examples of problems she likes to solve. Keep track of these responses by putting little tick marks on the top of your notes. I make three columns, the A on the left, B in the middle, and C on the right. When the candidate describes an individual contributor task, just put a tick mark under the A column. Put a mark under the B column for team-related work, and under the C for a management or leadership role. By the end of the interview, a definite and revealing pattern will emerge.

The use of "I" by itself is not indicative of an individual contributor, it's the type of project or work that counts. You might get lots of "I's" regarding team projects, so listen carefully. These could be B's, not A's. At the end of the interview, this collection of tick marks will provide insight into the candidate's preferred way of working. Lots of A's signal an individual contributor. A manager inclination would have more C's. The real team player would have a majority of B's.

How someone scores depends on the needs of the job. If the job is an individual contributor role (salesperson, technician, analyst, or consultant), make sure you hire someone who likes to work alone. If you need a manager to lead a group to get results be careful to observe this pattern. Be concerned if a candidate shows little balance or is too one-dimensional. Most jobs require some mix of all three. Pure individualists, dominant directors, and consummate team players can all be a source of problems. Remember no pattern is bad, it all depends on the needs of the job.

I once conducted a phone interview for a sales manager for a high-tech product line. The candidate was very aggressive and all his major accomplishments were related to him closing impressive deals. The "I" word was in every sentence. The "A" column had 75% of the tick marks. In this case, the person was a very strong, persuasive, individual contributor. While he was a top-notch salesperson, I couldn't recommend him for a management position. Toward the end of the interview, I asked him what he thought his greatest strength was. A "people person," was his immediate response. Although I wouldn't have categorized him this way, he believed being a strong people person meant having the ability to persuade and sell others. For me, someone has to have at least one-third of the ticks in the B column to merit this description. You'll learn a lot about interpersonal skills and flexibility by keeping track of accomplishments according to this ABC classification.

Personality should be used to exclude candidates rather than to include them. It's recognized that personality problems are a frequent cause of problems on the job. Conflict, ego, inability to work with others, and immaturity all result in friction, inefficiency, loss of morale, and turnover. These fatal flaws should immediately eliminate a candidate from consideration.

Most people are easy enough to work with, so if they don't have any of these flaws rank them at least a three. Rank them higher if their personality helps them do their job better. For customer service and salespeople, this is a critical need, so don't compromise here. A strong personality plus an appropriate ABC balance deserves a four or five. For most positions, it's best to remember that you're not hiring a best friend, but just a co-worker. Personality tests and reference checks will help you sort through this.

The Ten-Factor Candidate Assessment is as much a checklist of what a good interview needs to address as it is an evaluation tool. If you've measured all these factors during the interviewing process, your assessment will be extremely accurate. It's a great road map to identify the traits of top performers. Going through the process is the real key. You can't exclude or include candidates too soon. This approach will lead you to a balanced assessment, considering strengths and weaknesses in an objective manner. If your assessment is based on feelings rather than specific examples, you should re-interview the candidate.

While you might want to complete the Ten-Factor Assessment right after you meet the candidate, stay open-minded. Prepare a preliminary evaluation, and include in your notes why you ranked a candidates a certain way for each factor. Make sure you describe outstanding strengths and major weaknesses. Going through each factor will force you to review and consolidate your notes for each one of the factors. Update your evaluation of the candidate based on reference checks, additional interviews, testing, and the inputs of other interviewers. All these factors have to be considered before finalizing the assessment profile. This information and your notes provide the data for the formal written assessment.

■ SPOTTING FATAL FLAWS

Even apparently great candidates can have a fatal flaw. These are the less obvious traits that may cause a person to fail once on the job. An abusive personality, intolerance in some form, or an inability to make critical decisions under pressure are some common fatal flaws. These sometimes go unrecognized during the interview, either overlooked or masked by an offsetting strength. It's important for interviewers to recognize these flaws to prevent major hiring problems. Clues abound, but you must be observant and vigilant. Here's the lookout list. Raise the caution flag if you discover one of these tendencies or traits:

Fatal Flaws

➤ Great communicator, with lots of self-confidence, but management role doesn't seem to be growing. You may have found a great individual contributor or consultant-type person, but a weaker manager.

➤ Lots of drive and ambition, but too assertive. This could relate to ego problems, immaturity, or an inability to work in cross-functional teams.

➤ A dominant or stern personality. It might relate to assertiveness or indicate a negative attitude, lack of patience, or inability to persuade and motivate others.

➤ Extremes in any behavior—too analytical, too assertive, too friendly, or too persuasive. This usually leads to problems regarding lack of flexibility or balance.

➤ Lots of energy, great personality, but answers that are too general. This is a classic pattern—lots of sizzle, but little substance.

➤ Too many "I's" or "we's." This may indicate someone too hung up on himself, a predominant individual contributor or, in the "we" instance, a person who hasn't accomplished much on his own.

If you observe any of these signs, you must get proof to overcome the potential concern. The best way is to get an example of a significant example that disproves the potential fatal flaw. For example, if lack of team or management ability is the concern, get the candidate to describe his most significant management or team project. Get more than one example and make sure you get lots of facts, figures, dates, and names to substantiate the example.

For extremes in behavior, get examples of the opposite trait. Someone who is too friendly might not be strong-willed enough, and vice versa. Likewise, someone too persuasive might not be detailed enough. This is the typical salesperson problem. Get these people to describe some projects having to do with details or analytical work. Get the overzealous analyst or individual contributor to describe some important team projects. Then get specific examples of how she persuaded or motivated others to take actions against their better judgment. Reference checks and testing can help here. Do not ignore these caution flags. They can mean the difference between a great hire or a big problem.

This past year, we were involved in a situation with a candidate we placed who was very bright, assertive, and a great communicator. His references confirmed this, but indicated that he was only an adequate manager. He had the ability to hire strong people and then let them manage themselves, but even this wasn't high on his list. On the job, it became apparent that he didn't even want to spend the management time necessary to build a team. We were so excited about getting a candidate that was superb in all but one critical dimension, we minimized a potential fatal flaw. As a result, he was asked to leave within four months. You've got to do your homework with an open mind or else you miss or ignore the obvious.

Be especially careful when you evaluate the overuse of the "I" and "we" pronouns. This might indicate someone who is not team-oriented or a person who has few personal accomplishments. However, it could also just be the method the person chooses for communication. If the "I" usage relates only to personal projects, it reinforces this individual tendency. Just as frequently, however, it refers to a team project the candidate led, overriding the negative connotations. Be careful before you inadvertently eliminate a good candidate. Do some fact-finding to better understand the candidate's typical role in team projects. Conduct a similar analysis if the "we" dominates the discussion. In this case, look for the candidate's actual role in a number of different team projects. A lot of people get wrongly excluded or included for overuse of the wrong word. It's the substance that counts, not the manner in which it is described.

■ THE PROFESSIONALISM AND QUALITY OF THE INTERVIEW COUNT

Sometimes a weak assessment is more a result of bad interviewing skills than a weak candidate. You need to be a good interviewer to evaluate the candidate properly, and in the process you'll attract a better class of candidates. The best candidates want to work for great managers, and good interviewing skills should be an important showcase for a good manager. Candidates judge the quality of the company and the quality of their potential supervisor by the quality of the interviewing process.

Grading the quality and professionalism of the interview will highlight this important issue. Make sure you include all interviewers in this quality assessment. If you rely on the unexamined judgment of others and their skills are weak, the whole process may be compromised. I've seen highly qualified candidates lose out, because one or two interviewers missed the mark. The hiring manager has to be confident enough to override these flawed inputs. To help minimize this problem, you can give partial voting rights.

On a recent assignment, the CEO of a large financial organization wanted to reduce the scope of the inputs of a few members of the interviewing team, while still giving them the courtesy of having an input. We told this second round of interviewers that the CEO and CFO thought one candidate was the best prospect of the five they had already seen. They were told that their role was to determine whether there were any fatal flaws in the candidate that hadn't yet been detected. By limiting the authority of other interviewers this way, you can minimize the problems associated with weaker interviewers.

Sometimes the problem is the hiring manager's boss. This can be a serious issue if the boss is a weak interviewer or just wants to conduct a personality and fit interview. If you're ever in this position, it's best to write up why you want to hire the candidate beforehand, and ask your boss to validate one specific area only. The number one SMART objective is a good choice. By narrowing the scope of a less reliable interviewer, you can easily turn a personality contest into a mini-performance-based interview.

If the weak interviewer is the hiring manager, it's best to conduct a panel interview with some good interviewers taking the lead. This allows the hiring manager to participate. Lots of time is wasted and bad hiring decisions are made when incompetent interviewers influence the final decision. You must identify these problem people and establish alternative procedures ahead of time. Too much is riding on every hiring decision to allow controllable error to affect the outcome. Table 7.2 summarizes the factors that determine the quality and professionalism

Table 7.2 Assessing the Professionalism of the Interview and the Interviewer

Factor	Explanation	Rank
Level of Preparation	*Strong.* Read resume, prepared performance-based job description, conducted phone interview, and knew what to ask.	
	Good. Read the resume and reviewed the job spec.	
	Adequate. Looked at the stuff a few minutes before the interview.	
	Poor. Didn't look at anything before the interview.	
Length of Interview	*Strong* > 1 hour, multiple interviews.	
	Good. 45 minutes to 1 hour.	
	Adequate. 30–45 minutes.	
	Poor. < 30 minutes.	
Basic Interviewing Skills	*Strong.* Kept notes, listened 4 × more than talked, probed deeply, got lots of examples.	
	Good. Did some of the above, some of the time.	
	Adequate. Did a little of the above.	
	Poor. Relied more on emotions and gut feel.	
Length of time to make a decision to exclude or proceed	*Strong.* Took more than 40–45 minutes to be swayed one way or the other.	
	Good. Was pretty objective for the first 30 minutes.	
	Adequate. In about 15–20 minutes, knew this person could (couldn't) handle the job.	
	Poor. In less than 10 minutes, knew this person was a winner (a loser).	
Measurement of candidate's core traits—energy, talent, and team skills	*Strong.* Used Benchmark Experience pattern for the past 5–10 years for each job to measure core success traits.	
	Good. Partially measured core success traits, but less formally or for a shorter time.	
	Adequate. Spot checked core success traits.	
	Poor. Just took candidate's word or based assessment on energy shown during interview.	

(continued)

Table 7.2   *(Continued)*

Factor	Explanation	Rank
Benchmarks for the Top 3–4 Performance Ojectives	*Strong.* Used Benchmark Performance (anchor and visualize) pattern for the top performance objectives to determine competence.	
	Good. Compared a few critical job needs to candidate's past achievements.	
	Adequate. Made sure candidate could achieve at least one performance objective.	
	Poor. Did not compare performance objectives to candidate's past accomplishments.	
Overall Quality of the Interview	*Strong.* At least 4 of the categories rated Strong, the rest Good—interview is sound.	
	Good. At least 3 of the categories either Good or Strong—redo areas missed.	
	Adequate. Average mix of Adequate, Good, and Strong—redo areas missed.	
	Poor. One or two Poor categories. The quality of the whole interview is suspect.	

of an interview. Evaluate the quality of the interview/interviewer across these factors.

If you're not prepared for the interview, accuracy will suffer. Good preparation includes having and reading the performance-based job spec, reviewing the resume, and knowing the four core performance-based questions. If you have done all of this, rank yourself strong in this category. If you've done none of it, give yourself a poor rating. Many times, interviewers are woefully unprepared, yet they still get to offer input. Watch out for this. Thirty minutes is insufficient time to make a proper assessment. An interview this short is meaningless and justifies a poor rating. A strong interview needs to be at least an hour of substantive discussion. If you didn't take notes, talked too much, or weren't detailed enough in your fact-finding, interview quality suffers. To get to the top of the scale in this category, you have to be inquisitive and listen carefully as you probe for details.

Emotions also affect the quality of the assessment. Consider yourself in the top category if you're aware of your emotional triggers and can overcome them to remain objective. This is demonstrated by how long it takes you to make the hiring decision. If you can make a "yes/no" decision in less than 10 minutes, you rank in the lowest category of emotional control. You must remain objective for at least 30 to 45 minutes to conduct an unbiased interview.

The heart of a good interview is measuring core traits of success and job-specific performance. Energy and team leadership fall in the core category and are assessed using the impact/leadership questioning pattern for each past job. Job-specific performance is determined by anchoring and visualizing the SMART objectives. Rank yourself at the top if you used these four core performance-based questions and at the bottom if you didn't even consider them.

A competent interviewer needs to be "strong" in at least four of the six categories. If you're not at this level, the assessment of the candidate is suspect. Anything less than a strong rating will compromise the decision. Make sure that anybody giving advice on the selection of a candidate has at least a good rating or their influence will corrupt the process.

Asking for a written assessment is one way to ensure that other interviewers have conducted a thorough evaluation. Have them use the Ten-Factor Candidate Assessment as a guideline. For any rating other than a three have the interviewer provide some added substantiation. This should be in the form of written information citing actual examples used to support the weak or strong rating. On these written assessments, have the interviewer also indicate the length of the interview. In our half-day training session, we suggest that the interviewing team prepare the SMART objectives together and then divide them up. As a substitute, send a copy of the resume with the SMART objectives and a ten-factor rating sheet to each interviewer before meeting the candidate. This plus the written assessment will act as a catalyst to improve the value of the input of other interviewers.

■ MAKING THE HIRING DECISION

Just collecting the information about these ten critical job factors will lead you to the correct decision. In the process, you'll become a better interviewer. The quality of your decision will
always be compromised if you eliminate any one of the factors.
Watch out for the fatal flaws. These can easily sneak up and bite
you if you're not looking.

These assessment and interviewing techniques, while not
hard to apply, take some practice. The best opportunity is with
those candidates you wouldn't even think of hiring. Every now
and then, don't be surprised if you find a first-rate candidate
from this group. Emotional control and preparation are critical.
If you hire one of these people, these essential skills will be rein-
forced daily as you observe a valuable employee—a person you
normally would have never considered.

 THE FINAL CANDIDATE ASSESSMENT

✔ Don't short-circuit the assessment. Minimize conclusions
based on gut feelings and emotions. Get detailed examples of
past performance to assign a strength or a weakness for each
of the 10 critical assessment factors.

✔ Be prepared—before the interview, read the resume, know the
job, and stay inquisitive

✔ Make sure the candidate has a track record of initiative, team
skills, and positive attitude—the basic traits of all long-term
success.

✔ Look for a upward pattern of personal growth and development. Be concerned if growth has flattened or declined with a
resultant loss in motivation.

✔ Match the performance needs of the job by anchoring
each SMART objective. Look for comparable, not identical,
accomplishments.

✔ You'll be able to determine potential, talent, and thinking
ability through visualization questions.

(continued)

✔ The application or use of technical knowledge is a better predictor of success than an absolute level of knowledge.

✔ Compare the environment (complexity, growth, standards) of the candidate's prior companies with your needs to determine real compatibility.

✔ Great managers show a pattern of proactively building strong teams and developing strong people.

✔ Character and personality reveal themselves through performance.

✔ Use external means to validate your assessment. Reference checks, background checks, and testing strengthen your evaluation.

✔ Watch out for the fatal flaws—too bright, too dominant, too analytical, or too clever. Too much of anything can be a problem.

✔ A professional, well-run interview is as important to you as it is to the candidate. Strong candidates judge companies and managers based on the quality of the interview. Unless the interview is thorough, the conclusions obtained will be less reliable.

Chapter 8

Recruiting, Negotiating, and Closing

To be persuasive, we must be believable. To be believable, we must be credible. To be credible, we must be truthful.

—Edward R. Murrow

■ RECRUITING IS NOT SELLING AND OTHER MISCONCEPTIONS ABOUT THE MOST IMPORTANT PART OF HIRING

Recruiting is not something you do at the end of the interview. It starts the moment you begin the interviewing process. Interviewing and recruiting must take place in tandem. They're two sides of the same coin. The opportunity needs to seem immediately compelling to all candidates, especially the one you'll eventually hire. The mistaken belief that recruiting takes place after you've identified a strong candidate means you risk losing a first-rate candidate, and there are never enough of these to go around. You spend too much time in the assessment process to have a deal fall apart at the last moment. Good recruiting skills can overcome this problem.

Some managers think they can sell or charm a candidate into taking a job. This is not recruiting. Effective recruiting is indirect and subtle. While you need to convince a candidate to take a job given certain compensation restraints, you don't accomplish this with an order pad in hand and a superficial selling pitch. To do it right, the hiring manager needs a complete understanding of the job and a thorough knowledge of the candidate's competency, short- and long-term motivation, and compensation needs. A balance among these competing issues is the key in bringing a fair deal together. This takes time and strong recruiting skills. Open and honest communication is a prerequisite. None of this happens when you're selling.

Recruiting is more related to buying than selling, although many managers stop the evaluation and begin the selling process as soon as they find someone they like. Once you start selling, you stop the assessment process. You talk more and the candidate talks less. From this point onward, you won't learn anything new about the candidate other than what he or she wants you to know. You have lost control of the interview. This cheapens the job and makes the candidate more expensive. The candidate might not be good enough, but you'll never find out until he or she starts. You'll then wonder how you blew the interview. This is why a buying perspective is essential. Good recruiting ensures this open type of communication with the interviewer constantly evaluating the competency of the candidate. Just because you're favorably impressed with a candidate, doesn't mean you're ready to start selling or stop evaluating.

The Key to Recruiting

Stay the Buyer—Create a Compelling Opportunity and Make the Candidate Earn the Job!

Strong recruiting is necessary, but it's more effective if it's a marketing pitch, not a sales pitch. Talking about the great merits of your company *after* you've already assessed the candidate always comes across as selling, and it is inappropriate. From the candidate's perspective, this is the classic one-on-one hard sell.

When you say exactly the same thing *before* you know much about the candidate, it becomes marketing. There's much less pressure since you make the same presentation to all candidates, not any one in particular. This subtle change has a profound impact. If you present the job, without pressure, as a significant long-term and exciting opportunity, candidates will want to sell or convince you about their skills, instead of you having to sell them. They then tell you everything you need to know about them and you can close them on equitable terms. This is the essence of effective recruiting.

If you want to be a top manager, you need to be able to attract top people. Often this will depend on the quality of your recruiting skills. Many years ago, I worked with a strong candidate on an assignment with a company that had a rigorous selection process. The candidate was excited about the prospects and went to each interview ready to sell himself on why he was the best person for the position. He didn't get it, but he tried like heck. The job became more appealing the more difficult it was to obtain. This same candidate was turned off by another client that started selling him within 15 minutes of the first interview. This provides a valuable lesson: *If you make it too easy for someone to get the job, the person won't want it as much. If you make it challenging and harder to get, the candidate will want it more.* You increased the value of a job by making it more difficult to obtain. This is a basic principle of human nature, and the very heart of recruiting. The job has more value when it has to be earned. It has less value if it's too easy to get. This is why you always have to pay more if the job can't carry itself. Competition, real challenges, and opportunities to grow get candidates excited. Candidates sell you when confronted with opportunity. Strong candidates are proud of their accomplishments and want their potential new boss to know all about them. Your job is to set up the interview situation to allow them to discuss this information freely with you.

Most of the time, the circumstances surrounding a job are not perfect. You never have enough money, the best candidates generally have multiple opportunities, and you're always vulnerable to counteroffers. For strong candidates, you have to be able to present your job opportunity in a competitive position, without selling too soon or giving away the store. A good recruiter can level the playing field. Attractive opportunities need to be presented in an open, give-and-take manner. Every step of the way requires persuasion and understanding to overcome the natural resistance to moving forward. At the same time, you need to collect additional information about the candidate's competency. Putting the whole package together is the job of the hiring manager. The first step is to position the job to take the candidate's motivational needs into account. This way you'll increase the likelihood of getting a top person to join your team, despite the typical roadblocks, restraints, and hurdles you'll encounter along the way.

■ WHY CANDIDATES TAKE JOBS— UNDERSTANDING AND MANAGING MOTIVATION

Understanding candidate motivation is the first step in putting together an effective recruiting program. Candidates take offers for two fundamental reasons. The first we call a "going-away" strategy. It usually has to do with resolving or leaving an unfavorable job situation, such as a layoff or a spouse's relocation. Recruiting is relatively easy if the candidate's current situation is weak and current options are limited. Their standards are lower because of their personal circumstance. If you find strong candidates in this position, move fast. You have a nice, but temporary, advantage. Their opportunities will multiply very quickly. The "going-toward" strategy is the more common reason strong candidates take other positions. These people need some very compelling reasons to leave an already good position, or to compete with other attractive opportunities. For most candidates, the underlying motivation to change jobs is usually a combination of these two strategies. It's the interviewer's job to determine the degree of both and which one is most important.

Quickly find out which strategy is dominating the candidate's job-hunting efforts. Early in the interview, just ask why the candidate is considering a move at this time. This gets at the going-away strategy. Later on in the interview, follow up by asking what the person is looking for in a new job. This gets at the going-toward strategy. To get at underlying motivation, ask why these conditions are important to the candidate in accepting a new position. This requires an applicant to think at a deeper level and often reveals true motivation. You may need to use this information later in presenting the merits of the job. Compare the consistency between the going-away reasons with the going-toward strategy. For example, it makes sense if a person wants to leave a chaotic situation for more security. It doesn't seem logical though, if someone is leaving this same chaotic situation for more growth opportunity. Look for congruity at every level. Understanding motivation will help you make an insightful decision.

If the candidate is currently in a good situation, or has multiple opportunities, you must be more diligent. With these favorable personal circumstances, you need something very attractive to pull the candidate away. This is when you must rely on strong recruiting skills, especially if you want the candidate on your short list. Candidates with a going-toward motivating strategy take a new job for three reasons:

1. The quality of the company.
2. The quality of the hiring manager.
3. The challenge and excitement of the position.

You have to be able to address each of these during the interview. You need to develop a recruiting pitch around all three areas. Ask yourself why a strong candidate would want this job. Be specific and insightful, not general and superficial. Come up with four or five good ideas for each category. Base the company opportunities around the strategic plan—new products, new markets, and new systems work well. Make these the basis of your company's recruiting pitch, but don't present an opening 10-minute speech; instead, break it into 1-minute sound bites. Interject these opportunities before asking your questions. This creates interest and keeps the momentum of the interview at a high pace.

For example, telling a candidate about the company's plan for growth in a certain area has great appeal if you relate it directly to the importance of the job. Statements like this establish the foundation for long-term advancement and opportunity. By creating excitement, they challenge the candidate to rise to the occasion. Well-written SMART objectives are sufficient to address the position needs. During the questioning, state their strategic or tactical importance to make them sound even more appealing: *"The new IS system will help us get control of our rapid overseas expansion programs. Can you give me some examples of when you took the lead in setting up new complex systems like this?"* This type of question makes the job more important and more interesting. You're recruiting and interviewing in tandem with this approach.

Good candidates want to work for strong managers. This increases the likelihood that they'll grow, develop, and improve themselves by taking the job. The best evidence of this is the quality of the hiring manager's interviewing skills. Knowing the job, having high standards, asking tough questions, and openly listening to the responses in a nonjudgmental way provides insight into your leadership qualities. Make sure you understand what motivates the candidate, then suggest how this job will help her grow in this area. Give examples of what you've done for other people who have worked for you. Give their names and describe how they have advanced within the company. Even allow the candidate to talk to them. Recruiting is much easier if candidates want to work for you because you're a strong leader. This is one of the best ways to overcome many typical recruiting problems.

This three-pronged recruiting approach can overwhelm all competing opportunities. It needs to be planned out beforehand and integrated into the performance-based interviewing process. While there's a tendency and a need to attract and pursue great candidates, going overboard will usually misfire. Good recruiting provides the balance by making the job worth having and worth earning. On Table 8.1, list the four or five compelling attributes about the job, the manager, and the company.

As you complete this table, think how each factor will enable the candidate to grow and develop into a stronger person as a result of taking the job. Table 8.2 shows a chart for a marketing manager for a software company.

This information must be presented in small pieces throughout the interviewing process. Some of it can be told directly while you're asking questions, and some indirectly. This can be in the form of literature or an informative Web site, conversations with others who have worked for the hiring manager, or during a tour. Surprisingly, many major companies do a very poor job with this. If you don't constantly build up the importance of the job, the

Table 8.1   Attributes That Attract Candidates

The Job	The Hiring Manager	The Company
1.		
2.		
3.		
4.		
5.		

quality of the company, and the strength of the hiring manager, all you have left is the offer package. This is not the best way to attract top talent. You are much more likely to have success when the company, the job, and the hiring manager all meet some aspect of the candidate's motivating needs.

Table 8.2   Recruiting Pitch—Software Manager

The Job	The Hiring Manager	The Company
1. Critical game-breaker position—own the product line.	Strong leader and background with one of top software companies in United States.	Well-funded start-up with charismatic leader at the helm.
2. Establish strategic direction and distribution channels.	Great leadership style, allows subordinates to take on new challenges and grow fast.	Well-positioned in market space with new technology.
3. Develop new skills in the area of negotiating and business development.	A real team player, has demonstrated ability to build great teams everywhere.	Strong executive team ready with lots of relevant experience.
4. First multifunctional management job.	A high-potential person who's going places.	Big equity play to offset the inherent risk.
5. Learn new distribution channels in software.	Warm and personable, but with high standards.	Top-notch technical team that's been together.

If everything else is compelling, the financial aspects of the position become less important. This is how you overcome salary constraints and other typical problems. The candidate makes a personal strategic decision about all aspects of the offer, rather than a tactical one that relies wholly on a favorable compensation package.

■ RECRUITING AND CHALLENGING QUESTIONS CAN STRENGTHEN YOUR POSITION

You can increase candidate interest in a position through recruiting and challenging questions. Recruiting questions are no more than using the recruiting sound bites we mentioned earlier as prefaces to the standard questions. For example, *"We're creating a very sophisticated multimedia Web site, and are looking for aggressive salespeople to obtain advertising. Can you give me some examples of your most comparable sales accomplishments?"* It's important to state the strategic or tactical importance of a task and then ask the candidate to describe a related experience (the anchor) or how the task would be accomplished (visualize). Recruiting questions are effective because they create interest and pull the candidate toward the job.

Challenging questions create interest in an opposite manner by pushing the candidate away. For example, *"I'm concerned you don't have enough experience in developing international accounting systems. Have I missed something?"* This slight challenge increases the importance of this skill and requires a candidate to sell you. This approach, used judiciously throughout the interview, can increase a candidate's interest in a job. Valid concerns suggest areas where the candidate would be able to learn and grow on the job. Often applicants self-select this way. If the job is worthwhile, you'll sense the candidate's excitement and tenacity by how hard she pushes back. If the job is too challenging, she'll exclude herself from consideration.

Challenging can be abrasive when carried to an extreme. When combined with a compliment, it works well: *"While you have great experience in _____, it appears you haven't been exposed to _____. Is this true?"* Recruiting and challenging can also be combined.

Stressing the importance of a task and then mentioning concern about the candidate's apparent lack of skills in this area raises the standards of performance. A candidate needs to overcome a negative belief and sell harder if it's a critical area. Here's another example of this combined recruiting and challenging question: *"Developing the international market is essential for us in achieving our three-year plan. From your resume, I'm concerned you don't have enough European experience to handle this. What are your thoughts on this?"*

Try this process with some candidates you have doubts about to get their reaction. This will serve as useful practice. Recruiting and challenging questioning techniques are essential tools if you want to attract the best. It allows you to maintain balance with the strong candidates you want to attract by creating interest, determining motivation, and opening up the lines of communication.

■ END THE INTERVIEW ON A POSITIVE NOTE

The hiring manager should use the following as the last question at the end of the first interview. This is from the basic eight-question interview introduced in Chapter 4. It's a must for all finalists: *"Although we're seeing some other fine candidates, I believe you have a strong background, and we'd like to get back to you in a few days. What are your thoughts now about this position?"*

This is a good way to test the interest of strong candidates at the end of the first interview. By stating that you have other strong candidates you create supply, and make the job more desirable. Candidates get nervous about a job if they're the only one being considered. This strengthens your eventual bargaining position and improves the open flow of communications. Whether true or not, there's always the expectation that a flock of candidates will respond to great opportunities. Work with this and play it up.

A positive affirmation also is important. This feedback tells the candidate he's in contention. He'll think more about why he wants the job this way, not why he's not going to get it. This push-pull technique is a setup to get at the candidate's interest, the last and most important part of the question. You want to hear about interest and concerns. So try to uncover objections. If the candidate voices any, acknowledge the issues and suggest that you will discuss them at a later meeting (or discuss them briefly at this point). Encourage the candidate to call you back with more of his thoughts. This open two-way exchange of information will be important as you move into later interviews.

This is not intended to completely exclude the traditional selling side of recruiting. Most of the time, these are better ways to accomplish the same task without being so obvious. Being excited about a candidate and the merits of the open position is important. If you move too fast or sell too soon, you could lose both control and the candidate. The traditional approach attempts to sway reluctant candidates by directly selling the true worth of the opportunity. Once in a while this is okay, but once the candidate is convinced, go back to a buyer's position. Tell the candidate that while you want to convince her this is a great chance, you still need to complete your assessment. This approach allows you to strongly present your position, while maintaining underlying control. Often interviewers will move too fast after a candidate has been persuaded in the traditional way. They forget that they have not yet completed the evaluation process.

■ TESTING, MAKING, NEGOTIATING, AND CLOSING THE DEAL

We're now ready for the second interview. One of the short-listed candidates will ultimately be getting an offer, so you have to take care every step of the way. Use the techniques described in the rest of this chapter to make sure that the closing process moves along as smooth as possible.

Don't start too soon or wait too long to talk about salary. The best time is when both parties are somewhat serious. This is typically at the end of the first interview, or right before the second interview is scheduled. If you wait until the final offer stage to settle the details, it's too late. By then the candidate will know he is the finalist, and this gives him the upper hand. If you talk about salary too soon, before you and the candidate know each other, it creates an awkward situation. Then it's just a yes/no filter to determine if each party should proceed with the assessment. This precludes the chance of any trade-offs. This becomes a serious problem when you talk about salary before the first interview. I've seen lots of missed opportunities and good candidates prematurely excluded for superficial reasons.

The financial considerations are rarely why a deal falls apart. In the past 20 years in over 1000 different salary negotiations that I've been involved in, only 2 or 3% fell through because of compensation. If the job is great, candidates always compromise; and if the candidate is great, the company always compromises. My rule is to keep people talking about the importance of the job. The compensation package will then take care of itself. Both parties know enough about each other after the first interview, and it's important to begin the salary discussion then. Compensation becomes a secondary issue by this time, and you generally won't be too far apart anyway, especially if your open position is similar to the one the candidate is leaving. Candidates are always more realistic after they understand the opportunity, and companies are always more flexible when they meet a strong candidate. This further minimizes any potential salary gap.

We suggest developing the framework for an offer package early in the assessment process and in small steps. The process is smooth and painless this way. It minimizes the awkwardness of the typical negotiating session when you put everything on the table in the end. This approach also gives the candidate a stronger negotiating position. The key is to get concessions along the way, when you have leverage and something to offer. In addition to the financial package, you also want to get buy-in on some aspect of a final offer each time you invite a candidate back for another interview. You can negotiate pieces of the complete offer this way, rather than leaving it all to the end. You'll also be able to test sincere interest at each step. Using this parallel approach, you'll be assessing the candidate's competency at the same time you're recruiting and closing the deal.

One of my associates used this approach in negotiating an offer with a product manager for a health care products company. The candidate was very interested in the position after the first interview, and our client wanted to move quickly. We told the candidate that she was one of three people being invited back for a second round of interviews and the salary range was only slightly more than her current level. The job was an excellent career move for her and she agreed to come back knowing full well that if she were to get an offer it would be at a small increase. After a few more rounds of interviewing, it was clear she was the finalist, and at that time she upped her financial demands. We held firm though. We indicated to her that one of the reasons for proceeding was her prior agreement to continue the interview process knowing the tight financial situation. Although we didn't have any other candidates, we told her she would have to drop herself from consideration if she wanted to push the salary issue. She relented and accepted an offer consistent with our earlier discussions. This deal would have fallen apart or have become very uncomfortable if we hadn't discussed salary right after the first interview.

If you don't know the candidate's salary history, ask before you invite the candidate back for a second interview. If it's too high or if you have little room to maneuver, state your concern and ask if this is a serious issue. Another approach, if you don't know the salary, is to just state your salary range and say that you hope this fits in with the candidate's needs. In either case, any balking at this time is a good clue you may be light. A little probing helps. Keep your options open, and unless there's lots of resistance, get the candidate to come back in. Tell the candidate that while the salary could be an issue, there might be other things you can do to compensate for this, or that there are other significant opportunities worth exploring.

If the candidate agrees to come back, you know you've just established the condition of a potential offer. For candidates who are still reluctant, you can dangle some more carrots. A salary review in 3 to 6 months is an approach that works well. But don't go overboard. Salary, bonus, and equity opportunities can often move a reluctant candidate forward, but you don't want to play these cards too soon. I like to suggest to candidates that they shouldn't make long-term career moves without all the facts. Great opportunities can always offset short-term financial constraints. The key is to make the strategic opportunities overwhelm the tactical issues.

Use each subsequent interview session to gain more buy-in. If you sense sincere interest after the second interview, mention to the candidate what still needs to happen to get to an offer stage. This could consist of background and degree checks, reference checks, psychological testing, additional interviews, and a medical exam to ensure a drug-free workplace. Going forward is tacit acceptance to these conditions and the high likelihood the candidate is being straight about background data.

The benefit package can either be a lure or nonpositive information if it's not too strong. Conduct these discussions in casual conversations as you're arranging other meetings. By the time you're ready to make an offer, you will have already addressed many of the details. This approach removes some of the contentious elements from the offer process.

A few years back, I had a strong candidate for the CFO position at a retail store chain. After his second interview with the CEO, I told the candidate what the range of the offer would be (only a small increase over his current package) and the next steps in the evaluation process. This consisted of a meeting with two board members on the East Coast, a half-day session with an industrial psychologist in the Midwest, and then a dinner with the Chairman. This was before the medical and drug test, and a final meeting with the CEO. The candidate was very interested, but when he agreed to continue this arduous process, I knew the deal was done. Three weeks later, we finalized the package exactly as described. The candidate's decision to go forward under the conditions described was really a commitment, not just an inconvenience. This is a great model on how all offers should be made.

■ STEP BY STEP THROUGH THE OFFER

It's important to test each component of a formal offer before making it. Once you have formally extended an offer, you have limited options. Then the applicant becomes the buyer and the company the seller. Open communication stops. Candidates stop thinking about why they want the job and start thinking about why they don't want it. An offer extended when there is still doubt gets an *"I have to think about it,"* response. Thinking about an offer is fine, but once you've extended it your flexibility is weakened. It's better to have an applicant think about all aspects of an offer before you formally put it together. Before you extend a formal offer, you get unbiased information. Afterward, your same attempt to find out interest and what's happening comes across as harassment, pushiness, or overselling.

Contentious salary negotiations are awkward and stressful. Neither party wants to lose face. Deals often fall apart at this point for petty reasons.

Never make a formal offer until every aspect has been tested and agreed on beforehand.

Never make a formal offer until you have tested and reached agreement with the candidate on every aspect on the checklist shown in Table 8.3. This is the basic rule of making offers. By the time you're ready to get serious, you've already established the parameters of an offer, so it's easy to move into real negotiations. First, test general interest. This question allows you to differentiate between the job and the offer itself. *"Assuming an attractive offer, do the job and challenge appeal to you?"* This allows you to address any concerns about the job first. You'll eliminate a lot of bad fits this way.

People often take unappealing jobs because of great financial incentives. This is not the way to build a great team. By starting with job fit, you'll also be able to make the financial consideration a secondary component of the offer. Salary negotiations are usually easy if the candidate really wants the position for personal growth reasons. Go back to this throughout the negotiating process if you get in trouble. Find out why the candidate really wants the job and be sure to remind him about these points often.

"We're thinking of putting an offer together for you, but we'd like to know your thoughts now about the job" is a good way to make a preliminary offer test. Use the trial close with something like this to get more specific: *"What do you think if we could put a package together in the range of \$_____ to \$_____?"* You'll need to go back and forth with the candidate to test this range, but this gets both parties to start talking in an open manner. Don't let the candidate forget about the competition. Preface your remarks with, *"Although we're still seeing other candidates, I believe you'd make a great addition to our team. What do you think about something*

Table 8.3   Offer Summary and Checklist

Target Offer	Summary Details	Test/ Agree	Objections/ Comments
Salary			
Bonus			
Car			
Other Cash Comp			
Title—Position			
Benefit Package			
Options			
Relocation Package			
Next Review			
Vacation			
Other			

like . . . ?" Competition allows you to be a little stronger during the negotiating phase, and makes the candidate more realistic.

Table 8.3 is from the Recruiting Worksheet in the Appendix. Use it to guide you through preparing all terms of the offer using this testing process.

Hesitation on any item means there are other issues to be considered, so continue probing. Many objections at this stage have to do with lack of information. Don't move forward until you have addressed these concerns. You can make trade-offs at this time. Give something else if you can't meet a particular need, like a signing bonus instead of a higher salary. Also find out whether this item will be a deal breaker if you can't accommodate the candidate. Work these points until you obtain agreement. You'll discover this give-and-take process is easier if a formal offer is not on the table. When all the objections have been addressed in satisfactory fashion, you're ready to begin the final close.

■ THE CLOSE—PUTTING IT ALL TOGETHER

Once all the aspects of an offer have been agreed on, you're ready for a preliminary close. Don't make the formal offer yet. Use a close that gets the applicant to indirectly agree to the terms of the offer. Ask, *"If we could formalize this package in the next few days, when do you think you could start?"* In classic selling terms, this is called a secondary close, since acceptance of a less important criterion infers total acceptance. Make sure you get a specific start date. The lack of a start date often implies some other issues, usually external, that still must be resolved. Things like competing offers or counteroffers head the list. You'll never hear about these if you've already made a formal offer. At least now you can probe if the candidate is reluctant to provide a start date. This will uncover any other issues and give you time to address them. If you get a start date but still have doubts about sincerity, ask the candidate to walk you through the present employer's termination process. Find out how she'll tell her boss, the likely reaction, and the possibility of counteroffers. Leaving a company is difficult for many people, so provide some guidance and a helping hand.

Now you're ready for the final close. You're still testing, so don't hand over the offer letter quite yet. As you review the final terms of the offer with the candidate, ask *"If we could put this offer in writing today or tomorrow, when would you be in a position to give formal acceptance?"* Anything other than "immediately" is of concern. By this time, you've negotiated all the terms of the offer, the job scope, and provided streams of information on every point. Acceptance is assumed and you need to meet any backtracking now with serious concern. Find out the problem and attempt to address it using all the points previously noted. If the reaction is positive, you can certainly give the candidate until the next morning to get back to you with an official acceptance. But don't agree to more time than this.

The approach we recommend is an open and natural process with lots of give-and-take. If your sense is that the offer is fair and mutually agreed on, there is no reason the applicant still needs to think about it. All aspects of the thinking process should have taken place by the time you get to this point. If the candidate still needs to think about it for more than one day, step back, and withhold the offer. This will be infrequent. Hesitation at this late stage typically involves counteroffers. (This is discussed in more detail in the following section.) If you sense this is the case, tell the candidate that you are concerned and that you would like to understand what's happening. It's best to put every issue on the table so that you can discuss it in an open and frank manner.

This testing process is not a high-pressure approach. Making an offer and taking a job are critical decisions for both the candidate and the company. We want to give the candidate as much time as necessary to make a well-informed decision. That's why the informal offer and testing process is effective. It allows the candidate to do her research and consult with her spouse and other advisers. But we want this time to be on the candidate's watch, not the company's. This is a subtle difference. By delaying the formal presentation of the offer until acceptance is guaranteed, the company keeps the lines of communication open and stays in a stronger negotiating position. You'll gain more unbiased information this way and have more flexibility. Once the formal offer is extended, candidates are not as revealing in their comments, and you have less opportunity to respond.

There is no guarantee that all offers will be accepted or that everything will go easily, but more offers are accepted using this process and difficult problems often get resolved without it breaking down. This is largely due to the open communications aspect of the process. Neither party needs to lose face with the testing approach we recommend. It allows give-and-take on all issues with minimal conflict.

■ OVERCOMING OBJECTIONS—WHAT TO DO WHEN THINGS GO WRONG

Occasionally, the closing process hits a snag or two, especially in competitive areas like Silicon Valley with tight employment conditions. This is when some of the following recruiting techniques will come in handy.

➤ Close on an Objection

Use this technique with any of the following objections. It's a fundamental selling technique and it works well in closing a candidate. Once an objection has been stated, ask the candidate, *"I assume if we can resolve this issue, you're in a position to accept all the other terms of the offer?"* It pins the candidate down. If he squirms a bit, you know you have some other problems. Find these out first. It's best to get all the objections out in the open before you negotiate any of them.

We had a candidate who hesitated to accept an offer, stating he was concerned about the relocation package. We then asked if he would accept the rest of the package provided we could meet his needs for relocation. He still wouldn't commit and reluctantly admitted the problem was that his wife had a good job and really didn't want to move. We couldn't resolve this issue and were forced to drop an excellent candidate. Without this technique we would have spent many more hours on a useless cause.

➤ Not Enough Money

There's never enough money, so this is one reason I stress testing all offers before finalizing the financial package. This will surface and eliminate most problems before they become deal breakers. If the candidate balks at any time before you've made a formal offer, it's easy to just ask the candidate how flexible he is on this salary point. If he's open to discussion, your objective is to switch his interest in the job to the more strategic aspects. This could be better growth opportunities, more challenge, or more impact. An early review (less than a year) can sometimes compensate for a lower than desired starting salary. Sign-on bonuses are always popular and special bonuses can also meet some compensation targets. Make sure you review the benefit package in detail. These are often overlooked and they sometimes include some real gems.

If the candidate doesn't appear to be flexible on salary, pull the offer back as we did in the earlier example with the woman in the product marketing position. Since you haven't made a formal offer, it's easy to state that the compensation discussed is your limit: *"I don't think we can go any higher."* Get confirmation from the candidate: *"Are you suggesting that if we can't meet your salary needs, you're withdrawing yourself from consideration?"* If the answer is "yes," you can either say you'll see what you can do, or terminate the process. Problems can arise when all these issues are left to the end. By getting buy-in at each progressive stage of the interview, compensation can be negotiated in small steps.

Another way to negotiate salary is to introduce competition. Even if you don't have other strong candidates, you can still use the concept of indirect competition. A few years ago, I created a salary cap on a production manager's position in the food industry by telling the candidate that if we were to go any higher on salary we would be forced to look at candidates with more experience. The salary the candidate wanted was excessive. We had enough data to show him that the higher level was more consistent with directors than managers, and he had a few more years to go before he could get to this level. With this information and our strong stance, the candidate agreed to proceed within the salary range we had targeted.

Presenting an experience gap can overcome salary problems and create a compelling opportunity at the same time. I'm currently working with a strong candidate for a CFO position who doesn't have all the requisite experience. Her salary is high since she has a significant job in a Fortune 500 company. A move to a smaller company with a broader focus is an essential career move for her. It's worth it to give a little up on salary to eliminate this gap. The company let her know that they were willing to risk her lack of experience in these important areas, since she has so much potential, but they could not meet her initial salary requirements. She recognized the opportunity and agreed it was a fair trade-off. From her perspective, the job offers her something more important than salary.

To move past all these salary problems, you must create a long-term opportunity that overrides all short-term problems, have lots of direct and indirect competition, know the market, and not be afraid to discuss these points throughout the hiring process, even if it means taking the offer off the table.

➤ Counteroffers

You need to confront the candidate early if you sense the possibility of a counteroffer. Be wary if the candidate hesitates to commit to a start date or is vague about getting back to you with a final acceptance. Ask the candidate about the chance that the employer would present a counteroffer after giving a resignation. Be concerned if you receive shallow or general responses. Ask the candidate how she feels about counteroffers in general. Explore the character issues. You defuse the threat of a counteroffer by exposing it as an inappropriate means to keep an employee. The long-term relationship is often weakened when an employee threatens to leave and is then lured back with a counteroffer. Cite examples as proof. Also ask how she would feel if one of her employees had to be coerced into staying with a counteroffer. This is an indirect way of exposing the lack of integrity associated with accepting a counteroffer.

Counteroffers must be handled in a frank and direct manner. Most counteroffers occur during the period after a formal offer is presented, but not yet accepted. It's what happens during the *"I have to think about it,"* time period. If you delay the formal offer using the testing approach we recommend, you minimize the counteroffer problem. Since you won't present the formal offer until all objections are addressed, the candidate is less likely to put her current employer into a difficult counteroffer position. The candidate will either have to discuss the resignation beforehand without a formal offer, or state that a formal acceptance has already been given.

➤ Apparent Lack of Promotional Opportunities

Every good candidate wants a chance to grow and develop. Don't promise a promotion, though. This can get you into trouble if the candidate isn't as strong as expected, or if business conditions worsen. Good recruiting comes into play here since you've been describing many of the long-range opportunities within the company as part of your one-minute recruiting sound bites. To reinforce this, you can say that the candidate will receive as much responsibility as she demonstrates she can handle. Follow this up by stating that promotions go to employees who meet their performance objectives. If both the company and the candidate meet their objectives, these promotional opportunities will certainly develop for the candidate.

Describe other people under your direction who have received promotions this way. This approach presents you as a manager who can develop people and help them advance their careers. Your personal mentoring is an important aspect of why a candidate might take your offer despite other problems. Good people want a chance to grow and get promoted. If the candidate believes you'll strongly support her and that there are realistic opportunities within your firm, you'll score well on this point. This is a critical area for all top candidates. Bring it up during the interview even if the candidate doesn't. It can often offset problems with compensation or difficult working conditions. In many ways, presenting a realistic picture of how a candidate can grow, develop, and get promoted is the heart of effective recruiting. It is also the difference between building a good team or a great team.

➤ Job Isn't Big Enough or Not Enough Challenge

If a candidate contends the job isn't big enough, make it bigger. This doesn't mean you need to give a bigger title or larger staff. Just add more work. Adding special projects works well. Assigning one-time projects of a critical nature are a great way to expand the scope of a job. These one-time efforts provide real meat to a position and can often help sway a candidate to your direction. Find out what really motivates a candidate and assign an individual or team project that complements this interest. You can also tell the candidate that you'll assign special projects as soon as he gets up to speed. Be specific, since these projects are often why candidates accept jobs. If they're challenging, important, and offer high exposure and learning, they become great means to expand a job's scope.

You need to discuss the strategic and tactical importance of the position if the candidate believes it to be beneath his or her competency level. This is a significant issue, and you must deal with it directly. It affects the candidate's self-worth, so don't minimize it. Titles are important. If your title is not comparable to the candidate's previous title, make sure the comparability of the job is discussed. Higher visibility, exposure, and impact on the organization can offset an apparently lesser job. Make sure you use this technique to clarify a job's scope if the candidate perceives it to be too small. Of course, if the job is in fact a lesser position, you could have a real problem.

➤ Hesitating to Take the Next Step

A candidate's hesitation to come back is an obvious sign of a problem. If the candidate is a strong contender, it is worth the effort to find out the cause and possibly turn him around. Probe. Ask what is the problem or concern. Often it is lack of information about a specific issue or some rumor the candidate has heard. These can be addressed. Frequently, candidates remove themselves from consideration for the wrong reasons. By getting in the habit of testing interest, you'll uncover issues that you can easily address before they become deal breakers.

Here's an approach you should try. At the end of the interview, ask the candidate to rank his interest on a scale of 0–10. If it's in the 6–7 category, ask what one or two concerns prevent the job from being an 8 or a 9. This will tell you what you need to work on. *"Although we're still considering a few other strong candidates, I believe you're an excellent fit. From what you now know about the position how would you rank your interest level on a scale of 0–10?"* The key to good recruiting is an open back-and-forth exchange of information. Losing a strong candidate for the right reasons is acceptable, but often first-rate candidates get away because nobody bothered to find out and address their concerns.

The same problems can occur when you're inviting a candidate in for the first interview. You can often overcome strong objections with unusual opportunities. You have to position your presentation so that the candidate will explore it objectively. I remember a candidate who wasn't interested in a top job, closer to downtown Los Angeles, because he would have to move. I knew if I could just get him into the first interview, it was a done deal. The job would be a significant career move that would put the candidate into the big leagues. The job, the company, and the hiring manager were all representative of a world-class opportunity. I told the candidate he obviously wouldn't move unless this was a top 1% opportunity, so it was at least worth exploring. He agreed. He called me up the afternoon after the interview and loudly complained. It was a great job and he knew he was going to be moving away from the suburbs he loved. Strategically, however, it was the right move. Within five years, he became a senior-level executive with another Fortune 50 company.

➤ Lack of Apparent Long-Term Opportunity

You can minimize this problem by including some strategic objectives in the performance-based job description. If you include a performance objective like "prepare a long-term facilities plan to support annual growth of 25%," the candidate instantly recognizes the strategic importance of the job and the potential promotional opportunities. A good preplanned recruiting pitch can also help. Ask yourself why a top candidate would want this job. Forget the "mom and apple pie" stuff and be specific. Things like increasing market share by 5 points, introducing new technology, or helping to rebuild after a fall, are meaningful inducements for ambitious candidates.

Prepare a list of these recruiting ideas including the company's main long-range objectives. As you interview the candidate, describe how the job relates to these strategic needs. Again, it's best to break down this recruiting pitch into short sound bites that preface your actual questions. For example, here's a recruiting preface used at the beginning of a question for an accounting manager: *"The company is planning to enter Europe in a big way later this year. We see enormous growth potential in this market. In fact, we expect it to represent 25% of our business in three years. This is why we need a strong person to set up our complete international accounting system. Can you please describe some of your international accounting projects?"* This is a much better way of forming a question than the more common, *"Tell me about some of your experience in the international accounting area."* Not only do you send a strong message about the job, but the candidate will also talk more openly as she sells you on her qualifications for the position.

➤ The Take-Away to Address Hesitation or Resistance

Find out how hard a candidate pulls your offer back after you take it away. Use this tactic judiciously when it looks like a deal is about to break apart. Take the offer off the table. If the candidate has many significant objections or seems to be drifting away, it might be time for some drama. *"I don't think we'll be able to overcome your objections on these issues, perhaps we should just agree to stop discussing a possible offer,"* might do the trick. A candidate who is seriously interested in the position and wants to really work something out will pull it back. This could take the form of modifying his position or just agreeing to talk some more. Since you haven't made a formal offer, the take-away technique is a way to test interest in the case of some unreasonable objections. The take-away will put a cap on what you're willing to offer. If the candidate still expresses interest, he's basically accepted your package, with modest changes. Don't use this approach more than once with any candidate, and don't use it too soon. Use the take-away when it looks like the negotiations are about to fall apart. It can be the key to breaking a stalemate.

We used this approach with a hot product marketing prospect from a top consumer packaged goods company. The candidate was good and knew it. He kept on ratcheting up his offer demands until the situation got tenuous. I called the candidate and told him he just broke the bank. My client had just taken the offer off the table and couldn't go any higher. The candidate called back within four hours to accept the previous offer.

➤ The Push-Away to Demonstrate
Growth Opportunities

This is a good approach to convert a tactical weakness into a strategic strength. By raising doubt about competency in a certain area, you can often get the candidate to push back. This demonstrates an opportunity for growth and makes a job more appealing. For example, let's assume the financial package is a little tight. You might want to mention to the candidate that partly this is because of the candidate's lack of skills or experience in a certain area, such as international marketing: *"As mentioned during the interview, we're a little concerned about your lack of international experience. This is a critical area for us and will be a great area of personal growth for you. As you develop, we'll certainly compensate you accordingly, but right now we believe the offer is fair."* You've stated the importance of the area, and shown how the candidate can become a better person by developing this expertise.

Candidates will view this as a great trade-off for giving up a little salary. High standards encourage candidates to view the job as both a learning and developing opportunity, as well as a source of added compensation, once they have mastered the skills. You have to be able to balance both of these aspects as you put together a complete offer package. Many managers miss this area as they rush to the close. When you don't know enough about the candidate and ignore this vital area, you're left with compensation as the only negotiating lever.

■ DON'T STOP RECRUITING—FROM BEGINNING TO END

Don't forget the candidate after an offer has been accepted. There's a natural tendency to let your guard down at this point. Instead, be extravigilant. With tight employment markets, the best always have multiple opportunities.

Recently, an applicant called one night leaving an urgent voice mail—"I've got a problem. We need to talk." Since this candidate had already accepted an executive level engineering spot, but had not yet started, it was an unsettling call. It seemed that the candidate was getting a tremendous counteroffer that matched the salary and included a promotion. The candidate wanted my advice. The new position was a strategic move into a smaller company, but in a more impactful position. The counteroffer was a bigger individual contributor role at a large bureaucracy. The candidate knew this, but wanted reassurance. It was after 10:00 P.M., but I got my client, the CEO, and hiring manager, to call the candidate and discuss all the issues again. We reclosed the deal without any changes to the offer, just constant attention. On this one, the message is clear. Keep on recruiting until they show up. It probably doesn't hurt to keep it up after they start (but that's a different book).

There are some special things you can do to make sure the candidate stays closed. The key is to get the candidate involved in the job right away, even before starting:

➤ Jointly prepare the formal transition program right away. Meet a few times to review the job spec and prioritize activities. This clarifies the expectations before starting, something that rarely happens.

➤ Give the candidate an assignment before starting. One of my Silicon Valley clients had a candidate review the strategic and annual plan to better understand department objectives.

➤ Meet and call the candidate regularly and update her on the department status. This will give the new employee a strong understanding of what needs to get done before starting.

➤ Let the candidate see his new office. This allows the candidate to visualize his role and strengthens the bond to the company.

➤ Have the candidate meet all of the other staff members either in a formal or an informal manner before the start date. This makes her part of the team right away.

➤ Send over lots of reading material and new positive information. Get your new employee up to speed as rapidly as possible. He'll stay excited and be ready to make an impact right away.

➤ If convenient, send the candidate to a seminar or company event. We placed a sales manager who went to a company sales meeting before starting.

➤ Have a social event, such as a dinner with spouses. This loosens tensions, builds understanding, and develops a working relationship.

Keeping in touch with your new employee in these ways will help build a strong working relationship even if there's little likelihood the candidate would renege on an accepted offer.

■ HOW TO SHOOT YOURSELF IN THE FOOT AND OTHER RECRUITING BLUNDERS

It doesn't take much to lose a top-notch candidate. Recruiting is important, challenging, and difficult. Don't waste all this effort with some dumb mistake. There are enough land mines around without you having to create your own. The following checklist includes some of the biggest blunders I've seen in the past 20 years.

Recruiting Mistakes to Avoid

☐ Don't put a damper on the job. Don't tell a candidate that there are few long-term opportunities or that they'll have to stay in the same job for two or three years, or more. Maybe you think it's true, but jobs always grow and change. The best employees always seem to see their jobs expand regardless of the situation.

☐ If you're unprepared, appear unprofessional, and ask stupid questions, you'll drive away even average candidates. The best candidates want to work for effective managers. If you know the job, ask tough questions, and listen more than talk, you portray yourself and the company as a place where top people work.

☐ Don't sell too soon. You'll sound desperate if you start talking about the merits of the job within 10 minutes. This cheapens the job, you, and the company.

☐ Don't talk about money too soon or too late. In the beginning, money is only used to filter in or out candidates. In the end, it's just a negotiating point. It's better to start with small steps by the second interview. By the time you make the offer official, it will be already done.

(continued)

☐ Stay away from personal, ethnic, or family matters. Questions in these areas are against the law and in bad taste. If in doubt, ask your HR department for advice.

☐ Don't wait until the end of the interviewing process to make an offer. You've given up your bargaining position, because the candidate knows he's the only one left

☐ Don't wait until the end to recruit. Start the recruiting process with the first question in the first interview. Make the job compelling and the candidate important.

☐ Don't stop recruiting after the offer is made. These are tumultuous times. Great candidates are getting counteroffers and competing offers. Don't stop recruiting until the candidate starts.

■ RECRUITING BRINGS IT ALL TOGETHER

Recruiting is important for a number of reasons. First, by opening the flow of communications, it allows you to find out more about the candidate than you normally would learn. Second, it allows you to control the terms of the offer. Finally, it allows you to position your situation against all competing opportunities. This is why you have to be good at marketing. To recruit the best, you need to market yourself, the company, and the job as being valuable and worth having. The candidate has to know enough about the job to be in a position to trade off this opportunity against all others and against short-term financial needs.

Being a good recruiter is an essential component of good hiring. It's the key to building a strong team and the first step to becoming a top manager. Every college sports coach worth his or her salt is rated primarily on being a good recruiter. If you can get the talent, being the coach is relatively easy. But even a great coach can't compensate for weak talent. The same is true for management. You can't take recruiting and team building passively. Someone else isn't going to do it for you, especially HR. So don't blame them if things fall apart. Your personal success as a manager hinges on your ability to first build the team.

RECRUITING: THE HEART OF EFFECTIVE TEAM BUILDING

✔ Use the performance-based job description to create a compelling job. This sets the foundation for the recruiting process.

✔ Recruiting is not selling, it's marketing, and it needs to begin the first time you interview a candidate.

✔ Unless they're leaving a bad situation, candidates accept jobs for three reasons—the quality of the company, the manager, and the job. Make sure you present the merits of all three during the interviewing process.

✔ Create challenging opportunities and then let applicants tell you why they're qualified to hold the position.

✔ Stay the buyer throughout the interviewing process. You don't learn anything new if you're selling.

✔ Assess, recruit, and negotiate in parallel. If you make it a serial process, you telegraph to the candidate that she's the only contender and you weaken your position.

✔ Always lead the dance. Use challenging and recruiting questions to stay in control, create interest, and test motivation.

✔ Maintain competition. The job has more appeal, and you'll have a stronger negotiating position throughout the hiring process.

✔ Test all aspects of the offer before formalizing it. This allows for open communications.

✔ The testing process is a way to identify and overcome objections. If you make the offer too soon, you'll never really know the candidate's other options.

✔ Don't shoot yourself in the foot. Move slowly. Keep an open mind. Don't sell too soon. And ask only performance-based questions.

✔ You need to recruit from beginning to end. Stay in touch after the candidate has accepted the offer until the new employee is on the job. There's too much competition out there.

Chapter 9

Wide-Ranging Sourcing—
How to Find the Best

"Begin at the beginning," the King said gravely "and go till you come to the end; then stop."
—Lewis Carroll, *Alice's Adventures in Wonderland,* 1865

■ YOU CAN'T HIRE THE BEST UNLESS YOU'RE SEEING THE BEST

Sourcing is the process of getting enough candidates to interview. Although everything hinges on the quality of the sourcing program, it's usually the area in the staffing process that gets the least attention. Even without a good sourcing plan, you'll be able to hire a star every now and then. But if you want to hire stars regularly throughout your company at every level and at every function, you need a rock-solid staffing program. Sourcing is the sibling of recruiting. Sourcing gets the candidates in the door, recruiting gets them to stay.

"If you're only seeing turkeys, you'll hire a turkey." This is the hard truth. You can do everything else right, but if you're only meeting below-average candidates, you'll have to hire a below-average person. Sourcing is the most important link in the hiring

249

chain. Conversely, if you're doing everything else wrong, but you're only seeing the best, you'll eventually hire a top-notch candidate.

For example, Microsoft talks about their remarkable candidate assessment program. It is pretty sophisticated and worth emulating, but it's really nothing you couldn't do using the concepts in this book. Their sourcing, however, is truly amazing. They have the best developers and product managers and marketers in the country, probably in the whole world, knocking down their doors to get in. With this rich talent pool, they're bound to hire the best. Consistent great hiring eventually becomes a competitive advantage. It starts with superior sourcing.

■ YOU HAVE JUST ELIMINATED HALF OF YOUR SOURCING PROBLEMS

If you are using the techniques presented up to this point of the book, you have already solved at least 50% of your sourcing problems.

Now that you're measuring people's ability to do the job, rather than just get the job, candidates you formerly excluded are receiving serious consideration. These promising candidates were always there. You were eliminating them too soon for the wrong reasons. By controlling emotions, maintaining objectivity, and understanding the performance needs of the job, you now have the interviewing skills to get past the veneer and see the substance. This change alone will eliminate many of your sourcing problems and increase the number of qualified candidates.

Wendy Wimmer-Ross, the Director of Human Resources at Ruby's Restaurants in southern California described to me how using these performance-based approaches impacted their sourcing. Ruby's, a chain of 1940s-theme diners, has always had difficulty staffing their restaurants with enough managers and serving staff. We recently conducted a hiring seminar for their management team and stressed that they could broaden their pool of qualified applicants by reducing their emphasis on restaurant experience and highlighting performance requirements.

These had to do with team and organizational issues, the need to be proactive in dealing with people, and an ability to deal with the job's physical demands, among others.

As a result of these changes, the company has been able to fully staff each of their 40 restaurants, including store and regional managers. This is the first time in five years, this has ever happened. Wendy also said that no compromises were made on the quality of the people hired. All met the existing high performance standards of the company. To ensure that the emotional control component was neutralized, she conducted phone interviews before inviting candidates in for a personal interview. At this first interview, she would lead a panel interview with the store management. By controlling emotions this way, and changing the focus to performance instead of experience, Ruby's was able to staff itself fully within only six months.

Sourcing problems are cut in half when you focus on the performance needs of a job during the interview and in preparing ads.

You'll increase your candidate pool further by writing performance-based job descriptions for your classified advertising. Experience-based job specs are too narrow. These get turned into dull ads that discourage some of the best candidates from even applying because they're overly restrictive. And since the jobs sound boring, even those who meet the qualifications won't apply unless they desperately need a job. Performance-based ads that emphasize performing activities, instead of having experience, will attract well-qualified candidates. If the ad is compelling enough, you'll attract those with potential as well as some other great applicants sitting on the fence, waiting for just that right opportunity to present itself.

■ HOW TO WRITE A COMPELLING AD

The basic element of all sourcing programs is the ad. It doesn't matter where the ad is placed. At the beginning of every search, you have to tell a potential candidate you're out there looking. Start the rebuilding of your sourcing program with this lowly ad. It might turn out to be the only thing you'll need to do.

➤ The Traditional (and Not Very Effective) Ad

Ads are mostly written for people looking for work. The ad at the bottom of the page was picked out at random in CareerPath, the Times-Mirror Corporation Web site.

This style ad is representative of 90% of the 350,000 new jobs posted every month on this Web site. This is an important position within this company, yet the ad is a turnoff. There's nothing in it for the candidate other than a paycheck. No growth, no chance to make an impact, no career opportunity, just a job.

The traditional ad only attracts people who need jobs. These people are either underemployed or unemployed. Any job looks good to this group, since they need one badly. Although not by intention, traditional ads are written exclusively to attract this group. Surprisingly, every now and then a winner turns up using this technique, but it's a fluke. It's no way to build a company of stars.

Another differentiator of this type of ad is that it works better for lower-level and first-level managers, but it is less effective for senior-level positions. How many of your company's senior management responded or would respond to an ad like this? Probably not many. At lower levels, there might be a few more

---

Controller

Your 10–15 years experience in accounting will make you a major asset to our company. You will be responsible for financial and management accounting, SEC reporting, A/R, A/P, and internal controls. Must have at least 5 years as controller or asst., plus heavy SEC reporting and tax. Multi-unit consolidations is required. Must also have a CPA or MBA, and have excellent analytical skills and communication skills.

strong candidates responding. As you move higher up in the organization ads become less effective. In general if you want to attract the top group of candidates, those hard-to-find gems, typical ads in the typical places just don't cut it.

If you want to attract the best people, you need to write ads from a different perspective. Start by treating candidates as customers, not vendors. An ad is a marketing tool. Prepare it with this in mind. Strong people who have jobs need a compelling reason to leave their current and highly satisfying position. Most of the best people fall in this category.

Most ads mix a list of duties and responsibilities with some having-oriented prerequisites (e.g., have 10 years' experience, have a degree, have the same job, have the same industry background, have the same scope). People are surprised when they get weak response to an ad like this. Would you take another job at the same pay doing the same things over and over again? Not unless you needed a job. You're certainly not going to change jobs unless you think you'll become a stronger person as a result. Ads need to reflect this. You can use the performance-based job description to make ads broad and compelling. An example of the same ad rewritten from a performance and marketing perspective, appears on page 254.

➤ A Marketing-Driven Performance-Based Ad

This ad is written with the strong candidate in mind. It's the type of job a top person, with a going-toward strategy, would need to pry her out of a good job. Remember from Chapter 8 that a going-toward motivational strategy is based on a candidate's need to move to a significantly better job. This ad effectively describes a strong company, the growth opportunity, and the challenge of the position. Compelling opportunities like this attract the best. Start with the performance-based job spec to format the ad copy. Be substantive. Talk about the company strategy and challenges. Give enough information for the candidate to determine whether the job offers real growth.

To overcome the inertia of not responding and staying put, the job and the ad have to be different, interesting, and compelling. You want to attract as diverse a group of responses as possible. The profile of the person you're looking for changes once

---

Controller

We're a fast-growing player in our industry and need a leader to help get us under control. We need someone to build and manage the team to set up new forward-looking systems and help us define our performance reporting needs. This includes everything from SEC, reporting to tax and monthly analysis. You'll be using your MBA or CPA right away on some exciting new and challenging projects.

If you've got the horsepower to take over this critical department and grow fast with our company, send in your resume. Include a separate write-up describing your most significant team and individual accomplishments. We realize compensation needs to be very aggressive to continue to build an all-star team.

---

you know the true work that needs to be performed. The ad needs to take this into account by focusing on the outcomes, or performance needs, rather than the inputs, or experience requirements. This performance-based ad is a good model.

Review a few of your most recent ads. Which group of candidates do they attract, those needing work, or those open to explore new opportunities? I learned this fundamental rule about management from one of my candidates. He said, "If something isn't working right, don't keep on doing it. Keep on changing it until it works right." You might want to try this same technique with your ads if they're not pulling as effectively as they should. On page 255 is another ad this time from a popular newspaper. It's not bad, but the second version on the right has been rewritten from the candidate's perspective. For a strong candidate, the decision to proceed forward is not based on need, it's based on opportunity. This fundamental difference has been captured in the revised version. *Which ad treats the candidate as a customer?*

When you use performance criteria to write ads, you've come full circle. These are the same performance criteria you'll use to

• Marketing Manager •

As a world leader, we operate in 50 countries, serving the energy and chemical industries. If you are a highly motivated marketing professional with the talent, proven experience, and initiative to manage our marketing services and research functions, we would like to invite you to join our team.

You will be responsible for coordinating with Product Mangers on all outbound marketing activities, conducting market research for the VP of Sales & Marketing, and developing the advertising plans and budgets.

The ideal candidate will have the following:

- BS degree in marketing or business, or equivalent related work experience.
- Minimum of 4 years experience in marketing and/or public relations.
- Excellent written and oral communication skills.
- Working knowledge of Microsoft Office, primarily Word and Excel.
- Experience with database management.

• Marketing Manager •

As a world leader, we operate in 50 countries, serving the fast-changing energy and chemical industries. As a result, we need a progressive marketing pro to guide the launch of our major new ALPHA program. This critical person will manage all of our marketing services and research functions.

You will lead the effort with our Product Managers to develop innovative outbound marketing programs, develop marketing strategies with the executive team based on state-of-the-art market research, and develop broad, multi-channel advertising programs.

This is a career-building opportunity worth exploring. Give us a call if you have an international marketing background, know how to build market share in the industrial products arena, aren't afraid to try new ideas, and want to be on a fast-track growth curve.

Global Tech, Inc.
Creating careers, not jobs!

write job descriptions, assess competency, transition new employees into the company, monitor progress, write reviews, and reward and promote. This is what performance management is all about. At its core is the prioritized list of deliverables—the SMART objectives created in Chapter 2.

■ MULTILEVEL SOURCING—DON'T PUT ALL YOUR EGGS IN ONE BASKET

You always have to be looking, and you have to be looking everywhere. If you're just going to run an ad in your local paper, you're limiting yourself. Unless they're having a bad day, the best people generally don't look here for a job although they may glance at their trade magazines, business journals, and trade newspapers. The key is to try lots of different channels concurrently. This will increase your odds that the best people will hear about the opportunity. In addition, you need more than one finalist to protect yourself. Expect things to go wrong. There's always lots of competition for the best, and a strong economy aggravates a tough situation.

From a sourcing perspective, there are two types of candidates—those who are actively looking for work, and those who aren't. There are two general sourcing methods to reach these

Table 9.1   A Summary of Alternate Sourcing Approaches

Geared toward Candidates Looking		Geared toward Candidates Not Looking	
Name	**Comments**	**Name**	**Comments**
Traditional Advertising	Passive. Often the quickest and least expensive, but results mixed.	Direct Sourcing	Active. Internally develop lists of possible candidates.
Events	Active. Consists of job fairs and trade meetings. Good for high tech.	Direct Marketing	Active. Send letter to possible candidates to solicit interest.
Networking	Active. Internal referrals programs with employees, suppliers, and customers. Call, use or join trade associations and professional societies.	Contract Research	Active. These folks find those not looking and you pay them per hour. Formerly exclusive territory of recruiters.
Internet and High-Tech Approaches	Passive. Consists of Web sites, career sites, and resume scanning. Inexpensive, sometimes effective, and growing in popularity.	Recruiters	Active. You pay them to do all of this and they often guarantee results.

candidates—passive and active. With a passive approach, you wait for a candidate to call you, usually as a result of some form of advertising. This will only attract those looking for work. An active approach is much more forceful. You stir the pot and directly seek out the best of those looking and those who don't even know they're looking. There are a number of different techniques within each of these two broad categories. These are summarized in Table 9.1.

Any form of advertising, including the Internet, is a passive sourcing technique. You're hoping a top person will respond to your ad. While it sometimes works, it has the same 2 or 3% success rate as direct marketing so it's important to get as much coverage as possible. An active approach is more direct. This is what good recruiters use. They identify where the best people are and personally go after them. You need to consider both active and passive approaches as you create an aggressive, multilevel sourcing program. Each sourcing method has its own strengths and weaknesses. While some are more effective than others, it's important to know how to maximize the effectiveness of whatever approach you use.

■ SOURCING METHODS GEARED TO CANDIDATES LOOKING FOR A JOB

➤ Traditional Advertising

Take your compelling performance-based ad and put it everywhere. Consider local and national newspapers, trade and professional journals, and airline magazines. Outdoor signs work for some positions. We have a local company that uses some clever comments to lure production personnel. It seems like a fun place to work. They must get filled quickly. These ads are always gone within a week replaced with some new position. The college placement office is also a good place for ads. We hire researchers and administrative personnel through the local community college placement centers, and have found some fine people.

There's also an on-line service for the major colleges and universities. This is a more modern way of posting jobs at the college career center. Now you only have to post your ad once, and then select the schools where you want your advertisement to be seen. It's inexpensive. Just contact any university placement office to get the details.

Since advertising is a passive sourcing technique and only geared to those candidates looking for work, it should be conducted in conjunction with other approaches.

➤ Events

This is an active approach to get in the midst of people looking for work. Hiring events consist of job fairs, sponsoring booths at professional association events, and sponsoring special career days. Job fairs are effective when cosponsored by related companies trying to fill similar positions. When these are heavily promoted and advertised by the local newspapers, they can draw a number of qualified candidates. They're less effective in tight labor markets and when the breadth of job openings is too wide. They're best for high-tech positions, although you need to move quickly if you find a talented person.

Consider sponsoring a booth at a professional association meeting. We met a number of great HR managers and executives at one of their annual meetings. Talk to people in these fields to determine the best events to consider. Sponsor your own career fair and invite a few experts in to discuss various career topics. Consider a joint program with one of the major outplacement or employee service firms. They sometimes have experts who can draw talent to the event.

These events are more proactive than advertising, since you are going into the field to find people who are actively looking. They should be part of an ongoing sourcing program.

➤ Networking

This active sourcing approach gets everyone involved. We all know good people. At a minimum, set up an employee referral program. Pay a significant amount to your employees for anyone they recommend who ultimately gets hired. Of course, don't reduce your standards. Also network with your suppliers, professional service providers, and even your customers. Suppliers know experts in their field and if you need someone with special skills, they're a good source to tap into. A lot of firms ask their accounting firms for leads when they want to hire financial people. Expand this to include your bankers, legal advisers, consultants, and business associates. Make the approach formal. Send a quick note with a short summary of your job needs. Customers can also be a valuable source for leads. Few of these people will ever give you someone who is currently employed and happy, but most of the referrals will be well qualified and worthy of consideration.

Call or join the trade associations of people you want to attract. Material control people belong to the American Production and Inventory Control Society (APICS). Financial managers belong to the Financial Executives Institute and the CPA Society. Property Managers belong to the Institute for Real Estate Management (IREM). Get in touch with the local chapters and start spreading the word. Send letters to the officers of these groups. We've discovered that these are some of the best people. Ask them for referrals. The *Encyclopedia of Associations* (CD-ROM)[1] is a great place to find the names of these officers.

Get the names of the appropriate trade groups from the resumes you receive from your ads. There are too many organizations around to keep track of them all so this is a good way to get the names. We often run highly specific ads with the primary purpose to get these kinds of leads. We then call the trade group headquarters to get rosters, officer lists, and a list of members open to explore new opportunities. Outplacement firms are also a good place to start to look for mid- and upper-management personnel. Some of the larger outplacement firms have databases of all the candidates in their system, so they're easy to find.

➤ The Internet and Other High-Tech Sourcing Options

It's a brand-new world and new approaches are needed to attract superior people. The Internet is a hybrid of passive and active sourcing. The Internet and E-mail are two new tools that will profoundly alter hiring practices. Right now, the Internet is underutilized, just serving as an automated classified ad clearinghouse. In this way, it's another form of passive classified advertising. But

---

[1] Published by Gale Research. Available through AMAZON.com.

progress is being made steadily to make it more active, so get on the bandwagon.

More sophistication is being added in the form of mixing and matching resumes using key word searches. While these advances will help match job seekers and hunters more efficiently, there are problems. For one, it's too cumbersome. There are too many resumes from too many people that are even harder to read than the traditional paper resume. The sorting is still pretty rudimentary, so it's hard to find the best fit. Some on-line services provide a strong versus weak match based on criteria you select, and this helps. In a few years, I'm sure a short list of best-fit candidates will become available; the Times-Mirror group with their massive CareerPath Web site is working on this problem. So get on the Internet and become comfortable with this new recruiting tool. It will get better. The Internet still has one major problem that no amount of automation will solve. Only candidates looking for a job are represented there. The ones who are happy are not submitting their resumes for consideration. Until they do, you are still only going after the candidates who need or want a new job. While there are some top 10% candidates in this group, it happens only about 1% of the time. Contingency recruiters[2] are having a field day with the current system. They are running ads themselves and sorting through the responses to find the top candidates and then introducing these candidates to the companies looking for these types of people. This is an important service for both the company and the candidate. They are providing the automation and personal contact the system needs.

Here are a few simple things you can do to quickly go high tech. Right now, we're collecting E-mail addresses from every potential candidate, whether the person is interested in considering a job right now or not. We also try to get a short profile or resume to include in our database. We scan this information using Page-Keeper software (about $150). We also scan in promising unsolicited resumes. When an assignment comes up, we conduct a key word search (e.g., for a telecommunications engineer, we search for BSEE, telecommunications, hardware, ATM, access switching), and any resumes with these words show up in ranked order. We

---

[2] Contingency recruiters only get paid when a person they recommend is hired. They then earn 15 to 25% of the annual salary.

then call these people or send them an E-mail describing the merits of the job using a compelling ad to attract interest. While this is an active sourcing approach, it's small potatoes stuff. On the other hand, it's inexpensive and effective. It's also a good way to get started in high-tech sourcing.

If you're now familiar with the Internet, start your on-line recruiting at www.interbiznet.com. This web location (also referred to as a URL) offers a great selection of the top 100 Internet electronic recruiting sites. From this central point you'll quickly be able to start recruiting on-line. Here's a quick look at some of the ones we use regularly.

➤ *Career Mosiac* (www.careermosaic.com): This is probably the largest job hunting site on the net. Try out their resume search tool. This allows you to enter key words to search their database of thousands of resumes.

➤ *HeadHunter* (www.headhunter.net [note "net" not "com"]): I love this site. The first time I went to it I found a potential candidate for a sales manager for a telecommunications firm using their easy-to-use search engine. You can't post jobs, but you can advertise via an on-line banner. Check it out.

➤ *Job Center* (www.jobcenter.com): This is a great site that does it all—search resumes, post jobs at reasonable fees, and they'll even send you resumes (via daily E-mail) of the best candidates responding to your on-line ad. Since candidates have to pay to have their resumes included in their database, it eliminates some of the weaker applicants.

➤ *Monster Board* (www.monster.com): This well-known site for job hunters offers lots of guidance and exposure for companies searching for talent on the Internet. The fees are reasonable and it's a good place to get started.

➤ *JOBTRAK* (www.jobtrak.com): The site has formed unique partnerships with over 650 college and university career centers, MBA programs, and alumni associations nationwide. While the site is a bit passive (you post ads and then wait), it does tap into an important source of top candidates, and is worth trying out. Fees are reasonable.

On-line recruiting is the place to be. Start right away. See our site (www.cjapower.com) for some of the latest tips and practical guidance on using the Internet for sourcing. With the advances being made now, I estimate that in a few years you'll be able to fill 50% of your technical positions and 25% of your middle and senior level management positions on-line. Resume registries will even make it possible for you to find candidates not actively looking. The Internet will become a great, inexpensive source of candidates. Hustle and good recruiting skills will be the key to making it work properly for you and your company. You'll succeed with great ads, attractive web sites, compelling opportunities, and a determination to get the best candidates before anyone else.

■ HOW TO FIND THE GREAT CANDIDATES NOT LOOKING FOR A JOB

If you want to find the best talent in the field, you'll have to use some active and direct sourcing techniques. This is what recruiters do and that is how they justify their fees. The best people are not actively looking for a new job so you have to contact them directly. As a result, these approaches are always more expensive, but you are much more likely to find a top candidate. The following sections summarize some common programs used to find the best people.

➤ Direct Sourcing

All the techniques in this active category require direct sourcing. At the most fundamental level, this consists of identifying the best people doing the work you want done and then contacting each one personally. To get the names, you can buy professional society rosters, comb annual reports, and search the Internet. You can also ask those in your network for names of the best people they know in the field, not just those looking for work. You can also develop a network based on "one degree of separation."

Find people who work with the types of people you want to hire. We got the names of good medical device salespeople by calling local medical clinics. This is obviously only the first step. Next, you must contact these people and convince them that your position is worthy of consideration.

➤ Direct Marketing

Once you have the list of target names, you need to make contact. A direct-mail approach is one technique that works extremely well. It's inexpensive and effective. Just send a letter to each person describing your position in compelling terms and ask whether the person is interested in pursuing the opportunity, or knows anyone else who would be. You can also ask for other lead sources, and then send these people the same letter. Keep this chain-letter approach going. With this approach, you'll find some strong candidates you normally would not have met.

➤ Contract Researchers

Not all the names of the best people are publicly available, no matter how hard you look. To get these names, you have to identify your target companies, including competitors, and then identify the people in the appropriate position. You have to dig them out. This is how most recruiters find their best candidates. Contract researchers also do this, some better than others. They typically charge from $40 to $80 per hour. After identifying the name, they'll personally call the prospect and attempt to establish interest.

This is the first step in recruiting. The best people have to be convinced the opportunity is a great one. This requires a personal appeal. In my firm, we have to call 20 to 30 potential candidates who come close to the mark before we get one viable candidate. This means we must contact about 100 people to get three or four strong candidates—even more in tight markets like Silicon Valley. Some contract researchers only work for search firms, but more of them are going out on their own. Talk to your local HR professional societies for referrals.

➤ Recruiters

If you need a top person and can't find or attract one, consider using a recruiter or headhunter. They use all these techniques and charge anywhere from 20% to 35% of total compensation. Follow this basic principle that covers every position: Only pay a headhunter a search fee for a B+ or better candidate. Search fees should be an investment, not an expense. A strong recruit pays for herself or himself quickly: an A+ candidate within six months, a B+ person within a year or so. You can find B candidates easily enough on your own, so don't waste your money if all you need is a solid performer. Strong prospects need to be pried out of their current situations, and that justifies the fee.

This brings me to a second principle: you must use a recruiter for every strategic position if you don't have a few great leads for A+ candidates firmly in hand. These are the game-breaker positions you must fill with a top candidate. Don't compromise on this one. The cost to acquire this expertise is insignificant if the person needs to achieve a major business objective. It doesn't matter whether it's a senior engineer or a VP Marketing. When the success of the company rides on this person's shoulders, go all out. Don't nitpick the compensation, either.

You should use a retained recruiter[3] for every critical position over $100,000 per year, a contingency recruiter in the $50,000 to $100,000 per year category, and temporary-to-permanent[4] for all administrative positions. Top people expect to get their next job through a recruiter. They go out of their way to cultivate these relationships since recruiters are often the source of the best jobs.

I read an internal report prepared by American Hospital Supply (since acquired by Baxter-Travenol) in the early 1980s that addressed this issue. Their goal was to determine how their top talent was brought into the organization. They had a database of their high performers ranging from those with a few

---

[3] Retained recruiters sign a contract to find a person and get paid during the course of the search.

[4] Temporary to permanent. Many staffing and employment agencies offer programs to try out candidates before hiring them full time.

years with the company to senior executives. A quick review determined that about 60% of these best people came into the company through their college recruiting program. Of the rest, more than 80% came in as a result of a search firm or a referral, with the balance from ads. American Hospital was known to hire highly qualified people and had some very progressive HR programs, so this is not a fluke.

A quick check with some other companies reconfirms this trend even today. A significant difference is the reduced reliance on internal promotions. Although still high, all the downsizing and restructuring in the late 1980s and early 1990s has increased the need for companies to go outside for senior managers much more than before.

The key to effective sourcing is to use a combination of passive and active approaches consistently. All this takes a lot of hard work. It's necessary if you want to reach the people who aren't aggressively looking for a job. Don't rely on one technique. If your number one candidate falls apart, you've lost the advantage of time. Once you become desperate, your standards fall and you hire on basic needs not superior performance.

The conclusion is obvious. If you want to consistently hire good people you need to develop them internally, use recruiters to find them, or go after the best directly yourself. The other way is to establish yourself as a leader in your field (e.g., Microsoft and Intel), and the best will come to you. The latter approach doesn't work as well, however, for upper management and executive level spots. Top people in these positions still have to be identified and pulled away. So until there's a way to get ready access to the group that's not looking, it seems that recruiters, or at least recruiter's techniques, are here to stay.

■ INNOVATIVE SOURCING—THE CISCO APPROACH

If any company has the sourcing process figured out, it's Cisco, the $6.4 billion Silicon Valley networking giant. A September 29, 1997, *Fortune* magazine article, "Cisco's Recruiting Edge," describes some of Cisco's innovative sourcing approaches. It starts with CEO John Chamber's strategy of only hiring the top 10 to 15%. To achieve this, much of the company's efforts must involve direct sourcing techniques to find candidates not actively looking. Cisco is in a hot telecommunications field and to get the best requires some unusual methods. Here's a sampling of some of their more remarkable sourcing techniques:

➤ Enticing newspaper ads advertise the company's Web site, not specific jobs. Once here, the job seeker can review hundreds of open positions.

➤ Company recruiters look for prospective candidates at unusual congregating places. For example, the company will go to the local home and garden show to meet young homeowners. The up-and-comers typically go to these events and Cisco attempts to contact them in this unusual setting.

➤ The company matches up potential candidates with current employees who can provide firsthand information about the company. Candidates learn more about the company this way before they get heavily involved in the interviewing process. Candidates learn about this "friends" program through local movie theater advertising.

➤ The company recently launched an on-line resume program called Profiler, which captures critical aspects about a candidate's background. If the candidate is at work, there is also a kill button to clear the screen quickly.

➤ They'll buy talent. Cisco is acquisition minded, and they have acquired a number of companies to obtain top engineering and management talent. Rather than design and develop a product from scratch, it's often easier to find a successful group of talented people already in the business. This approach also eliminates the competition.

The key to all of Cisco's efforts is in developing new techniques to go after the best people, who aren't aggressively looking for new jobs. Most people are willing to talk about an exciting career opportunity, even if they are currently happy with their existing position. Cisco has made this a strategic objective and has developed some successful tactics to implement it.

■ BUY SOME TIME—A STAFFING PLAN CAN ALERT YOU TO NEEDS AND PROBLEMS

As your need to fill a spot increases, your standards drop. The lack of time is your enemy, and the candidate's (and headhunter's) friend. You will compromise, ignore negative data, pay more for less, and ultimately weaken your staff. There are only a few ways to overcome this critical problem and each one requires you to be proactive. Here's a quick review of some alternatives with pointers.

A staffing plan should be a subset of every annual operating plan. This identifies all the new positions you'll be adding over the next year. There are no excuses for failure to plan this way. This allows you to begin the recruiting process six months ahead of time for new positions. People quitting is a different situation. If turnover is predictable, say 10% per year for engineering designers, there aren't many excuses. Just plan on adding 10% new people like this each year, and always be on the lookout for qualified candidates.

Even if turnover isn't predictable, weaker and marginal people have a tendency to leave. In some way, they're driven out. You can plan for this. In fact, you should build your plan to take into account the need to upgrade the quality of your staff. Don't wait for staff changes to happen. Make them happen. Work toward replacing the bottom 20% of your staff each year if they're not cutting it, and work on ensuring that the top 20% stays. Good employee development programs can help minimize unnecessary turnover of these top performers.

Enfish, the hot new software company located in Pasadena, CA, recently established an annual staffing plan. To support growth, the company has had to upgrade all aspects of its hiring. A performance-based job description is required for all new positions, and managers must document the candidate's ability to meet the performance outcomes before hiring. As a parallel effort, they decided to develop an annual staffing plan based on their annual business plan, sales forecasts, and production plans.

Louise Wannier, the founder and CEO, told me this was of tremendous help since it made all managers aware of their needs well before they became critical. She hired a full-time recruiting person just to handle the anticipated growth. As a result they were able to fill positions much more quickly than normal, without making the typical compromises. Their forward-looking staffing program has enabled Enfish to support its rapid development schedule. They have discovered that planning staffing needs is as important as planning any other long-term activity.

A CFO I recently interviewed told me that the staffing plan was an essential part of his company's annual planning process. By tying in staffing requirements and all other resource needs (capital, facilities, working capital) to the sales and production forecast for the year, the company was able to accurately predict its financial position. Since the company updated the sales forecast monthly, they were better able to anticipate changes long before the need arose. An upturn in forecasted sales due to a hot new product line allowed the company to hire and train the customer support staff before the orders arrived. The same planning process prevented the company from hiring additional design engineers and production staff when the sales forecast indicated an unexpected downturn.

A good staffing plan can be prepared using a simple spreadsheet that line managers upgrade regularly based on any new information. Table 9.2 shows a section of a typical staffing plan that

Table 9.2 Anticipation of Staffing Needs by
Linking to Sales Forecasts

Plan to Forecast Comparison	July	August	September	October	November	December
Annual Plan Unit Sales	10,000	10,500	11,000	11,500	12,000	12,000
Current June Forecast	10,000	11,000	12,000	14,000	16,000	18,000
Difference	0	500	1,000	2,500	4,000	6,000
Customer Service Staff						
Department Manager	1	1	1	1	1	1
Shift Supervisors	2	2	2	2	3	3
Total Telephone Service Agents	8	8	9	10	12	14
New Telephone Service Agents	0	0	1	1	2	2
Replacements (25% turnover)	1	0	1	0	1	0
Total New Agents/Month	1	0	2	1	3	2

has been tied to the sales forecast. This one reveals the need for more customer service staff to handle a forecasted pickup of current levels in orders four months ahead. This gives the department manager and HR the time needed to effectively source candidates.

Build replacements into the staffing plan, as shown in Table 9.2. There should never be a surprise when someone important leaves and needs to be replaced. You'll find clues months in advance, if you look. Lack of open communications is a big clue. Staying in touch with your staff is an important aspect of management. Remember that good candidates leave jobs because the other job, company, and hiring manager offered more. Evaluate your staff's satisfaction along these same dimensions. Think about the individual team members. Would they take their current job under the current conditions if you offered it to them again? If not, it's time to take some action. Determine if salary and working conditions are competitive. Is the job content challenging enough? Are you being a mentor or a jerk? What makes the company special? Has the quality of your staff's work product declined? What about the spouse and his/her possible relocation? Clues abound to potential turnover problems. Don't wait for them to happen. Be proactive. It's difficult to replace a top performer. It's far easier to prevent it from happening.

You're not going to anticipate or prevent every staffing problem. Sometimes you'll just have to go into the market and find a replacement. You'll do a much better job if you're anticipating rather than reacting. There are always two or three essential positions in every department. Do you know which ones they are? Is the quality of the people in these positions top-notch? If not, put upgrading these positions into your staffing plan. For those who are strong, make sure that you've addressed any potential morale or motivation problems.

Next, develop some alternatives. Reallocation of duties is my favorite. Prepare a performance-based job description for each position in your department. Mix and match some of these critical SMART objectives based on the strengths of each of your team members. Try work-type profiling for additional help, by restructuring jobs and dividing up tasks. This way you can minimize the catastrophic problem of a critical person leaving.

This approach will help cross-train others in your group in case someone does leave. Also, someone might give second thoughts to leaving if the job content has improved. Reallocating critical performance objectives of a job across a department in this way minimizes unnecessary turnover. In addition, you may want some of your team members to develop their own SMART objectives for their jobs. This will allow you to customize a job to meet the strengths of the individual. Simply planning ahead this way, to anticipate staffing needs due to turnover, can sometimes prevent it.

■ NEVER STOP LOOKING

In 1975, when I worked for a living, this is how I got an important job. I was a Director of Business Planning with Rockwell's Consumer Electronics operations (one of the companies that originated the hand-held calculator). Our business dropped from $10 million per month to $5 million in a matter of months and losses were mounting. It was time to think about leaving.

A month before, a group president of another company I had met at a business meeting the prior year, called and asked if I was interested in another opportunity. We had had lunch a few times during the year, so it was not an unexpected call. He had been keeping me informed of opportunities at his company regularly, and now the timing was right for me. I called him back, met again, and started with his firm a few weeks later in a similar position. Within two years, I was a VP and general manager of one of their business units. After starting, I learned that this contact program was something the group president had been doing his whole career. He told me he was always able to fill about 50% of his open positions this way. He developed a career plan for all his staff, and could roughly predict when open positions would become available for these prospects.

Always be on the lookout for good people. Keep a database of people you know, who could be potential team members. The timing for people is never exactly right. A great person you know will rarely be available exactly when you need to fill the appropriate position. But if you know three or four people, you'll often find one when the timing is right for both of you. This is what recruiters do. We're always on the lookout for top people. We cultivate and maintain these relationships. When an opportunity arises, these are the first people we call.

On a smaller scale, you can do the same thing. Keep track of the best people you know. Tell them to keep you aware of their career needs and personal situations. Be open to referrals from them. Develop your own network and database of these top people. Staffing is important to your personal success. You can't leave it to the last minute. Go out of your way to develop some unique personal database sourcing programs. They'll pay enormous dividends.

One of my clients is a senior executive at one of the large entertainment companies. He's established a policy with some of the search firms in the area. Because he wants to take the pulse of the Los Angeles employment market, he'll meet any strong candidate even if he doesn't have a current open position. This executive has been in the entertainment industry for about 10 years, and prior to this moved up rapidly at one of the large Fortune 100 consumer products companies. Over the past few years, he's been instrumental in placing at least 20 senior-level managers and executives from these referrals and other past associations. He's typically able to fill even difficult positions within a few weeks. The quality of his staff is world-class as a result. But it wasn't due to luck. He planned it out long ago and continues working at it every day.

■ SELECTION—HOW TO REVIEW A RESUME (IN 30 SECONDS OR LESS)

Using performance criteria, we've cast a wider net with more broadly defined parameters. It will result in getting more candidates. Don't complain about too many resumes, even if they don't all meet all your specs. They're easy to screen. You'll only need about 30 seconds to a minute for each resume, but you need to use a performance-based filter not an experience-based one. The key is to focus on comparable change. Look for changes the candidate implemented and changes in the scope and title of the jobs held compared with your needs. These are the most important clues to superior performance.

We're a relatively small executive search firm and get about 50 unsolicited resumes per day. I personally look at least 50% of them. It takes me about 30 seconds to discard a resume and 1 minute to decide to input the resume into our scanner system. If I don't have a job in mind, here's what I look for:

> A professional looking resume. If it's not, it gets dumped within 10 seconds. The resume represents the candidate's work product. It's a business communications piece. Sloppy work is not acceptable.

> The quality of the companies. Credible accomplishments at solid companies are a big plus.

> The tenure at each organization. Turnover is a big concern. People who can get lots of jobs are great at the interviewing, but not so great at the doing. Be concerned about a long-term pattern of turnover. But don't be too quick eliminating those caught up in the merger and acquisition activity of the late 1980s and early 1990s. Turnover as a result of corporate restructuring is understandable.

> A track record of increasing responsibility. Promotions at a few different and strong companies are a strong indicator of a top candidate. This is probably the most important factor to consider. A number of lateral moves is indicative of a plateaued career. (I'm not too concerned with this if the candidate is still energetic.) A break in service is okay, too, if preceded by a solid track record.

> Solid academics.

> An unusual, but not gimmicky cover letter. This could include an in-depth description of a candidate's major accomplishment, or a more insightful presentation of why the candidate is looking. While this is not a dealmaker, it will add some points.

> Strong or unusual competence in a specific area.

If there is a specific job we're considering, we add the following additional screening factors:

> Job-specific accomplishments comparable to the top two or three SMART objectives. This is the key difference

when screening for accomplishments compared with screening for experience. The SMART objectives represent the real work that needs to get done. For example, you don't need 10 years of industry experience if you're hiring a manufacturing manager. You probably need someone who can lead the upgrading of manufacturing systems, build a strong team of supervisors, and increase productivity. Look for this in the resume, regardless of the industry, as long as the accomplishments and technical knowledge are reasonably comparable.

➤ The comparability of the jobs is a critical factor. You need to consider the scope of the assignments, the size of the organization in dollars and people, the relative position of the job within the organization, and the complexity of the business.

If the candidate meets these criteria on paper, it's time to conduct a phone interview.

■ SOURCING—IT'S THE STRATEGIES, NOT THE TACTICS, THAT WILL ULTIMATELY DETERMINE YOUR SUCCESS

You have to be seeing good prospects, to hire good employees. You can be great at doing every other aspect of staffing and hiring, and still be a failure if you're not seeing enough qualified candidates. Compensation can't be excluded from the sourcing plan. Don't expect to hire top candidates if your overall compensation package is below average. You might be able to sneak in one or two people this way, but it won't work as a long-term strategy.

Compensation is a sourcing issue. Candidates learn quickly which companies don't pay well, and which ones do. If you have a reputation as a low-paying company, you won't see some of the best people. They won't even consider applying. As Catherine Meek, the well-known compensation expert, once told me, "Over the long term, an aggressive compensation program based on performance is essential, if you want to build a world-class company with world-class people."

We've presented a lot of sourcing tactics in this chapter, but it's the strategies that are really important. The need to be proactive heads the list. You have to spend time at sourcing and your company has to dedicate the appropriate resources. If you want to build a strong team at every level and department in the company, sourcing can't be an "as required" or passive activity. Active sourcing is essential. The best aren't looking. You have to go after them. Planning is a prerequisite. This buys you the time needed to do it right. If you treat candidates as potential customers rather than future subordinates, a whole shift in attitude takes place. This impacts advertising, priorities, the time spent on the process, the allocation of resources, and the quality of the interviewing and recruiting process. Great staffing starts with great sourcing.

Together, these strategies and tactics will help you do it right. Remember, you might already be seeing some great candidates, you just don't know it, yet. Once you begin using performance-based interviewing, you'll probably discover hidden talent in your current crop of candidates. In fact, the number of candidates will increase just by eliminating overly restrictive conditions that exclude some of the best.

Sourcing is the critical make-or-break component of the hiring process. The quality of the candidates interviewed will directly affect the quality of the candidates ultimately hired. When you get to the point where you're only seeing top-notch people for every position, you won't need to worry about anything else.

SOURCING—HOW TO GET THE BEST INTO YOUR OFFICE

✔ You're already seeing top people. You just have to follow some of the hiring principles in this book to find them.

✔ Develop direct sourcing programs to go after the strongest candidates. These people already have good jobs and need to be pried away. Develop a college recruiting program since some of the best people are easier to attract right out of school.

✔ Build your sourcing program around the "treat candidates as customers" concept. You want these great candidates to "buy" your company. This requires compelling ads, personal contact, and attention.

✔ Identify what motivates the candidate—a going-away or a going-toward strategy. A going-away strategy means that the candidate's current situation is bad and he is actively seeking a new job. Most top performers have a going-toward strategy and have to be lured away from a good situation. Write ads from this perspective.

✔ Three primary reasons motivate top candidates to take a new position—the quality of the job, the quality of the company, and the leadership qualities of the hiring manager. A sourcing, recruiting, and interviewing program needs to address all three issues concurrently.

✔ Ads need to be compelling with some sizzle around the top one or two SMART objectives. It's better to focus on the opportunity and challenge to draw the best candidates in. Minimize passive verbs like "having" and "responsible for" unless you want to attract average candidates.

✔ Things will always go wrong, so don't put all your sourcing eggs in one basket. Multichannel sourcing is the best technique. Run ads everywhere. Develop formal referral networks including your employee network.

✔ Reach out and touch someone. The best people are rarely looking so you have to grab their attention. Direct mail and E-mail campaigns can help. Be original. Get trade group rosters and contact some of the members.

✔ Networking and referrals are still the way to go. This is what recruiters do, and it works. Use your employees, vendors, customers, trade associations, and professional service corporations to get names of top people *not* looking. Then go after them with a personal pitch.

✔ Use recruiters if you can't find a top person through a referral network. The fee is worth it if you get a first-rate candidate. Make sure that recruiters are going after people who are not aggressively looking. Half your fee is going to finding people you can't find on your own. The other half is for keeping the deal together.

(continued)

(continued)

✔ Anticipate your needs. A forward-looking staffing plan can pinpoint staffing requirements months in advance.

✔ Annually, plan on upgrading the bottom 20% of your staff, and ensuring that the top 20% stays.

✔ You can sometimes avoid turnover problems if you anticipate the needs of your best employees. Make sure you have open communications and that their jobs continue to be challenging and fulfilling.

✔ Cross-train and reallocate the critical jobs throughout your team. Give the best team members bigger challenges and get everyone else involved in meeting the critical group SMART objectives. In case someone does leave, you'll still have coverage. You'll also minimize the need for a top employee to leave to find growth elsewhere.

✔ Always look for promising candidates, even when you don't need them. Build your personal network of potential employees when you don't need to hire anyone. It will be readily available then when you do.

✔ Review all resumes with performance, not experience, as the selection criterion. A track record of success at a few highly regarded companies is the best piece of information on a resume. Look for comparable performance, not identical experience.

✔ Sourcing must be a high-priority strategic process with forward-looking staffing plans and a well-thought-out compensation program. This will allow you to anticipate staffing needs, rather than having to react to surprises.

Chapter

Implementing Performance-Based Hiring

There are no secrets to success: Don't waste time looking for them. Success is the result of perfection, hard work, learning from failure, loyalty to those for whom you work, and persistence.

—Colin Powell

■ CHANGING STRATEGIES DRIVE THE NEED FOR NEW, RESPONSIVE STAFFING SOLUTIONS

Over the past 10 years, business conditions have profoundly affected every aspect of managing. The link connecting strategy, structure, and staffing has tightened. The pace of change is accelerating and those companies wanting to remain competitive must stay current. Strategies have been reworked and overhauled to meet the challenge. To meet the needs of rapidly changing strategies, old line hierarchical organizations have had to be replaced by more responsive and flexible organizational structures. Downsizing, reengineering, and constant improvement have made continuous reorganization a prerequisite for growth. Organizations now must recycle and rebuild themselves every few

277

years to stay competitive. Flexible teams, employee leasing, virtual corporations, and outsourcing of anything but core competencies are now commonplace. Every day, we read about another joint alliance, strategic partnership, merger, or acquisition that changes the very nature of the traditional organization. The restructuring of the corporate infrastructure has begun, replaced by fast, responsive, and customer service-oriented organizations.

The impact on staffing has been equally profound. Tenure-based promotions are now part of history. Lifetime employment has been replaced by three- to five-year assignments. Teams are rebuilt and replaced by new teams every few years. Management layers have been removed, and every employee is expected to work harder and smarter. In the face of this constant change, the manager's job is more challenging. Staffing has become more important. Every hiring decision has a bigger impact than before and there are more of them. New techniques are needed to address the changing importance of staffing and management. If asked individually, most managers would say that building a team is one of the most important contributors to their personal success. Despite this, few companies have formalized the hiring process so it really can make an impact.

■ THE POWER STAFFING SYSTEM—FIVE STEPS TO BETTER HIRING

What's surprising is that most companies have rigorous and well-supported systems for just about every process—from product development to order entry—except hiring. Hiring seems to have been ignored from the massive process reengineering effort of the past 10 years. A possible reason is that an effective hiring system takes more than just good interviewing skills. It involves people, emotions, budgets, time, negotiating, and job knowledge. These things are hard to systematize, especially when everything should have happened yesterday.

The POWER Staffing system addresses all aspects of hiring from finding candidates, determining best fit, to closing the deal. This five-step performance-based system links together every component of effective hiring into a system that can increase accuracy into the 80 to 90% range. None of the steps are hard to understand or difficult to use. The challenge is doing them all together. As shown in Figure 10.1, everything has to be done concurrently and implemented the same way. While each step is practical and easy to grasp, the process is severely weakened if any step is eliminated or compromised. It's the integration of these five steps that makes the process so effective.

Following is a quick review of each of the POWER components and how they link together. When hiring falls short it can always be attributed to a breakdown in one of these steps:

Performance-Based Job Descriptions. Define superior performance by writing out the top five or six deliverables or SMART objectives. These will drive the sourcing campaign, guide the interview and assessment, and serve as the foundation for the new employee transition program.

Objective Interview and Evaluation Process. Preplanned interviews and written assessments are prerequisites to

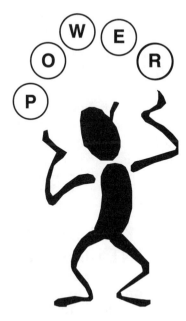

Figure 10.1. While the hiring steps are easy, you need to juggle lots of different objectives at the same time. Drop just one and the hiring process will be compromised.

accurate hiring. The influence of perceptions, biases, and emotions is minimized once everyone knows the performance needs of the job.

Wide-Ranging Sourcing Plans. Don't wait for candidates to call you. Go out and get them. You have to see good people before you can hire them. Good sourcing starts with a compelling ad based on performance needs, not experience.

Emotional Control. Cut hiring errors dramatically by waiting until the second half-hour of the interview to make a yes or no decision. You have to break the emotional link between yourself and the candidate and use the SMART objectives to judge competency. Bite your tongue and force yourself to take at least one full page of notes before you decide anything.

Recruiting Right. Stay the buyer. If you sell too soon, you cheapen the job and lose your negotiating position. Use the performance-based job description to create a compelling job. Candidates will be more open and will want to tell you why they're qualified.

■ IMPLEMENTING THE POWER STAFFING HIRING SYSTEM

Table 10.1 summarizes each of these steps in the hiring process and lists the associated forms, with the specific chapters in which they are discussed. (Copies of these forms are included in the Appendix.) The order shown is reasonably time-sequenced. It's not perfect since some activities overlap or are done concurrently.

■ THE POWER CHECK REVIEW—HOW GOOD ARE YOUR CURRENT HIRING METHODS?

Use the following questionnaire to determine what stage your company's hiring practices have reached. For each of the 20 steps, rank your current level.

It is best to implement a hiring system in four stages. These correspond to Column 2 in Table 10.2.

Table 10.1 Steps in the Hiring Process

Implementation Step	Associated Templates	Chapters
Preparing the Performance-Based Job Description	1. SMART Objectives Worksheet	2
	2. Performance-Based Job Description	
The Sourcing Plan		9
The Interviewing Process and Controlling Emotions	3. Emotional Control Worksheet	3
	4. Fact-Finding Worksheet	4
	5. Basic Eight-Question Interview	4
	6. Comprehensive Interview	6
	7. Phone Interview	4
	8. Performance Interview	4
The Assessment Process	9. Work-Type Profiling	5
	10. Reference Checking Worksheet	6
	11. Candidate Assessment Worksheet	7
Recruiting, Negotiating, and Closing	12. Recruiting Guide and Worksheet	8

1. *The Traditional System.* This includes just the basics—an approval process with some type of formal justification.

2. *The Performance-Based Hiring System.* This is the traditional system combined with performance-based job descriptions, preplanned interviews, and written assessments.

3. *The POWER Staffing Hiring System.* This stage incorporates all the components of the POWER Staffing hiring process with the addition of recruiting and sourcing. Company-wide implementation starts with a formal training program for hiring managers.

4. *The Advanced POWER Staffing Hiring System.* This stage adds refinements at each critical step to increase the level of effectiveness of the hiring process. Performance-based hiring is linked to the management process by using the SMART objectives to transition the new employee into the job.

Table 10.2   POWER Check—The Performance-Based
Hiring System Survey

Hiring System Criteria	Stage	Survey Questions Description	Status* (0–5)
1. A basic hiring system.	1	Is some type of formal hiring system in place with written guidelines?	
2. Formal hiring requisitions with justification.	1	Is a formal justification including needs and cost/benefit analysis required for each new position?	
3. Background verification and reference checking.	1	Are complete background checks performed, including degree and employment verification? Does this include reference checks conducted by the hiring manager?	
4. Performance-based job descriptions for all new positions.	2	Are performance objectives clearly written and included on each job description? These should be in the form of SMART objectives describing the top 5–6 deliverables for the position.	
5. Written summaries of all interviews.	2	Are written summaries of each interview required justifying a yes or no decision based on the candidate's ability to meet the performance requirements of the job?	
6. Use of preplanned job-specific written interviews.	2	Are interviews preplanned and are the same questions asked of all candidates for the same job?	
7. Use of techniques to minimize emotional biases.	2	Are all interviewers aware of their biases and how this can affect their assessment of candidates?	
8. Established interviewing guidelines on how to treat candidates.	3	Is a process in place that describes the importance of hiring and how to treat candidates being considered for employment?	

*Rank each area on a scale of 0–5, 5 being complete, 0 incomplete.

Table 10.2   *(continued)*

Hiring System Criteria	Stage	Survey Questions Description	Status* (0–5)
9. Formal written assessment.	3	Are assessments balanced, considering all strengths and weakness across the spectrum of job requirements?	
10. Use of formal questioning techniques by other interviewers.	3	Are other interviewers required to assess job-specific factors or are they left to their own measurement criteria?	
11. Compelling ad campaigns.	3	Are performance-based ads prepared that are compelling, focusing on the doing not the having?	
12. Formal approval cycle and testing of all offers.	3	Are all aspects of the offer tested and agreed upon throughout the interviewing process, or is everything quickly put together at the end?	
13. Interview training for all managers.	3	Are all managers required to undergo interview training before hiring any team members?	
14. Psychological/competency testing.	3	Is testing used to confirm, rather than predict, performance? (Rank lower if used before meeting candidate or to replace performance-based interview.)	
15. Panel interviews, take-home case studies, and use of similar evaluation tools.	3	Are expanded interview or validation techniques used to supplement the one-on-one interviewing process?	
16. Effective recruiting program with marketing slant.	3	Is the recruiting process clearly understood? Is negotiating leverage maintained through use of challenging and recruiting questions, or are applicants sold too soon?	
17. Work-type analysis matching performance needs to candidate's interests/ability.	4	Are SMART objectives categorized into the four work-types (strategist, entrepreneur, manager, technical) and are candidates evaluated in each of these categories?	

(continued)

Table 10.2   *(continued)*

Hiring System Criteria	Stage	Survey Questions Description	Status* (0–5)
18. Forward-looking staffing plan—based on annual plan or forecast.	4	Are detailed annual staffing plans made for each department based on the annual plan or forecast?	
19. Formal multi-level sourcing plan coupled with direct sourcing.	4	Is a comprehensive sourcing plan in place targeting different applicant sourcing pools? Are programs designed to directly go after the best?	
20. Formal transition program for new employees.	4	Is the performance-based job description used as the framework of a formal new employee transition program? Are performance expectations clear and are new employees given frequent feedback?	
Total Score			

Give yourself a five (5) if the step is a formal part of your current hiring process. Assign it a three (3) if it's ad hoc, or informal. If it's a rare event, give yourself a zero (0) or a one (1).

Add the scores and compare with 100. If you score above a 50 you're doing well. Even a plain vanilla Stage 1 hiring process with minimum standards will eliminate many hiring errors. A systematic and disciplined process reduces much of the emotional component of a bad hiring decision. If you have a strong company, above-average compensation, and a strong labor pool, this type of system will provide a solid hiring foundation.

No matter what point you have reached in this hiring process, you don't need to do everything on the list to see significant improvement. You will reduce errors and improve accuracy with each incremental addition. Use the four-stage implementation process as an overall guideline to begin upgrading your hiring systems. Spend at least a few months at each stage before moving on. This allows buy-in from everyone involved. You can transition to the next level when people get comfortable with the process and improved results are obvious.

■ STAGE 1. THE TRADITIONAL TENURE-BASED HIRING SYSTEM

Stage 1 consists of a traditional formal hiring system, including management approval of all new hires, using some type of written requisition process. There should be written guidelines, a compensation review before making the offer, and a written job description, at least one page long. At a minimum, the job description should include an overview of the position, an organization chart, a list of duties and responsibilities, and the ADA (Americans with Disabilities Act) requirements. Sometimes this includes the candidate profile listing educational needs, required skills, and experience. While we don't like this format because it doesn't describe performance needs, it's a beginning. Formal background verification and reference checking are also required. The offer itself needs approval before it is extended to the candidate.

These guidelines will get your hiring under control. Discipline through the approval process prevents line managers from moving too fast. This eliminates some of the emotions involved. It's a fairly typical system used in most companies.

We have some significant concerns with the basic system. For one, it doesn't address the critical factors on hiring we've talked about in this book—the focus on getting the job, not doing it; the need to weigh performance over experience; buying in too soon; losing control over the applicant; boring ads; lack of enough good candidates; and superficial assessments. Nonetheless, any system with some type of controls will have a positive impact.

■ STAGE 2. THE BASIC PERFORMANCE-BASED HIRING SYSTEM

Shifting to a performance-based hiring system can eliminate many classic hiring problems. For Stage 2 implementation, you need to:

➤ Write performance-based job descriptions including SMART objectives.

➤ Understand how to control emotions by measuring performance first.

> ➤ Use the anchor/visualize and the impact/leadership ques-
> tions together with fact-finding techniques to uncover
> core and job-specific success traits.

> ➤ Require a written summary of the candidate's responses
> to the preceding questions.

Stage 2 benefits include a dramatic reduction in hiring mistakes, fewer mismatches, higher quality candidates, improved
communications, and less need to rely on perceptions and stereotypes.

Myron Manufacturing in New Jersey is a good example of a
company just beginning the Stage 2 implementation. The company is a large family-run company with heavy international operations. Jim Adler (no relation), the COO of the company, used
these techniques a few days after attending one of our YPO
(Young Presidents Organization) presentations.

On an airplane trip to Europe, he prepared the performance-
based job spec for an international marketing manager. Since it
was his first attempt, it took him about a hour to fashion a clear
understanding of the key performance objectives of the position.
To conduct a comprehensive interview, he needed only this list of
SMART objectives plus the impact/leadership and anchor/visual-
ize questions. Jointly with two other managers over the next few
days, he conducted panel-type interviews for three candidates.

Here are a few of his observations:

> ➤ The process of fact-finding and drilling down allows you
> to better understand the candidate's real role in the ac-
> complishment. The candidate's competency and experi-
> ence levels were readily apparent.

> ➤ The quality of management and team skills was evident
> after the candidate drew the organization chart, ranked the
> quality of the team members, and then discussed in detail
> some of the staffing and management changes made.

> ➤ The other interviewers in the room quickly picked up on
> the fact-finding technique and were significant contribu-
> tors within 20 minutes.

> ➤ The process makes it easy for people who don't naturally
> interview well to quickly become better interviewers. By

talking about real accomplishments, a good candidate overcomes any initial nervousness.

➤ Getting lots of details about specific events minimizes exaggeration. People who were just good talkers didn't fare too well when they had to substantiate their claims.

➤ By having candidates visualize a few of the SMART objectives you quickly see how a person will think through issues and interacts with others once on the job.

➤ It turned out to be a great recruiting tool. The top candidate wasn't too interested at the beginning, but when she learned about the key performance objectives for the position she was excited by the challenge and wanted to be part of the team.

➤ The subsequent psychological testing was 100% consistent with the findings from the interview.

➤ The process is really more about management than interviewing. If you know the real needs of the job, hiring is just a step in the process of getting it done right.

Stage 2 is easy to implement. Everything moves smoothly once the performance-based job description is created. To get the process started, the CEO or the head of the HR department has to champion the need for the SMART objectives to be incorporated into the job description. Job requisitions shouldn't be approved unless these performance requirements are attached.

Jack Lantz, the President of Unitek, a Southern California manufacturing company, has been using performance-based job descriptions for a number of years with great success. He told me that every new management position requires the preparation of a job spec listing the top six to eight performance objectives. The management committee agrees on all of them before the job is approved. This way, everyone involved in the interviewing process clearly understands the performance needs of the position. As a result of this process alone, Jack indicated that hiring accuracy has increased by 200%. In three years, there have been no bad hires and no surprises. The strengths and weaknesses of each new employee were clearly known before the person was hired.

The company also uses the Wonderlic Comprehensive Personality Profile and Wonderlic Personnel Test during the interview process. Further evaluation is conducted if these tests reveal any inconsistencies with the performance-based interview. The use of these tests as a confirming indicator helps Jack and his management team pinpoint potential performance problems before hiring a new employee. As Jack told me, the personality issues become less important when everyone knows and agrees to the performance criteria of the position.

We've found that everyone using the process gets better results, without exception. The key is preparation of the performance-based job specification. The first time, it will take over an hour to get it right. After a few tries, it will drop to about 45 minutes for new positions. Updating an existing position takes only 20 to 30 minutes. Once you have a clear definition of the job in mind, interviewing becomes a natural process of fact-finding and benchmarking performance. Then, there is no need to substitute biases, emotions, and stereotypes as the selection criteria.

■ STAGE 3. THE ADVANCED PERFORMANCE-BASED HIRING SYSTEM

While you have made major strides in Stages 1 and 2 in upgrading the hiring process, you have paid little attention to other aspects of hiring, particularly sourcing and recruiting. Stage 3 incorporates these important components. Good sourcing is essential. Things frequently go wrong with your top candidate. For one thing, these best candidates always seem to have multiple offers. You have to attract enough of these strong candidates to have a fair shot at landing one of them. Once these strong candidates are identified in the interviewing process, you then have to be able to convince them to join the team. That's why good recruiting skills are needed to complement a strong sourcing program.

In addition, everyone needs to be on the same page in terms of interviewing competence. Strong candidates can then view the hiring process as representative of a sophisticated company with the same high standards at all levels.

➤ Make Hiring an Integrated System

In Stage 3, we broaden the scope of the staffing process from just a very good interviewing system, to a complete hiring process used by every manager in the company. Here are some of the key steps needed to make this transition:

➤ Train all managers in the basic concepts of performance-based hiring and the POWER Staffing hiring system.

➤ Write ads based on performance needs, not experience. Target sourcing programs to attract different pools of top candidates.

➤ Install some type of scheduling process and adhere to it. Make candidates feel important during the hiring process, and don't ignore lunch if the candidate will be at your location during this time. This is important, but often overlooked. Make sure interviewing schedules are formalized and that each interviewer has a copy of the resume, the SMART objectives, and preplanned questions geared to address specific performance needs of the job.

➤ Expand external testing and additional evaluation techniques such as panel interviews, take-home case studies, and psychological testing to confirm competency. Over the long term, interviewing accuracy will directly reflect the depth and breadth of the evaluation techniques used. Expand the written assessments to include all factors associated with job competency.

➤ Make recruiting a formal process of marketing the job and company, not a sales campaign. Make sure there is a formal process of testing all components of an offer before you approve it and formally extend it.

Trammell Crow, the nationally known property management company, headquartered in Dallas, does a great job of training all their managers in the basics. Hazel Lockett, Zita Maclean, Donna Bernardi-Paul, and Jayne Kuhn lead a sophisticated HR Boot Camp for managers. All managers are required to attend these two days of intense training covering employment practices, management, staffing, and Hattie Hill-Storks' diversity program. I have worked with Trammell Crow for many years in this program, and collectively, we've trained over 1000 managers in performance-based hiring concepts.

During some of the more recent programs, many new managers have come up to me describing their shock in learning that these very same interviewing techniques were used on them when they first interviewed with the company. As candidates, their reactions were very positive. They said this type of interviewing allowed them to better understand the real job needs before starting. This approach has dramatically reduced a major source of hiring problems. To the candidates, these jobs appeared more challenging and the hiring managers seemed more knowledgeable. Managers also seemed sincerely interested in them and their comparable past accomplishments.

This has made Trammell Crow a more attractive place to work. All the new managers I have met are also top-notch people—informed, curious, attentive, and proactive. This type of program goes a long way in allowing a company to upgrade the quality of its personnel. It seems to be working at Trammell Crow.

With a Stage 3 staffing program in place, you really show your current employees and candidates that hiring great people really is the number one priority of management. This discipline and attitude will quickly translate into better hiring results. A decline in turnover and a more upbeat and professional group of new employees are signals that you have arrived.

■ STAGE 4. THE COMPLETE POWER STAFFING PERFORMANCE-BASED HIRING SYSTEM

Stage 4 is the pinnacle. You will know you're here if you have a strong pool of candidates for every position, sophisticated standards and measurement systems are in place that every manager uses, positions get filled quickly, and the closing process moves along without a hitch. If you find yourself reacting to staffing needs rather than anticipating them, it could be an indicator that some improvements in the sourcing program are necessary. Managers always compromise their standards when desperate to fill a position. Stage 4 addresses this and a few other areas to strengthen the hiring and management process:

➤ Develop a proactive sourcing process.

➤ Make the assessment process more bulletproof.

➤ Integrate the hiring system directly into the management process.

Sourcing is still the most challenging of all the POWER Staffing components. The whole hiring process falls apart if you're only seeing weak candidates. Microsoft, Intel, and Procter & Gamble have sourcing aced. The best people want to work for them. Compensation is well above average when equity is considered, and the consistent growth of these companies creates opportunity. With this formula for success, it's not hard to understand why the best come in flocks. One-third of Microsoft's candidates come across the Internet, responding to posted jobs. Even if the assessment process is faulty, you still wind up with a top-notch hire.

Take the best, throw them in over their heads, and pluck the survivors for promotion. This was the PepsiCo staffing model of the 1970s and 1980s, now updated for high tech. It takes more than sourcing to achieve this lofty level, though. Exciting products, tremendous opportunity, and competitive compensation also help. A good sourcing plan is essential to nurture any growing business.

If great people aren't regularly knocking at your door, you have to make the sourcing process more proactive. You should forecast your staffing needs at least three to six months into the future, although a year is even better. This will buy you the time to hire smart. In addition, proactive sourcing means directly going after the best people, rather than passively waiting for them to apply to your ad. A fundamental shift in thinking is required to pull this one off. It requires dedicated resources, direct personal contact, and extra handholding. Every line manager from the CEO on down has to elevate the importance of the hiring process in word and deed if you want this to happen.

If you're a company of sufficient size, you have to have a dedicated, senior-level person in charge. I can always tell how important staffing is in a company by finding out the management level of the person in charge of it, where sourcing is placed on the priority list, and how much time and money is spent on it.

If you want to further upgrade the assessment process, work-type profiling is a simple and useful tool. It combines the need for good fact-finding with the intuitive hiring decision. The work-type approach is a unique means to match job needs with a candidate's interests and abilities even when the jobs are seemingly unrelated. Many intuitive interviewers mentally do this anyway, so while it's an advanced assessment technique, it's very natural. It allows the technical interviewer to become more intuitive, and the intuitive interviewer to become more technical. Technical interviewers tend to get too much of the wrong information, and intuitive interviewers don't get enough of the right information. Although work-type profiling has been included as a formal part of the Stage 4 implementation, you can begin using it anytime you want to upgrade the quality of the assessment process.

Work-type profiling pinpoints the best predictors of future performance for a specific job, guiding all types of interviewers to the right answer. It minimizes the tendency to eliminate high-potential candidates because they don't have enough experience. Work-type profiling minimizes the "right person, wrong job" problem, by looking at work from a different perspective.

Performance-based hiring is a subset of performance management. The final piece of Stage 4 is the integration of hiring into this cycle. Essentially, this has to do with the use of the performance-based job description as a management tool. As a first step, it can serve as the basis of the new employee transition program. The SMART objectives were created to define the key performance objectives for the first year on the job. Since these were discussed with the candidate during the interviewing process, it's only natural to use them when the candidate starts. Update them to reflect changes and renegotiate them with the candidate as necessary. This helps clarify expectations and improve communications.

Not only do new employees feel more comfortable with this approach, it eliminates one of the primary reasons good people fail—lack of clear expectations. As time progresses, you should use these same performance objectives to track the new employee's performance on a regular basis. They can also serve as the basis of the annual review process. In fact, there's no reason why the preparation of SMART objectives is exclusive to the hiring process. Job descriptions for all current employees should be written this way and updated on a regular basis, quarterly or semiannually. This is what performance management is all about.

Every great manager I've met has a clear understanding of the performance requirements of each subordinate's job. Sometimes it's prepared jointly, but in the end, it represents an unambiguous vision of the work that needs to get done. The value of the process is that by preparing it, a manager not only hires better people, but becomes a better manager.

Hollis Bascom, the CEO of Orcon, is leading a Stage 4 implementation. Orcon is a medium-size manufacturer of industrial products located in Fremont, California. The company is now developing performance-based job descriptions for all positions and updating them regularly. Bascom recognized early in the process that the key to the program's success was the preparation of performance-based job descriptions first for every new position. He told me that before he used this process his hiring was completely random. He was never sure how a new employee would work out. By focusing on performance requirements, Hollis experienced a 100% improvement in hiring accuracy. He can now predict with a high degree of certainty a candidate's likely performance once on the job. Based on this success he's now taking the approach to another level. By writing performance-based job descriptions for all positions and updating them regularly, he expects to see better understanding and improved achievements throughout all levels of the company.

Tom Geiselman, the VP of Human Resources at Orcon, agrees that the preparation of the performance objectives, or the critical success factors, drives the program, but some adjustments need to be made when using them for all jobs. His perspective on moving from Stage 2 to Stage 4 is slightly different from Bascom's, since he's responsible for the implementation. He indicated that all managers must now justify their hiring decisions based on a candidate's past comparable performance. As a result, companywide hiring accuracy has increased about 50% and retention is up about 25%, so far. Tom believes much more progress is possible. In addition, the number of interviews managers need to gain confidence has decreased significantly, due to this focused process.

According to Geiselman, Orcon experienced another added and unexpected benefit. By bringing in more capable people, the training budget has been redirected toward more advanced development, rather than just the basics. He did add a cautionary note. There is a temptation to make the performance-based job description more than it is. While it's a great tool for hiring, he believes it doesn't need to be too precise with respect to the timing issues or the specifics. To address this, the company now writes performance-based job descriptions for all new and existing positions, but those for existing positions are more in-depth.

This is appropriate. As a hiring tool, the purpose of the performance-based job description is to uncover the critical performance drivers for the position. If more than one objective requires the same underlying ability, like team building, you only need to include the more important one on the SMART objective list. On the job, however, you want them both, since each task needs to be accomplished. After starting, the candidate and the hiring manager can review all the performance objectives and jointly prioritize and negotiate them. With this approach, the performance-based hiring concept transitions naturally to on-the-job performance management. Negotiate these tasks with the new employee once on the job. Getting complete agreement this way helps the new employee take ownership of the performance objectives.

■ THE UNDERSIDE VIEW—START AT THE BOTTOM AND LOOK UP

As stressed earlier in this book, hiring is too important to personal and company success for employers to depend on random chance. Despite the obvious benefits, hiring, somehow, commonly becomes a reactive process that is less important than the manager's other activities. As a result, performance standards are reduced, real job needs are oversimplified or replaced by misleading guidelines, interviews are considered impositions, candidates are ignored, decisions are shallow—and after it's completed, we wonder what went wrong.

In this book, we have proposed a substitute for every major hiring problem. By now, you've probably tried some of the techniques suggested here and discovered that they work. They work because we developed POWER Staffing backward. We found everything that worked first, and then put it all together into a systematic hiring process. When you work with hundreds of managers for over 20 years, you eventually find techniques that work most of the time. Mixing and matching, adding and discarding, and trial and error eventually led to a focused set of tools and techniques for every position, every job, every company, and every industry.

Even with some great techniques, the process is not bulletproof. This is a linked system comprising separate, but integrated activities, each dependent on the other. While none of the segments are difficult to implement, doing them together consistently is challenging. This is why company-imposed procedures can help. When performance-based job descriptions and written candidate assessments are mandatory, it prevents the hiring manager from taking shortcuts when some other more urgent activity crops up. Unless we intervene with formalized procedures, urgency will always take precedence, even over importance.

Hiring is a whole-brain process. This is both the problem and the solution. While the yes/no decision needs to be an intuitive one, the data collection process to make that decision needs to be logical and analytical. Combine this conflict with the emotional pull of first impressions, the need factor, stereotypes, and personality, and it's easy to see why hiring can fall apart. The POWER Staffing system overcomes these obstacles resulting in a consistent, well-informed hiring decision that balances the needs of candidate and hiring manager alike. It becomes a simple, commonsense approach, once you cut through the overgrowth and see the clear path. The path will stay clear as long as you recognize the importance of hiring to your personal success.

Bottom line, good hiring is no more than changing the selection criteria from getting the job toward doing the job. Everything changes when we make this switch. We stop hiring people that are great at interviewing, but weak on substance. And we reconsider those great candidates reduced to temporary incompetence by the glare of the spotlights. Turn them off and talk about real work. You'll find some overlooked stars in the shadows. It's substance, not style, that really counts. As Red Scott said, "Hire SMART, or manage tough."

■ THE TOP SIDE VIEW—HIRING AND THE BIG PICTURE IMPACT ON YOU AND YOUR COMPANY

Effective staffing should not be left to the competency of the individual hiring manager. The impact on the organization is too profound. The program described in this book provides the tools and techniques to make staffing a repeatable systematic process with far-reaching benefits. They are summarized in Figure 10.2.

The impact of good staffing using the POWER Staffing process on the line manager is immediate and important. This is the foundation of the performance management process. Every subsequent step in management depends on the creation and use of the SMART objectives. Managing this way allows the group to be more effective and responsive to the other needs of the organization.

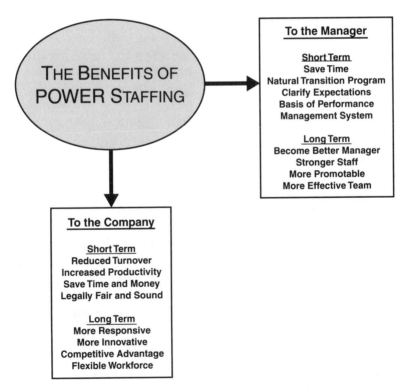

Figure 10.2. The impact of effective hiring.

The quality of a manager depends on the quality of the staff. Managers are effective when they can implement change, not maintain the status quo. If you spend most of your time managing your group to meet basic needs, you're wasting your time. You can't push a group to success, you can only lead it there. This is why good staffing needs to be the primary criterion for promotion.

Multiply each staffing decision 10-fold to appreciate the impact good staffing has on a company's success. The cost savings are the most obvious. From reduced turnover and elimination of wrongful terminations, to increased productivity, hiring the best people you can makes economic sense. Most managers would contend that the positive impact of a top person is at least 3 to 4 times that of the average employee and 10 times more than the marginal employee. On a long-term basis this translates to improved, higher quality products, produced more efficiently and delivered with flair. This is how a strong staffing system contributes to a competitive advantage.

From this perspective, the implementation of a performance-based hiring system like POWER Staffing needs to be a company-wide strategic decision. Staffing has always been the basic building block of every successful organization. To keep up with a rapidly changing global marketplace, effective staffing must now become the foundation.

IMPLEMENTING PERFORMANCE-BASED HIRING BEST PRACTICES

The following list summarizes and cross-references all the most important points in this book. Here are the *Hire With Your Head* hot tips and techniques.

Preparing Performance-Based Job Descriptions (Chapter 2)

✔ Create SMART objectives (**S**pecific, **M**easurable, **A**ction verb, **R**esult-based, **T**ime-bound) that describe the five or six most important deliverables or expected outcomes for the job.

✔ These SMART performance objectives represent the DOING, not the HAVING, and cover all critical aspects of the job

(continued)

(continued)

including major and interim objectives, problems, needed
changes, and technical and management issues.

✔ Assign the SMART objectives into one of the four work-type
profiles (visionary, entrepreneur, improver, technician) to
better understand underlying job needs.

✔ Using performance-based SMART objectives improves understanding and communications, clarifies expectations, allows
candidates to self-select, is more fair and legally sound, and
acts as a great transition program for the new employee. This
is what performance management is all about.

Controlling Emotions (Chapter 3)

✔ Wait 30 minutes before making a yes or no decision. More errors are made in the first 30 minutes than at any other time.

✔ Use the hiring formula—measure performance first, then determine character and personality.

✔ Recognize your hot buttons. Keep track of why and when you
make the hiring decision and then fight to stay objective. If
you're relaxed or bored within 15 minutes, you've made an
emotional decision.

✔ Stay the buyer as long as possible. If you decide too soon, new
data will have less value than older data.

✔ Change your frame of reference. Ask more challenging questions for those you like, and go easier on those you don't.

✔ Measure first impressions again after 30 minutes. This way
you won't be seduced. Compare the objective measure of first
impression to the original emotional determination. Be concerned if it got worse.

Interviewing and Assessment (Chapters 4–7)

✔ Don't compromise on personal energy and team skills. They
represent the core traits of all top performers. Use the im-
pact/leadership questions to develop a trend of these traits over
the past few jobs.

✔ Fact-finding is critical. Peel away the onion and probe deeply.
By understanding the real details in a candidate's top five or
six accomplishments, you'll know everything you need to
know to make a well-informed hiring decision.

✔ Anchor and visualize each SMART objective. A candidate's ability to organize a task before starting combined with a tangible comparable (not identical) accomplishment is a great predictor of subsequent performance.

✔ Ask for examples of everything. This is how you turn generalities into specifics.

✔ Use panel interviews and take-home tests to make the interview more representative of real work.

✔ To prevent classic mismatches (great candidate, but wrong job), assign the candidate's major accomplishments into work-type categories and compare them with the SMART objective profile.

Recruiting (Chapter 8)

✔ Recruiting is marketing, not selling. First create a compelling vision of the job, and then the candidate will sell you, rather than you selling the candidate.

✔ Stay the buyer from beginning to end so that additional data will have the same value as preliminary data.

✔ A job has more value when it's earned, than when it's given away. Don't move too fast. Make the candidate earn the position.

✔ Break long recruiting pitches describing the company into one-minute sound bites. Use these at the beginning of each question to describe the importance of the job. This is marketing.

✔ Question (challenge) the applicant's experience in certain critical areas. This raises the standards of performance and the candidate will see areas for personal growth.

✔ Never make an official offer until you're 100% sure it will be accepted. Test each component first throughout the interviewing process. Don't wait until the end. Just ask, "What do you think about . . . ?"

✔ Good recruiting can overcome budget restraints by switching the candidate's emphasis from short-term needs to long-term opportunities.

(continued)

(continued)

Sourcing (Chapter 9)

✔ Write ads and screen candidates based on SMART objectives. You'll eliminate or ignore the best candidates if you write experience-based ads. Performance counts in everything. Add sizzle.

✔ Be proactive. Anticipate hiring needs by preparing a staffing plan.

✔ Use several sourcing methods. Advertise everywhere—the Internet, trade publications, B-schools, society rosters, and newspapers.

✔ Use direct sourcing techniques—the personal touch—to find those not looking. The best candidates need to be persuaded on a one-to-one basis. Recruiters and contract researchers work best.

Appendix

List of Templates

Note: E-mail (coach@cja-careers.com) or send a letter with your address and we'll send you a free full-size set of each of these templates. Address letters to Template Offer, CJA-The Adler Group, 17852 17th St., #209, Tustin, CA 92780.

POWER Staffing™ Objectives Worksheet

Creating the Performance (SMART) Objectives

©1997 by Lou Adler, from his book *Hire With Your Head.* Part of the POWER Staffing™ "best practices" worksheet series, summarizing great hiring tips from some of the top managers in the US. Call 1-800-559-2559 for more hiring hot tips and tools.

Position:	Department:		Hiring Manger:		Date:

Instructions for Creating the Performance Criteria for Any Position

☐ Every job has five or six major things that need to get done (performance objectives) for the new employee to be successful.
☐ Make all objectives **SMART** - **S**pecific, **M**easurable, **A**ction Oriented, **R**esult-based, **T**ime Bound.
☐ Ignore job spec. Use macro approach to develop performance objective for each major area of job. Follow template below.
☐ Use micro approach (over) to convert traditional experience/skill spec to performance. Find out what's done with each criterion.
☐ Use benchmark approach (over) by finding traits and capability of people now in the job known to be competent.
☐ Prioritize the top 5-6 performance objectives and include on performance-based job description.
☐ ANCHOR and VISUALIZE each SMART objective to determine competency (over and Fact-Finding Worksheet).

Determine Performance Objectives using the Macro Approach

Job Factor	Example of HAVING vs. DOING	Comments and Descriptions	SMART Objectives
Major Functional Objectives	<u>Misleading</u>: Have 10 years OEM sales experience. <u>BETTER</u>: Increase OEM sales by 15% in year 1 and build new team.	Objectives need action verb (e.g., increase, change, improve) and measurable objective (e.g., 10% in 90 days).	
Subordinate Objectives	<u>Misleading</u>: Have good planning skills. <u>BETTER</u>: In 90 days submit plan and hire 3 people.	Include the sub-steps necessary to achieve key objectives. Ask for examples.	
Management & Organizational Issues	<u>Misleading</u>: Have good management skills. <u>BETTER</u>: Assess and rebuild the team within 120 days.	Provide measurable objectives to determine quality of management skills needed.	
Changes and Improvements Necessary	<u>Misleading</u>: Be an agent of change. <u>Better</u>: Upgrade the client contact tracking system before the next promo.	Be specific regarding the needed changes and upgrades. It's easier to compare applicant's accomplishments this way.	
Problems to Be Solved	<u>Misleading</u>: Be a problem solver. <u>BETTER</u>: Work with IS to eliminate customer service bottleneck before May.	Describe actual problems needing work and then ask applicants how they would solve them.	
Technical Skills in Actual Situation	<u>Misleading</u>: Have good PC skills. <u>BETTER</u>: Develop PC-based tracking system by June.	Provide specific example of how technical skills will be used. It's better to have open discussion of real work	
Team Skills in Actual Situation	<u>Misleading</u>: Have good team skills. <u>BETTER</u>: Jointly develop inventory reduction plan with sales and manufacturing.	Describe situations that demonstrate good interpersonal/team skills and get similar examples from the applicant.	
Deliverables- Tactical, Strategic &Creative	<u>Misleading</u>: Have good strategic thinking and planning skills. <u>BETTER</u>: Develop a long range product plan.	Cover anything that hasn't been addressed above. Also describe actual examples of creative and strategic projects.	

CJA-The Adler Group, Inc.   *"Are You POWER Hiring^{sm} Yet?"*   Dallas • San Jose • Los Angeles
17852 17th, #209, Tustin, CA 92780 • 714/573-1820 • FAX 714/731-3952 • 800/559-2559 • www.cja-careers.com

POWER Staffing™ Preparing SMART Objectives Worksheet

Create Performance Objectives with the Micro Approach

Traditional Job Spec Skills and Experiences	**Performance Criteria** What's the outcome of each skill?
1)	1)
2)	2)
3)	3)
4)	4)
5)	5)
6)	6)
7)	7)

Advice: Convert each skill, experience, responsibility or trait into a measurable objective. Ask "What will the person do with this that determines competency?" For example, for strong PC skills, indicate what they'll do with the PC skills, e.g., "Set up detailed project tracking system."

Benchmark the Best

What do the best people do who have held this position?
Create performance objectives by comparing to the "best in class."

1)

2)

3)

4)

5)

6)

Advice: This is a great technique for process oriented jobs. Think about what the best people in this job do that makes them best. Seek these traits. Reverse this and avoid those traits of the weaker people. Some examples, "handle angry customers," "accurately input data for 6 hours per day."

Prioritize the Objectives

Use this Checklist to Prioritize the Top 5-6 Objectives and Transfer to the Performance-based Job Spec

☐ Check those objectives that must get done.
☐ Rank the impact on the company on ABC scale.
☐ Are there any alternatives? If so you might want to eliminate an objective or lower its priority.
☐ Don't duplicate. Be broad. Make sure final list covers all important job criteria.
☐ Get appropriate balance between management and individual contributor.
☐ Are technical objectives properly placed?
☐ Have interpersonal and culture issues been covered in the objectives?
☐ Make sure there's a balance on the technical, tactical and conceptual (strategic) level.
☐ Include thinking and intellectual skills in one of the objectives.

The Preliminary List - Top 8-10 Performance (SMART) Objectives
Summarize Major Objectives from Macro, Micro and Benchmark Approach Here

Objective (Summarized)	Check if a Must Have	ABC Ranking of Importance	Eliminate Duplicates	Management or Individual	Balanced Thinking	Priority Ranking

Performance-based Job Description

To Hire Superior People First Define Superior Performance

©1997 by Lou Adler, from his book *Hire With Your Head*. Part of the POWER Staffing™ "best practices" worksheet series, summarizing great hiring tips from some of the top managers in the US. Call 1-800-559-2559 for more hiring hot tips and tools.

Position Information

Title: .... Manager: .... Date: ....

Deparment:... Prepared By: .... Comp: ....

Other: ....

Position Summary - General Overview of Duties and Responsibilities	Instructions and Hot Tips
Prime Duties: .... Responsibilities: .... Key Issues:	**Position Summary:** Provide quick overivew of job and importance in meeting company objectives. **Notes:**

Organization Chart - Include titles of subordinates and supervisor and brief duties	Organization Chart: Graphical overview is important. Have candidate prepare matching org chart for comparison. **Notes:**

Supervisor's Title

Position Title

Title: # People: Duties:	Title: # People: Duties:	Title: # People: Duties:	Title: # People: Duties:	Title: # People: Duties:	Other

Comments: ....
....

SMART Performance Objectives - List 5-6 Deliverables in Priority Order	SMART Objectives - Make job needs Specific, Measurable, Action verb, Result, Time. During interview ask candidate to provide best comparable accomplishment.
1. .... 2. .... 3. .... 4. .... 5. .... 6.	Prepare Performance Objectives for: • Major and Sub-Objectives • Technical Objectives • Management and Team Issues • Problems and Needed Changes

Work-Type: _____ Technical _____ Organizer _____ Entrepreneurial _____ Creative/Strategy

Assign SMART Objectives to Work-Type and Indicate Dominant (1) and Secondard (2)

Categorize SMART objectives into Work-Types to tap into motivation, improve fit and avoid mismatches.

Skills and Experience Summary - Basic Skills and Experiences Required	Skills: It's better to convert these skills into SMART objective. Ask, "What will candidate do with this skill or experience?"
Education : .... Years: .... Industry: .... Skills: .... Other:	If over specify, you'll lose opportunity to attract candidates looking for growth.

CJA-The Adler Group, Inc. *"Are You POWER Hiring*^{sm} *Yet?"* Dallas • San Jose • Los Angeles

17852 17th, #209, Tustin, CA 92780 • 714/573-1820 • FAX 714/731-3952 • 800/559-2559 • www.cja-careers.com

POWER Staffing™ Emotional Control Worksheet

Tools, Tips, and Tactics to Minimize Hiring Errors

©1997 by Lou Adler, from his book *Hire With Your Head.* Part of the POWER Staffing™ "best practices" worksheet series, summarizing great hiring tips from some of the top managers in the US. Call 1-800-559-2559 for more hiring hot tips and tools.

Name:	Company:	Date:

The "Yes/No" Buying Switch

Stay the buyer as long as possible by keeping your buying switch open in the "maybe" position.

Yes — Maybe — No

We stop evaluating once buying decision is made.

Emotional Control Checklist

- ❏ Delay the Buying Decision
  - • collect all info before decision
- ❏ Recognize Your Hot Buttons
  - • these force decision too soon
- ❏ Get Examples to Prove Point
  - • get real facts to support feelings
- ❏ Measure Performance First!
  - • measure fit and personality last
- ❏ Measure 1st Impression After Waiting 30 Minutes
  - • increases objectivity and accuracy
- ❏ Change Your Frame of Reference
  - • neutralize 1st impression by taking opposite position

- ❏ Walk the Floor
  - • talk about real issues or problems
- ❏ Turn Off the Spotlight
  - • make interview a normal discussion
- ❏ Treat the Candidate as a Consultant
  - • delay judgment - listen
- ❏ Don't Compete - Don't Posture
  - • this minimizes initial friction
- ❏ Stay Inquisitive
  - • probing stops after you buy
- ❏ Conduct a Phone Interview First
  - • minimizes 1st impression biases
- ❏ Use Pre-planned Interviews
  - • evaluations are the same for all candidates this way

Emotional Control Self-Evaluation - Determine Your Interviewing Type and Hot Buttons

The key to better hiring is to delay the buying decision as long as possible. Recognizing why and when you make a "Yes" or "No" decision can help. Circle the key traits that affect your judgment to identify your hot buttons and interviewing type.

Type	Description	"Yes" Hot Buttons	"No" Hot Buttons	Comments/Advice
Emotional Yes or No within 5 minutes	Makes decision in less than 5 minutes based on first impressions. Tends to oversell, under listen, look for facts to justify emotional decision, minimize negatives if "yes" and positive data if "no."	Affable - Articulate Assertive - Appearance Confident - Hand Shake Poise - Interest Eye-contact	Nervous Short answers Clammy No eye-contact Quiet Sloppy	
Intuitive Cloner Yes or No within 5-15 minutes	Makes decision within 5-15 minutes based on a few traits considered essential to success by the interviewer (or lack of these traits), then begins to sell, under listen, globalize strengths or weaknesses.	Intelligent - Intuitive Initiative - Assertive Good questions Confident - Extroverted In-depth answers Good communicator Specific talent Character Commitment	Poor communicator - shallow or general responses indicating apparent lack of intelligence, commitment initiative. Quiet - Introverted Too analytical or too detailed. Not tough enough	
Mechanic Technical No in less than 15 minutes, but Yes in 1-2 hours or longer	Makes "no" quickly (like an intuitive) due to lack of specific skills, technical knowledge, or experience, but takes over 1 hour to determine depth of technical competence or process approach.	Experience - Education Credentials - Skills Process approach Thinking - Analytical	Lack of specific technical knowledge or direct experience. Uses different methods to accomplish task. Different work and management style.	
Performance Interviewer No within 30-45 minutes, but Yes takes 1-2 hours or more	Delays decision until determine level of core success traits and comparability of accomplishments to job needs.	Energy - Team skills Talent - Management Anchor and visualize key job objectives. Commitment Cultural fit	Lack of core success traits - despite positive or negative first impression. Lack of comparable job specific accomplishments or inability to visualize SMART objectives.	

CJA-The Adler Group, Inc. *"Are You POWER Hiring™ Yet?"*   Dallas • San Jose • Los Angeles
17852 17th, #209, Tustin, CA 92780 • 714/573-1820 • FAX 714/731-3952 • 800/559-2559 • www.cja-careers.com

POWER Staffing™ Emotional Control Candidate Tracking System

Name	Position	Yes or No	Time to Decide	Key Factors for Yes/No	Performance Job Spec?	Pre-planned Interview?	1st Impression	1st Impression after 30 min	Length of Interview	Comments

Use this form to keep track of your emotional response to applicants. Note time in minutes to make the "Yes/No" buying decision. Note if a performance-based job spec and a pre-planned interview were used before the interview. Compare the initial "real" first impression (good, poor, average) with the objective first impression. The objective is to delay the buy-ing decision as long as possible. This allows the interviewer to conduct a complete evaluation. Often this evaluation is "short circuited" and incomplete if the "Yes/No" buying decision is made too soon, before a complete assessment is done.

POWER STAFFING™ Software

Automates hiring - prepares job specs, generates interviews, tracks and evaluates candidates

---

The POWER Staffing™ System - Worksheets and Forms

☐ The POWER Staffing™ Quick Reference Guide
☐ The Performance-based Job Description
☐ Creating SMART Objectives
☐ The Sourcing Plan
☐ Fact-Finding and Basic Performance Questions
☐ The Basic 8-Question Interview with Hot Tips
☐ Emotional Control - Tracking Hot Buttons

☐ The 10-Question Interview with Hot Tips
☐ The Entry-Level Performance-based Interview
☐ The Comprehensive Interview
☐ Reference Checking - How to Do It Right
☐ The Candidate Assessment
☐ Multiple Candidate Comparison
☐ Recruiting, Closing and Making Offers

POWER Staffing™ Fact-Finding Worksheet
Using the Four Core Question to Validate Past Performance

©1997 by Lou Adler, from his book *Hire With Your Head*. Part of the POWER Staffing™ "best practices" worksheet series, summarizing great hiring tips from some of the top managers in the US. Call 1-800-559-2559 for more hiring hot tips and tools.

Candidate:	Position:	Interviewer:	Date:

Part 1 - The Benchmark Experience Two-Question Pattern for Each Past Job

#1: Overview and Impact - Give me a quick overview of your job, the company, and describe the biggest impact you made. (You can also ask for examples of initiative or get greatest accomplishment.)	#2: Organization Chart and Team Project - Have candidate draw an org chart and describe a team or management project and specific role. (If a manager find out how candidate built and developed the team.)
Title Most Recent: _____ Dates: ____	Titles of Direct Reports or Team Members:
Title Prior #1: _____ Dates: ____	Titles of Direct Reports or Team Members:
Title Prior #2: _____ Dates: ____	Titles of Direct Reports or Team Members:

Overview

Part 1 on this side relates to job history. Part 2 on the other side determines candidate's ability to meet the performance objectives of the position.

Fact-finding Checklist

Get this info for each accomplishment to validate it.

- ☐ Overview of the accomplishment.
- ☐ Actual title and size of organization and reporting relationship.
- ☐ Bottom line or business impact.
- ☐ When it took place - the year and duration in years and months (even actual dates are OK).
- ☐ Get candidate to describe actual role.
- ☐ Ask the candidate what his/her leadership role was - how did he/she develop program and implement it.
- ☐ Find out the biggest challenges or most difficult aspects of the task. Ask "What were the constraints that needed to be overcome?"
- ☐ Ask "Why do you consider this the most significant work in this job?"
- ☐ Ask for the key steps or major deliverables involved in accomplishing the task.
- ☐ Ask "Describe the people challenges and give me some examples."
- ☐ Get details about the team - names and titles. Find out the reporting relationships. Who was in-charge?
- ☐ Get some examples when the candidate had to change the opinion of others and in dealing with conflict.
- ☐ Ask "How did you grow or change as a result of this effort?"
- ☐ Ask if the task was completed on time and if this was difficult.
- ☐ Ask why/how was the candidate chosen for this role.
- ☐ Find out how the candidate ranks the overall success of the task and why.
- ☐ Ask "What aspects did you enjoy (dislike) the most and why?"
- ☐ Ask "What was your real contribution or value-added to this task?"

CJA-The Adler Group, Inc.   *"Are You POWER Hiring℠ Yet?"*   Dallas • San Jose • Los Angeles
17852 17th, #209, Tustin, CA 92780 • 714/573-1820 • FAX 714/731-3952 • 800/559-2559 • www.cja-careers.com

POWER Staffing™ Fact-Finding Worksheet - Part 2

Benchmark Performance - Determining Ability to Meet SMART Objectives

ANCHOR	VISUALIZE	SMART Objectives
State the performance (SMART) objective and ask the candidate to describe their most comparable accomplishment. Use the Fact-finding Checklist to validate each accomplishment.	Ask the candidate how they would achieve the objective if they had the job. First ask the candidate what information they would need. Then how they would organize and implement the task.	Prioritize the top 5-6 deliverables or performance objectives for the position. Make them SMART. For example, "Within 6 months improve factory performance by 3%."

SMART Objective 1:

SMART Objective 2:

- Specific
- Measurable
- Action Oriented
- Result-based
- Time Bound

Consider all the job factors as you prepare these performance objectives - major objectives, interim objectives, team and management issues, problems, technical issues, changes needed, and interpersonal problems.

ANCHOR

It's important to get a comparable past accomplishment to determine a candidate's ability to achieve the SMART objective. Use the fact-finding techniques on the front. Keep notes on this page under the specific objective.

SMART Objective 3:

VISUALIZE

All good candidates can anticipate the needs of the job before starting. Get into a give-and-take discussion with the candidate by asking how they would implement the task. You only need to do this for two or three SMART objectives. Here's some additonal questions to ask.

- ☐ What are the critical issues involved?
- ☐ Is the time schedule realistic?
- ☐ What other resources would be needed?
- ☐ What other information would you need to obtain before beginning?
- ☐ What would you do in the first week or two?
- ☐ What types of people would you need to complete the task on time?
- ☐ What's the critical success factor?

SMART Objective 4:

Look for these important clues:
- the quality of the questions
- the depth of insight
- organizational skills
- alone or with a team
- ability to identify critical issues

SMART Objective 5:

The ability to ANCHOR and VISUALIZE is a strong predictor of success. Be careful of good ANCHORS only. These people are too structured. Good VISUALIZERS only are good consultants, but have never done it.

POWER Staffing™ Objective Interview

The Basic 8-Question Performance-based Interview

©1997 by Lou Adler, from his book *Hire With Your Head.* Part of the POWER Staffing™ "best practices" worksheet series, summarizing great hiring tips from some of the top managers in the US. Call 1-800-559-2559 for more hiring hot tips and tools.

Candidate:	Position:	Interviewer:	Date:

Use This Interview When the Performance Objectives Are Known

The Deliverables - Performance (SMART) Objectives	Hot Tips and Fact-Finding Checklist
List SMART Objectives (Specific, Measurable, Action verb, Result, Time-bound) Example: *Improve product margins by 5% within 6 months.* 1. .... 2. .... 3. .... 4. .... Work-Type: ___ Technical ___ Organizer ___ Entrepreneur ___ Strategist/Creative Assign SMART Objectives to Work-Type and Indicate Dominant (1) and Secondary (2)	1. Be inquisitive. Get examples to turn generalities into specific responses. 2. Get trend of personal growth, energy, and team/management skills over time. 3. Listen 4X More Than Talk! Get this info for each accomplishment to validate it. ☐ Get overview of the accomplishment. ☐ Get actual title, size of team, titles of supervisor and subordinates, dates and duration of task. ☐ Ask for bottom line, business impact. ☐ Ask the candidate what his/her leadership role was - how did he/she develop program and implement it. ☐ Find out the biggest challenges or most difficult aspects of the task. Ask "What constraints needed to be overcome?" ☐ Ask "Why do you consider this a significant accomplishment?" ☐ "What were the key steps and major deliverables involved in accomplishing the task?" ☐ Ask "Describe the people challenges and give me some examples." ☐ Get names and titles of staff and rank their performance. Get examples of how people were developed. ☐ Get some examples when the candidate had to change the opinion of others and in dealing with conflict. ☐ Ask "Was the task completed on time, and was this difficult?" ☐ Ask "Why were you chosen for this role?" ☐ "How would others (peers, subordinates, supervisors) describe you and your style?" ☐ "How would you rank the the overall success of the task and why?" ☐ Ask "What was your real contribution or value-added to this project?" ☐ "If you had a chance to do it over, what would you change?" ☐ Ask "How did you grow or change as a result of this effort?"

Opening Question (Recruiting and Setting Performance Tone of Interview)

(First provide 1-2 minute overview of company and importance of job, and then ask...) *Please give me a quick overview of how your background and experience has prepared you for this type of leadership position.*

Benchmark Experience Question Pattern (ask these two questions for the past 2-3 jobs.)

Please give me a quick overview of your (current/prior) position and describe the biggest impact (change) you made (or when you took the initiative).	Describe your organization (draw org chart) and tell me how you developed, and managed your team (or tell me about some team project and describe your role).
Current/Most Recent Position - Title:	**Yrs:**
Prior Position #1 - Title:	**Yrs:**
Prior Position #2 - Title:	**Yrs:**

CJA-The Adler Group, Inc.   *"Are You POWER Hiring℠ Yet?"*   Dallas • San Jose • Los Angeles

17852 17th, #209, Tustin, CA 92780 • 714/573-1820 • FAX 714/731-3952 • 800/559-2559 • www.cja-careers.com

POWER Staffing™ 8-Question Interview
The Basic Performance Interview - Part II

Candidate:	Position:	Interviewer:	Date:

Benchmark Performance (ask these two questions for each SMART objective)		**Hot Tips - Assessing the Answers**
ANCHOR: (State objective) *Describe your most similar past accomplishment.* Objective 1: Objective 2: Objective 3: Objective 4:	**VISUALIZE:** *How would you accomplish this task?* (O.K. for just top two objectives) Objective 1: Objective 2:	**Key:** Use fact-finding to learn everything about top 4-6 accomplishments and then use these tips to evaluate answers. **Work-Types:** Assign responses to these categories and compare to job needs: ☐ **Creative/Strategist**: long range, visionary, new ideas, concepts, strategy. ☐ **Entrepreneur/Builder**: risk taker, fast-pace, persuasive, energetic. ☐ **Improver/Organizer**: manager, upgrades, improves people and process. ☐ **Technical/Producer**: analytical, detailed, quality, executes process. **Team and Management - ABC Rule:** Assign responses to Alone (individual contributor); Belonging (part of team); or in-Charge (as manager). Determine patterns and compare to job needs. **Scope and Size - The 6S Rule**: During fact-finding evaluate companies and jobs according to - Span of control, Speed (pace of change), Sophistication, Standards of performance, Size, Scope and complexity of the work. **Focus - Internal or External**: Assign major accomplishments according to Building the Business - External, or Running the Business - Internal. **Breadth of Thinking**: Assign major accomplishments into Strategic (long range), Tactical (current), or Technical (process). **Functional or Project Focus**: Assign responses to task, department, function, multi-function, or total business. **Personality**: Look for honesty, self-awareness. **Close**: Don't go too fast. Make the job worth earning. Create competition to test true interest.
Character and Values (if not already answered) *Tell me about a time you were totally committed to a task.*		
Personality and Cultural Fit *What three or four adjectives best describe your personality? Give me examples of when these have aided in the performance of your job and when they have hurt.*		
Closing - Use this to create supply and determine interest *Although we're seeing some other fine candidates, I think you have a very strong background. We'll get back to you in a few days, but what are your thoughts now about this position?*		

Summary and Assessment Notes

Trend of Impact, Energy and Initiative - Up, Flat or Down	
ABC Rule for Team/Management Skills - Alone, Belonging, in-Charge	
Technical Competency and Ability to Learn - Strong, Adequate, or Weak	
Work-Type Fit - Dominant and Secondary Match, Partial, or None	
The 6S Rule Scope and Size of Prior Jobs - Comparable, too big, too small	
Focus - Internal (Running the Business) or External (Building the Business)	
Breadth of Thinking - Strategic, Tactical, Technical	
Functional or Project Focus - Task, department, function, multi-function	
Personality - Self-aware and open or misleading	

POWER Staffing™ Comprehensive Interview
The Complete Performance-based Interview

©1997 by Lou Adler, from his book *Hire With Your Head.* Part of the POWER Staffing™ "best practices" worksheet series, summarizing great hiring tips from some of the top managers in the US. Call 1-800-559-2559 for more hiring hot tips and tools.

Candidate:	Position:	Interviewer:	Date:

Use This Interview When the Performance Objectives Are Known

The Deliverables - Performance (SMART) Objectives

List SMART Objectives (Specific, Measurable, Action verb, Result, Time-bound)
Example: *Improve product margins by 5% within 6 months.*

1. ....
2. ....
3. ....
4. ....

Work-Type: ___ Technical ___ Organizer ___ Entrepreneur ____ Strategist/Creative
Assign SMART Objectives to Work-Type and Indicate Dominant (1) and Secondary (2)

Opening Question (Recruiting and Setting Performance Tone of Interview)

(First provide 1-2 minute overview of company and importance of job, and then ask...) *Please give me a quick overview of how your background and experience has prepared you for this type of leadership position.*

Benchmark Experience Question Pattern (ask these two questions for the past 2-3 jobs.)

Please give me a quick overview of your (current/prior) position and describe the biggest impact (change) you made (or when you took the initiative).	*Describe your organization (draw org chart) and tell me how you developed, and managed your team (or tell me about some team project and describe your role).*
Current/Most Recent Position - Title:	**Yrs:**
Prior Position #1 - Title:	**Yrs:**

Work-Type Profiling (assign repsonses to work-types and compare to job needs)

Think about a favorite work experience, a one-time event, that gave you a great deal of personal satisfaction. Please describe it and tell me why it was important to you.

Please describe your most significant accomplishment. (If not answered above.)

What types of problems do you like to solve? Please give me some specific examples.

Interviewing Hot Tips

1. Be inquisitive. Get examples to turn generalities into specific responses.
2. Get trend of personal growth, energy, and team/management skills over time.
3. Listen 4X More Than Talk!

Fact-Finding Checklist

Get this info for each accomplishment to validate it.

- [ ] Get overview of the accomplishment and specific clarifying example.
- [ ] Get some measurements - when? why? what was quantitative impact?
- [ ] Scope it out - get actual title, size of team, titles of supervisor and subordinates, dates and duration of task.
- [ ] Get background of company - size, growth rates, complexity of systems, standards of performance, quality of senior management.
- [ ] Ask for bottom line, business impact.
- [ ] "What were the biggest challenges and major deliverables involved in accomplishing the task?"
- [ ] If manager, get names and titles of staff and overall quality of department.
- [ ] "Describe some techniques and examples of how you managed this team through a challenging time."
- [ ] Ask "Why were you chosen for this role?"
- [ ] "How would you rank the the overall success of the task and why?"
- [ ] Ask "What was your real contribution or value-added to this project?"
- [ ] "If you had a chance to do it over, what would you change/"
- [ ] Ask "How did you grow or change as a result of this effort?"

Work-Types Comparison

Assign responses to these categories and compare to job needs:

- [ ] **Creative/Strategist**: long range, visionary, new ideas, concepts, strategy.
- [ ] **Entrepreneur/Builder**: risk taker, fast-pace, persuasive, energetic.
- [ ] **Improver/Organizer**: manager, upgrades, improves people and process.
- [ ] **Technical/Producer**: analytical, detailed, quality, executes process.

CJA-The Adler Group, Inc.   *"Are You POWER Hiring℠ Yet?"*   Dallas • San Jose • Los Angeles
17852 17th, #209, Tustin, CA 92780 • 714/573-1820 • FAX 714/731-3952 • 800/559-2559 • www.cja-careers.com

POWER Staffing™ Comprehensive Interview
The Basic Performance Interview - Part II

Candidate:	Position:	Interviewer:	Date:

Benchmark Performance (ask these two questions for each SMART objective)		Hot Tips - Assessing the Answers
ANCHOR: (State objective) *Describe your most similar past accomplishment.* Objective 1: Objective 2: Objective 3:	**VISUALIZE**: *How would you accomplish this task?* (O.K. for just top two objectives) Objective 1: Objective 2:	**Key:** use fact-finding to learn everything about top 4-6 accomplishments and then use these tips to evaluate answers. **Team and Management - ABC Rule:** assign responses to Alone (individual contributor); Belonging (part of team); or in-Charge (as manager). Determine patterns and compare to job needs.

Character and Values (if not already answered)

Tell me about a time you were totally committed to a task.

Future goals are important, particularly when significant past goals have already been achieved. Please describe the biggest goal you've already achieved. What's the biggest new goal you've set for yourself?

What are the key things you're looking for in a new position? Why is having these important to you?

Scope and Size - The 6S Rule: During fact-finding evaluate companies and jobs according to - Span of control, Speed (pace of change), Sophistication, Standards of performance, Size, Scope and complexity of the work.

Focus - Internal or External: Assign major accomplishments according to Building the Business - External, or Running the Business - Internal.

Breadth of Thinking: Assign major accomplishments into Strategic (long range), Tactical (current), or Technical (process).

Functional or Project Focus: Assign responses to task, department, function, multi-function, or total business.

Personality and Cultural Fit

What three or four adjectives best describe your personality? Give me examples of when these have aided in the performance of your job and when they have hurt.

How has your personality and relationships with others changed over the past few years? Are there certain areas you'd like to see further growth?

Personality: Look for honesty, self-awareness.

Close: Don't go too fast. Make the job worth earning. Create competition to test true interest.

Closing - Use this to create supply and determine interest

If you were to take a position like this, how would you approach it in the first few weeks and months? What kind of impact do you think you could make in the first year?

Although we're seeing some other fine candidates, I think you have a very strong background. We'll get back to you in a few days, but what are your thoughts now about this position?

Candidate Assessment Summary - Circle Most Representative Term and Compare to Job Needs	
Trend of Performance - Up, Flat or Down	Focus - Internal (Running the Biz) or External (Building the Biz)
ABC Team/Management Rule - Alone, Belonging, in-Charge	Breadth of Thinking - Strategic, Tactical, Technical
Technical Competency/Ability to Learn - Strong, Adequate, or Weak	Job Focus - Task, department, function, multi-function, the whole biz
Work-Type Fit - Dominant and Secondary Match, Partial, or None	Character/Goals - Solid/committed, adequate, questionable
The Scope and Size of Prior Jobs - Comparable, too big, too small	Personality/Fit - Balanced/good, neutral/okay, self-absorbed/caution

POWER Staffing™ Phone Interview

The 20-Minute Performance-based Phone Interview

©1997 by Lou Adler, from his book *Hire With Your Head*. Part of the POWER Staffing™ "best practices" worksheet series, summarizing great hiring tips from some of the top managers in the US. Call 1-800-559-2559 for more hiring hot tips and tools.

Candidate:	Position:	Interviewer:	Date:

Always Conduct a Phone Interview Before Meeting a Candidate

The Deliverables - Performance (SMART) Objectives

List SMART Objectives (Specific, Measurable, Action verb, Result, Time-bound)
Example: *Improve product margins by 5% within 6 months.*

1. ....
2. ....
3. ....
4. ....

Work-Type: ___ Technical ___ Organizer ___ Entrepreneur ___ Strategist/Creative
Assign SMART Objectives to Work-Type and Indicate Dominant (1) and Secondary (2)

Opening Question (Recruiting and Setting Performance Tone of Interview)

(Spend two minutes describing company, job, yourself.) *Please give me a quick overview of your current situation and a general overview of how your background is related to our needs.*

Benchmark Experience Question Pattern (ask these questions for last most significant job)

Please give me a quick overview of the position and company and describe the biggest impact or change you made.	*Describe your organization (draw org chart) and, 1) tell me how you developed, and managed your team, or 2) tell me about some team project and describe your role.*

Current/Most Recent Position - Title: Yrs:

Most Significant Accomplishments (if not already answered above)

Please describe your most significant individual accomplishment. (typically a one-time event, an analytical, technical, special study or project)

Please describe your most significant management or team project and clearly define your role.

Hot Tips

Objective: Save time. Use this interview to determine if it's worth personally meeting the candidate. It addresses initiative, talent, span of control, team and management issues and interest.

Key Points

1. Be inquisitive. Get examples to turn generalities into specific responses.
2. Get trend of personal growth, energy, and team/management skills over time.
3. Listen 4X More Than Talk!

Quick Fact-Finding Checklist

Get this info for each accomplishment to validate it.

☐ Get overview of the accomplishment and specific clarifying example.
☐ Get some measurements - when? why? what was quantitative impact?
☐ Scope it out - get actual title, size of team, titles of supervisor and subordinates, dates and duration of task.
☐ Get background of company - size, growth rates, complexity of systems, standards of performance, quality of senior management.
☐ Ask for bottom line, business impact.
☐ "What were the biggest challenges and major deliverables involved in accomplishing the task?"
☐ If manager, get names and titles of staff and overall quality of department.
☐ "Describe some techniques and examples of how you managed this team through a challenging time."
☐ Ask "Why were you chosen for this role?"
☐ "How would you rank the the overall success of the task and why?"
☐ Ask "What was your real contribution or value-added to this project?"
☐ "If you had a chance to do it over, what would you change/"
☐ Ask "How did you grow or change as a result of this effort?"

CJA-The Adler Group, Inc.   *"Are You POWER Hiring℠ Yet?"*   Dallas • San Jose • Los Angeles
17852 17th, #209, Tustin, CA 92780 • 714/573-1820 • FAX 714/731-3952 • 800/559-2559 • www.cja-careers.com

POWER Staffing™ Phone Interview
Use the 20-Minute Phone to Minimize Impact of First Impression

Candidate:	Position:	Interviewer:	Date:

ANCHOR the Most Important SMART Objective (if not answered already)

(State performance objective) *Describe your most comparable past accomplishment.*

Personality and Cultural Fit

What three or four adjectives best describe your personality? Give me examples of when these have aided in the performance of your job and when they have hurt.

Closing and Recruiting - Use this to create supply and determine interest

Although we're evaluating some other good candidates, you seem to have a strong background. Is this position something worth considering?

What are you looking for in a new position? Why is having _____ and _____ important to you?

Let's set up a personal interview. Please bring a separate write-up of your most significant technical or individual contributor accomplishment, and your most significant team or management accomplishment (about 1/2 page each).

Quick Assessment - Circle Most Representative Response

Energy Level and Initiative - High, Moderate, Low	
Trend of Growth and Impact - Up, Level, Down	
ABC Rule - Team/Management - Alone, Belonging, in-Charge	
Technical Competency - Strong, Adequate, or Weak	
Work-Type Fit - Dominant and Secondary Match, Partial, or None	
The Scope and Size of Prior Jobs - Comparable, too Big, too Small	
Focus - Internal (Running Business) or External (Building Business)	
Breadth of Thinking - Strategic, Tactical, Technical	
Job Focus - Task, Department, Function, Multi-function	
Personality Fit - Positive, Neutral, Weak	

Hot Tips - Assessing the Answers

Key: Use fact-finding to learn everything about top 4-6 accomplishments and then use these tips to evaluate answers.

Work-Types: Assign responses to these categories and compare to job needs:

☐ **Creative/Strategist**: long range, visionary, new ideas, concepts, strategy.
☐ **Entrepreneur/Builder**: risk taker, fast-pace, persuasive, energetic.
☐ **Improver/Organizer**: manager, upgrades, improves people and process.
☐ **Technical/Producer**: analytical, detailed, quality, executes process.

Team and Management - ABC Rule: Assign responses to Alone (individual contributor); Belonging (part of team); or in-Charge (as manager). Determine patterns and compare to job needs.

Scope and Size - The 6S Rule: During fact-finding evaluate companies and jobs according to - Span of control, Speed (pace of change), Sophistication, Standards of performance, Size, Scope and complexity of the work.

Focus - Internal or External: Assign major accomplishments according to Building the Business - External, or Running the Business - Internal.

Breadth of Thinking: Assign major accomplishments into Strategic (long range), Tactical (current), or Technical (process).

Functional or Project Focus: Assign responses to task, department, function, multi-function, or total business.

Personality: Look for honesty, self-awareness.

Close: Don't go too fast. Make the job worth earning. Create competition to test true interest.

Write-ups: It's best if candidate is prepared to discuss most significant accomplishments in depth.

Notes, Comments, and Recommendations

POWER Staffing™ Performance Interview

The Basic Performance-based Interview for All Positions

©1997 by Lou Adler, from his book *Hire With Your Head*. Part of the POWER Staffing™ "best practices" worksheet series, summarizing great hiring tips from some of the top managers in the US. Call 1-800-559-2559 for more hiring hot tips and tools.

Candidate:	Position:	Interviewer:	Date:

Use This Interview When the Performance Objectives Are Unknown

Benchmark Experience Question Pattern (ask these two questions for the past 2-3 jobs.)

Please give me a quick overview of your (current/prior) position and describe the biggest impact (change) you made (or when you took the initiative).

Describe your organization (draw org chart) and tell me how you built, developed, and managed your team (or tell me about some team project and describe your role).

Current Job Notes:

Previous Job Notes:

Most Significant Accomplishments (ask these two questions if not already answered above)

Please describe your most significant individual accomplishment.

Please describe your most significant team or management accomplishment and describe your role.

Favorite Work Experience (if not included above)

Think about a favorite work experience, a one-time event, that gave you a great deal of personal satisfaction. Please describe it and tell me why it was important to you.

Favorite Problems (ask this when candidate says "I'm a problem solver," or anytime)

Everyone says they're a problem solver. Can you give me a few examples of the types of problems you like to solve.

Hot Tips and Fact-Finding Checklist

HOT TIP: Ask for Examples to Turn Generalities into Specific Responses

Get trend of personal growth, energy, and team/management skills over time.

Get this info for each accomplishment to validate it.

- ☐ Get overview of the accomplishment.
- ☐ Get actual title, size of team, titles of supervisor and subordinates, dates and duration of task.
- ☐ Ask for bottom line, business impact.
- ☐ Ask the candidate what his/her leadership role was - how did he/she develop program and implement it.
- ☐ Find out the biggest challenges or most difficult aspects of the task. Ask "What were the constraints that needed to be overcome?"
- ☐ Ask "Why do you consider this a significant accomplishment?"
- ☐ "What were the key steps and major deliverables involved in accomplishing the task?"
- ☐ Ask "Describe the people challenges and give me some examples."
- ☐ Get some examples when the candidate had to change the opinion of others and in dealing with conflict.
- ☐ Ask "How did you grow or change as a result of this effort?"
- ☐ Ask "Was the task completed on time, and was this difficult?"
- ☐ "If you had a chance to do it over, what would you change/"
- ☐ Ask "Why were you chosen for this role?"
- ☐ "How would others (peers, subordinates, supervisors) describe you and your style?"
- ☐ Find out how the candidate ranks the overall success of the task and why.
- ☐ Ask "What was your real contribution or value-added to this project?"

CJA-The Adler Group, Inc.   *"Are You POWER Hiring℠ Yet?"*   Dallas • San Jose • Los Angeles
17852 17th, #209, Tustin, CA 92780 • 714/573-1820 • FAX 714/731-3952 • 800/559-2559 • www.cja-careers.com

POWER Staffing™ Basic Performance Interview

Part II - When Performance Objectives are Unknown

Candidate:	Position:	Interviewer:	Date:

Initiative and Leadership (always get 3 examples, if short. Everyone can come up with 1-2)

Can you give me a few examples of when you took the initiative (or a leadership role) in accomplishing something over and above expectations?

Most Significant Creative or Strategic Accomplishment (if not included above)

Please describe the most significant project or accomplishment when you had to do some long-term planning (or be strategic or be creative).

Most Intense or Pressure Packed Project (if not included above)

Think about a real intense or pressure packed situation. Can you tell me about it and describe your role and what you accomplished?

Character and Values (if not included above)

Tell me about a time you were totally committed to a task.

Closing

Although we're seeing some other fine candidates, I personally think you have a very strong background. What are your thoughts now about this situation?

Hot Tips - Assessing the Answers

Key: Use fact-finding to learn everything about top 4-6 accomplishments and then use these tips to evaluate answers.

Work-Types: Assign responses to these categories and compare to job needs:

- ☐ **Creative/Strategist:** long range, visionary, new ideas, concepts, strategy.
- ☐ **Entrepreneur/Builder:** risk taker, fast-pace, persuasive, energetic.
- ☐ **Improver/Organizer:** manager, upgrades, improves people and process.
- ☐ **Technical/Producer:** analytical, detailed, quality, executes process.

Team and Management - ABC Rule: Assign responses to Alone (individual contributor); Belonging (part of team); or in-Charge (as manager). Determine patterns and compare to job needs.

Scope and Size - The 6S Rule: During fact-finding evaluate companies and jobs according to - Span of control, Speed (pace of change), Sophistication, Standards of performance, Size, Scope and complexity of the work.

Focus - Internal or External: Assign major accomplishments according to Building the Business - External, or Running the Business - Internal.

Breadth of Thinking: Assign major accomplishments into Strategic (long range perspective), Tactical (current performance), or Technical (process).

Functional or Project Focus: Assign responses to task, department, function, multi-function, or total business.

Summary and Assessment Notes

Trend of Impact, Energy and Initiative - Up, Flat or Down	
ABC Rule for Team/Management Skills - Alone, Belonging, in-Charge	
Technical Competency and Ability to Learn - Strong, Adequate, or Weak	
Work-Type: Strategic/Creative - Entrepreneur - Improver - Technical	
The 6S Rule Scope and Size of Prior Jobs - Comparable, too big, too small	
Focus - Internal (Running the Business) or External (Building the Business)	
Breadth of Thinking - Strategic, Tactical, Technical	
Functional or Project Focus - Task, department, function, multi-function	

POWER Staffing™ Work-Type Profiling

Matching Job Needs with Candidate's Abilities and Interests

©1997 by Lou Adler, from his book *Hire With Your Head*. Part of the POWER Staffing™ "best practices" worksheet series, summarizing great hiring tips from some of the top managers in the US. Call 1-800-559-2559 for more hiring hot tips and tools.

Candidate: Position: Interviewer: Date:

Comparing the Position and Candidate Work-Type Profile

SMART Objectives	Work-Type				People		
Assign objectives into a dominant(D) and secondary(S) work-type. Give 2 pts. for "D" and 1 pt. for "S". Also A-Alone, B-Belonging (team), C-in-Charge (management)	P/ T	O /I	E/ B	C/ S	A	B	C
1.							
2.							
3.							
4.							
5.							
6.							
TOTALS							

Listen to Candidate Responses and Assign to Categories

Candidate Responses	Work-Type				People		
Assign these to work-types - 2 pts for dominant, 1 pt. for secondary. Also assign to A: Alone, B: Belonging (team), C: in-Charge (management)	P/ T	O /I	E/ B	C/ S	A	B	C
Most Significant Accomplishment							
Most Significant Team Accomplishment (use 2nd most significant if used above)							
Most Significant Individual Accomplishment (use 2nd most significant if used above)							
Favorite Work Experience (ok to use again, ask why favorite)							
Best examples of types of problems candidate likes to solve							
Best three examples of initiative taken							
TOTALS							

Instructions and Hot Tips

All work can be categorized into four work-types: Assign SMART objectives and candidate responses into these objectives.

Creative/Strategy Phase (C/S): Ideas, products, and concepts start here. Includes visionaries, consultants, strategists, and creators.

Entrepreneurial/Builder Phase (O/I): This is where the idea becomes reality. The world of risk and change. Includes salesman, deal-maker, entrepreneurs, and turn-around specialists.

Improver/Organizer Phase (I/O): Running, improving, and upgrading the business. The world of tactics, plans and implementation. Includes managers, organizers, and planners.

Producer/Technical Phase (P/T): Where the work gets done - the process or transaction level. In a broad sense we label them producers, technicians, analysts, and administrators.

Work-Type Profiling

1. Assign each SMART objective to a dominant (2 pts.) and secondary (1 pt.) work-type.
2. Total scores to develop a work-type profile.
3. Prepare a candidate work-type profile by assigning major accomplishments into dominant and secondary work-types.
4. Compare the candidate and job work-type profiles to determine best fit.

ABC Interpersonal Skills Analysis

Categorize each accomplishment into:

    A: Alone or Individual Contributor

    B: Belonging or Team Role

    C: in-Charge or Management Role

Compare candidate's work-type to job needs.

Work-Type Comparison

Use this table to summarize the Candidate's Work-Type Profile and ABC Analysis

Best Fit - Dominant and Secondary Match

Next Best Fit - Dominant and Secondary Reversed

Factors	Work-Type		ABC
	Dominant	Secondary	
Job			
Candidate			
Summary			

CJA-The Adler Group, Inc.   *"Are You POWER Hiring℠ Yet?"*   Dallas • San Jose • Los Angeles
17852 17th, #209, Tustin, CA 92780 • 714/573-1820 • FAX 714/731-3952 • 800/559-2559 • www.cja-careers.com

POWER

POWER Staffing™ Work-Profiling and Job Fit
Compare Job Fit Across All Job Related Factors

Candidate: Position: Interviewer: Date:

Category	Work-Type Dominant Secondary		ABC Relationships	Span of Control	Management Level	Compare Environments
Description	Assign job and candidate to dominant and secondary work-types as described on other side of this work-sheet.		Compare job candidate for: Alone, Belonging (team) or in-Charge (manage).	Compare job to candidate for number and type of staff, and management level.	Is candidate staff, supervisor, manager, director, VP or GM (see below)?	Compare current environment to candidate's for: pace, systems, complexity, size, quality, and growth rates.
The Job						
The Candidate						
Summary Comments						

In above chart compare the job and candidate across all factors. For Management level consider this: staff: executes work, supervisor: oversees staff, manager: improves process, director: leads complex change, VP: applies strategic thinking, GM: directs multiple functions.

Notes and Conclusions

Areas of Best Fit:

Areas of Least Fit:

Comparability Analysis:

POWER Staffing™ Reference Checking

Use Performance-based Hiring to Build Great Teams

©1997 by Lou Adler, from his book *Hire With Your Head*. Part of the POWER Staffing™ "best practices" worksheet series, summarizing great hiring tips from some of the top managers in the US. Call 1-800-559-2559 for more hiring hot tips and tools.

| Candidate: | Position: | Interviewer: | Date: |

Use Reference Checks to Address Concerns and Confirm Strengths

Part 1 - Qualifying the Person Providing Reference

☐ Determine the relationship to the candidate. Ask for titles of both, years known, and most recent contact.

☐ Ask reference about current situation - company, title, how long, and scope of job.

☐ Determine what the environment was like – pace, standards of performance, quality of people.

☐ Ask the reference how tough a rater they are, and the basis of their rating system.

Reference Check Background Information

Name: _____

Working Relationship: _____

How Long Worked Together? _____

Current Position of Reference: _____

Was was environment like when worked together? _____

How do you judge performance? _____

Other: _____
_____

Part 2 - Qualifying the Candidate

(Select from this list based on the relationship to candidate.)

☐ *Please give me a summary of strengths and weaknesses.*
☐ Get examples of accomplishments to support major strengths.
☐ *How do the weaknesses affect job performance?*
☐ *Can you give me some examples of initiative?*
☐ *How would you rank this person as a manager?*
☐ *What's was his/her biggest management accomplishment?*
☐ *How strong was this person in building/developing teams?*
☐ *How would you rank this person's overall technical competence in (job specific) area?* Get specific examples.
☐ *Is technical competence a real strength? Why?*
☐ Get example of best work for top 1-2 SMART objectives.
☐ Team and interpersonal - get examples of group projects.
☐ Determine timeliness - get examples when under pressure.
☐ *How strong are his/her verbal and written communications? How were these measured?*
☐ Find out ability to handle pressure, criticism. Get example.
☐ *How strong a decision-maker? Can you give me some examples and how they were made?*
☐ *Can you give me an example of commitment?*
☐ *What's one single area that candidate could change in order to be more effective?* (to get at weaknesses)
☐ *Would you rehire the candidate? Why or why not?*
☐ *How would you rank this person's character and personal values system? How did this affect performance?*
☐ *How would you compare this candidate to others at the same level you know? Why is _____ stronger (or weaker)?*
☐ *What about potential? How far can this person go? Why?*
☐ *How would you rank overall performance on a scale of 0-10? What would it take to move up 1 point?*

NOTES and COMMENTS

CJA–The Adler Group, Inc.   *"Are You POWER Hiring™ Yet?"*   Dallas • San Jose • Los Angeles

17852 17th, #209, Tustin, CA 92780 • 714/573-1820 • FAX 714/731-3952 • 800/559-2559 • www.cja-careers.com

POWER Staffing™ Reference Checking

Use Targeted Reference Checks to Validate Strengths and Weaknesses

Plan Specific Areas to Discuss with Each Reference	Hot Tips and Advice
☐ Ask supervisors about the quality of the work and the results.	☐ All good candidates have good references.
☐ Ask subordinates about management and leadership skills.	☐ First validate the quality of person giving the reference.
☐ Ask peers about team projects, cooperation, and support.	☐ The best candidates have the best references.
☐ Inquire about potential weaknesses uncovered by testing.	☐ Get examples to substantiate generalities.
☐ Look for fatal flaws and extremes in behavior.	☐ Use fact-finding techniques to understand candidate's role.
☐ Find out the limits to the candidate progressing higher.	☐ Ask for areas of improvement to uncover weaknesses.
☐ Be clear about dates and reporting relationships.	☐ Use subordinates, peers, superiors equally.
☐ Ask about any concerns in achieving performance objectives (see below)	☐ Be skeptical.

Use References to Address Concerns About Ability to Meet the Performance Objectives

Rank the candidate's competency for each major objective. Confirm these with each reference as necessary.

Performance Objectives - Use generic ones listed, or substitute specific SMART objectives	Competency (Strong, Adequate or Weak (S to ?)	Reference Check Summary and Confirmation
1. Necessary motivation and drive in critical areas	S A W ?	
2. Achieve major performance objective of position	S A W ?	
3. Persuade, manage, organize, and motivate others	S A W ?	
4. Ability to achieve objectives based upon technical competence and knowledge	S A W ?	
5. Ability to solve typical problems inherent in the job	S A W ?	
6. Ability to lead change and organize necessary improvements	S A W ?	

Summary - Comments - Conclusions

Quality and Importance of the Reference:

Overall Quality of the Candidate Based on this Reference:

Comments and Recommendations:

Ten-Factor Candidate Assessment

©1997 by Lou Adler, from *Hire With Your Head.* Part of the POWER Staffing™ "best practices" worksheet series, summarizing great hiring tips from some of the top managers in the US. Call 1-800-559-2559 for more hiring hot tips and tools. A-3/98

Candidate: _____ Position: _____ Interviewer: _____ Date: _____

Trait/Factor	Scale - Weak(1) to Strong(5)					Score
	1	2	3	4	5	
Energy, Drive, Initiative	Little energy shown in any previous job. Passive work performance.	Generally consistent performance, but never exceeds expectations.	Consistent level of good performance with spotty periods of high levels of energy.	Generally highly motivated, but some brief periods of below top performance.	Consistent self-starter. Many examples of exceeding expectations in all jobs.	
Trend of Performance Over Time	Growth trend is spotty and inconsistent with the basic needs of the position.	Trend of growth is down, but candidate meets the basic needs of the position.	Trend of growth has flattened, but still consistent with needs of position.	Trend of growth is strongly upward although candidate might not be quite there.	Upward pattern of growth and increasing track record of performance.	
Comparability of Past Accomplishments (Anchor SMART Objectives)	No job needs are directly met. The gap is too wide to overcome.	Only one or two SMART objectives are met, but too many voids to address quickly.	Key SMART objectives are met with some voids that can be addressed.	Majority of SMART objectives are met with only little compromise needed.	Past accomplishments are strong and compare directly to all SMART objectives.	
Experience, Education and Industry Background	Weak fit on all standard measures: not enough experience or education.	Adequate experience, education. A stretch to meet minimum standards.	Solid education and experience, consistent with needs of position.	Direct education and experience exceeds current job needs.	Very strong comparable experience with good industry and educational fit.	
Problem Solving and Thinking Skills (Visualize SMART Objectives)	Structured thinking. Inability to adapt knowledge to new situations.	Some ability to upgrade and modify existing methods and processes.	Able to understand basic issues and come up with some alternative solutions.	Has ability to understand most issues and develop new solutions.	Has ability to understand all issues and develop and communicate new creative solutions.	
Overall Talent, Technical Competency and Potential	Little direct technical competence and inability to learn within reasonable time.	Some technical ability and talent, but might take too long to come up to standard.	Technically competent. Reasonable ability to learn. Narrow focus on job only.	Technically strong, smart, ability to learn quickly. Broader focus. Sees related issues.	Very talented, learns quickly, strategic, tactical, and technical focus. Very broad perspective.	
Management and Organizational Ability	Little relevant management experience or unable to organize similar projects.	Some management ability, but insufficient to make contribution anytime soon.	Reasonable management experience. Will have to grow to become more effective.	Solid manager and organizer. Exceeds the needs of the position.	Has strong ability to manage and organize groups of similar size and type of staff.	
Team Leadership - Persuade/Motivate Others	Little evidence of persuading or leading others. Tends to be more individualistic.	Some evidence of team skills, but inconclusive. Generally more individualistic.	Solid team leadership skills or potential, but not completely apparent.	Seems to have very strong team leadership, but not completely tested.	Strong track record. Has the ability to motivate and develop others. Positive Attitude.	
Character – Values, Commitment, Goals	Questionable values and integrity. Self-serving. Misleading.	Reasonably solid values and ethics, but questions remain regarding candor.	Appropriate values and ethics. No significant problems and no unusual strengths.	A committed person. Good character, values, and attitude.	High integrity, committed person with strong values and ethics. Frank and candid.	
Personality and Cultural Fit	Fatal flaw or some imbalance or poor attitude and fit with existing team.	Adequate fit, but could cause some degree of conflict or might have negative impact.	All around solid person. Will fit with group without causing much conflict.	Generally positive attitude. Personality will help in performance of job.	A person with a balanced ego, positive attitude, flexible and can work with others.	
Total Point Score	Rank each trait on a 0-5 scale as noted. Reinterview the candidate if insufficient information available for any of these categories. Multiply total score by two (x2) to compare to 100.					

CJA - The Adler Group, Inc.   *"Are You POWER Hiring^sm Yet?"*   Dallas • San Jose • Los Angeles
17852 17th, #209, Tustin, CA 92780 • 714/573-1820 • FAX 714/731-3952 • 800/559-2559 • www.cja-careers.com

POWER Staffing™ Recruiting Worksheet

How to Recruit Candidates and Negotiate and Close Offers

©1997 by Lou Adler, from his book *Hire With Your Head*. Part of the POWER Staffing™ "best practices" worksheet series, summarizing great hiring tips from some of the top managers in the US. Call 1-800-559-2559 for more hiring hot tips and tools.

Candidate:	Position:	Hiring Manager:	Date:

Develop a Three-Step Recruiting Plan/Pitch

Develop compelling evidence for each category why move has strategic importance. Semi-customize for each finalist. When presented directly/indirectly during sessions compensation becomes secondary concern.

The Job	The Hiring Manager	The Company

Recruiting and Interviewing Questions

Opening - (Provide quick overview as to importance of job and company plans.) How has your background prepared you for this type of position?

Recruiting Question - (Job objective) is of critical importance since (state importance to company). Tell me your most significant accomplishment in this area.

Challenging Question - While you're strong in (candidate strength), I'm concerned about your experience in (area of concern). Have I missed something in your background?

Determine Motivation - Why are you considering leaving? What are you looking for in a new position? Why is having (a) and (b) important to you? What would be your biggest concerns in taking a new position?

Closing (at end of 1st interview) - Although I'm seeing some other strong candidates, I also think you have a very strong background. What are your thoughts now about this position?

Closing in On Compensation

Determine Salary - after the first interview or later.

☐ Our compensation range for this position is in the range of ($x-y). If this meets your needs I'd like to arrange another interview.
☐ What's your current compensation? (get base, bonus, other compensation, tie out to W-2).
☐ If higher - I really like your background, but your compensation is above our target. Aside from the compensation, is this a job that seems interesting? Knowing our range is it worth continuing these discussions?
☐ Negotiating Test - I really like your background, but I've got another candidate with a bit more experience, but at a slightly higher comp. Since you're a little lighter experience-wise, but with great potential, would you consider compensation below this?

Get Concessions at Every Stage of the Interview Process

☐ I'd like to invite you back for another interview. First, I'd like to review our interviewing process. It consists of ...(ref checks, drug tests, testing, background verification, criminal and credit check). If this makes sense to you let's set up another interview.

Recruiting Hot Tips

This worksheet will guide you through every phase of the recruiting, negotiating and closing process. Good recruiting - increases motivation, improves communications, overcomes compensation constraints, allows interviewer to maintain control.

Basic Rule #1 - Applicant control is the key. Always stay the buyer! Once you start selling you've lost control and the job has less appeal.

Recruiting: Don't oversell. Over buy! Create compelling opportunity and make candidate earn the job. A recruiting pitch is O.K., but break it into short prefaces for each question to create interest.

Opening Question - Give 1 minute overview of the importance of the position and company plans. Then have candidate describe most relevant accomplishments.

Recruiting Questions - Use recruiting prefaces throughout the interview to maintain interest. State importance of task and ask candidate to justify competency.

Challenging Questions - Push candidate away. Increases control and determines interest and confidence.

Uncover motivation and interest throughout the interview. Determine going-away strategy (why leaving) and going-toward strategy (new job attraction) to position opportunity.

Closing - Create competition and interest - This makes the job more compelling and keeps you in control.

Test Salary After First Interview But not sooner. Too soon and you might exclude for wrong reasons. Too late and you've lost negotiating edge.

CJA-The Adler Group, Inc.   *"Are You POWER Hiring℠ Yet?"*   Dallas • San Jose • Los Angeles

17852 17th, #209, Tustin, CA 92780 • 714/573-1820 • FAX 714/731-3952 • 800/559-2559 • www.cja-careers.com

POWER Staffing™ Recruiting and Closing Worksheet

Testing Offers and Overcoming Objections

Target Offer	Summary Details	Test/Agree	Objections/Comments
Salary			
Bonus			
Car			
Other Cash Comp			
Title - Position			
Benefit Package			
Options			
Relocation Package			
Next Review			
Other			

Testing the Offer
Use this form to guide you. Prepare a preliminary offer and test every aspect before making it formal. The worst thing you can do is to extend an untested offer and then wait for a response. You've lost control and prevented open communications.

Get Concessions at Every Stage - As candidate advances in interview get agreement on aspects of offer at every step. This way closing is natural throughout the interview process, not just at end when you have less leverage.

Don't move too fast. This can frighten away good candidates. A job change requires thought. Don't push too hard. Let candidate absorb the opportunity.

Salary - Delay salary discussion until after the first meeting or when inviting back for second. Use acceptance of salary range as price to come back for next interview.

Overcoming Objections

Typical Objections/Concerns	Overcoming Objections
Not enough money	Change focus to long-term opportunities from tactical short term issues - ask if making a tactical or strategic decision."
Competing Offer	Create comparison balance sheet highlighting strategic strengths of the two positions.
What are the promotional opportunities?	"Promotions are based on your performance and business opportunities. You'll be given as much as you can handle."
Job isn't big enough	Focus on what needs to get done and job importance. Review and/or add performance targets.
Hesitating to move on to next step	Bring concerns on the table. "It seems like you have a concern with this. Let's discuss it."
The long term opportunity doesn't seem strong enough	Bring candidate back for strategic overview. Get senior exec to describe company growth plans.

Overcoming Objections - Expect for things to go wrong. The purpose of testing is to uncover objections. You're then in a position to negotiate the item in an open non-confrontational style. You won't close everyone this way, but you'll close more. You'll also know why someone didn't accept your offer. Once the offer is extended open communications cease.

Testing Offers - Just ask for the candidate's thoughts after stating one of the offer terms.

"I have to think about it." - If you hear this it means you've moved too fast. You want candidate to think about it, but when you're in control, not the candidate - before the offer.

Acceptance - This approach results in immediate acceptance, or the next day. Do more probing and delay if offer can't be accepted right away. Too many things can go wrong once offer has been extended.

How to Test the Offer

- ☐ Trial Close - (Describe job or specific term of offer area) *Is this job something of interest?*
- ☐ Testing Offers - *Although we're still considering other candidates, we're thinking about putting an offer together for you in the ranges discussed. What are your thoughts?*
- ☐ Differentiating between job and offer - *Assuming an attractive offer, how does the job scope and challenge appeal to you?*
- ☐ Closing Upon an Objection - *If we could meet you on that point, are you in a position to accept an offer?*
- ☐ Secondary Closes - *If we could put an attractive package together as described, when could you start?*
- ☐ Final Close - *If we could get the offer approved at the terms agreed upon, when could you formally accept?*

Biggest Don't

We'd like to make an offer of (describe package). What are your thoughts? If you hear *"I have to think about it,"* offer was made prematurely. Test all aspects before formally extending offer.

POWER Staffing™ Hiring Hot Tips

Five Steps to Better Hiring Decisions

POWER Staffing™ "best practices" summarizes great hiring tips from some of the top managers in the US. The POWER Staffing system can be implemented with our Windows™ hiring software system or template-based Hiring ToolKit. © 1997 by Lou Adler.

1 Performance Job Specs

Build Job Specs on the DOING not the HAVING!

- Ask, *What does this person need to DO to be successful!?* Prepare a prioritized list of 4-6 deliverables, consider:
  - Major Objectives & Projects
  - Enabling or Sub-Objectives
  - Management/Org Issues
  - Strategic/Tactical Objectives
  - Technical Projects
  - Interpersonal Issues
  - Problems and Changes
  - Convert skills into projects
- Benchmark: Include the traits of the best people now doing the work.
- Create **SMART** Objectives (Specific, Measurable, Action oriented, Result, Time-based) for above, e.g., *"Within 6 months develop an on-line factory performance reporting system tracking major costs."*

2 Sourcing Candidates

Multi-Level Sourcing

- Be proactive, anticipate needs, always look.
- Network with employees, customers, vendors.
- Post everywhere - signs, colleges, internet.
- Use direct sourcing to find candidates not currently looking.

Write Compelling Ads

- DOING not HAVING.
- Don't add "Must have..."
- Add sizzle.
- Ask for extra write-up re: most significant impact.
- Broad, not narrow.

Filter Resumes On

- Track Record.
- Impact/Changes Made.
- Quality of Companies.

3 Controlling Emotions

Measure Performance First! - Before Personality

- Don't exclude or buy-in too soon, keep an open mind.
- Make sure new data can have same impact as previous data.
- Stay inquisitive, be skeptical.

How to Control Emotions

- Recognition: know your "hot buttons." If uptight or relaxed, you're less objective.
- Change Frame of Reference: be tougher on those you like and easier on those you don't.
- Conduct Phone Interview First!
- Wait 30 Minutes: measure 1st impression again, objectively.
- Treat Candidate as Consultant: listen 4X more than talk, and assume candidate is an expert.
- Talk About Real Work: walk around, discuss real issues.

4 Performance Interview

Opening Question/Recruit (create excitement about job)

- Provide exciting overview of job and ask candidate to describe relevant background.

Impact/Leadership Pattern (get this info for past 2-4 jobs)

- Get OVERVIEW of job and ask for significant IMPACT.
- Get ORG CHART and most significant TEAM and/or management project.

Job Competency (ask for top 3-5 SMART Objectives)

- ANCHOR: State objective. Ask for related accomplishment.
- VISUALIZE: Discuss objective and how to accomplish it.

Closing Question/Recruit (create supply/demand & test interest)

- Although we're seeing other strong candidates, you have a very fine background. What are your thoughts now about the job?

5 Recruiting Candidates

Stay the Buyer

- If you "buy" too soon or move too fast, you oversell, cheapen job, lose control and stop evaluating.

Create Compelling Vision of Job

- Make the candidate earn job. It has more value, and candidates then sell you!

Recruit

- Market the job by describing its importance before each question. It creates demand.

Challenge

- Push away, question level of experience. It makes the job worth having - tests interest!

Test Interest/Offers

- Always ask ... *"What do you think about an offer of ...?"*
- Test every aspect this way before formal offer is made.

Hiring DO's and DON'Ts

Don't Ask About

- Age or anything related that can determine age.
- Race, nationality or related issues.
- Clubs, social groups, or where living.
- Anything about arrest record.
- Children or family issues, now or in the future.

To Comply with ADA

- Use performance job spec.
- Objectives must be essential.
- You may ask person with disability how they would accomplish task.
- No need to lower standards, but you may need to provide accommodation.

You May Ask About

- Academic background if job related.
- Ability to travel if job related.
- Professional groups, certifications.
- Felony convictions and details.
- Ability to work unusual hours if job related.

Fact-Finding: Peel the Onion
Increases Accuracy & Reduces Exaggeration

- Get lots of info about top 4-6 accomplishments.
- Conduct the same interview whether you like or dislike the candidate.
- Get examples to support generalities.
- Ask .. Why? When? How? How long?
- Quantify; ... get dates, facts, figures.

CJA - The Adler Group, Inc.   *"Are You POWER Hiring℠ Yet?"*   17852 17th, #209, Tustin, CA 92780 • 800/559-2559 • FAX 714/731-3952 • www.cja-careers.com • Dallas • San Jose • Los Angeles

POWER Staffing™ Hiring Tools, Tips and Techniques

How to Conduct a Reference Check

☐ Get overall summary of strengths and ask for best example to validate.
☐ Ask for best example of initiative, self-motivation, ability to lead change.
☐ Management/team projects - ask about ability to hire, manage, motivate, develop others.
☐ Find out ability to handle pressure, criticism - get circumstances.
☐ Decision-making - determine process, pace, significance, and get realistic examples.
☐ Commitment - get best example to prove level of commitment. Find out frequency.
☐ Ask *"What motivates or drives the candidate to success?"*
☐ Ask *"Would you hire/rehire?"*
☐ Get overall summary - *"How would you compare this candidate to others you know at the same level?"*
☐ Ask *"How would you compare this candidate to others you know at the same level?"*
☐ Get overall summary - *"How would you rank overall performance on 0-10 scale? What would it take to move up 1 point?"*

Key: Remember to get specific examples to support generalities and glowing statements. This reduces exaggeration.

Fact-Finding Techniques

✔ Narrow & Deep, not Broad & Shallow
✔ Get as much info as you can about 4-6 major accomplishments
✔ Get Examples to Support Generalities

Ask/get this information for each accomplishment

☐ Get Info about company:
 - size: sales, # of people
 - rate of change
 - quality of systems
 - budget
☐ Quick overview of task
☐ Quantify major objective and get results
☐ Get list of required deliverables (quantify)
☐ Time: when and how long the project took
☐ Key challenges and how addressed
☐ How would you rank quality of results?
☐ What were the biggest challenges you faced?
☐ How did you overcome these challenges?
☐ Describe specific role

☐ How would others describe your effort and results?
☐ Get 3 examples of initiative for each project.
☐ Get: title, titles of staff, and supervisor's title
☐ Rank quality of staff
☐ Describe people development issues
☐ How did you grow and change?
☐ How could it have been done better?
☐ What was bottom-line business impact?
☐ Why were you chosen for role?
☐ What was your value-added?
☐ Why did you like it?

Performance Hiring

"Focus on the candidate's ability to do the job, not get the job."

Performance Job Descriptions
Objective Interviews
Wide Ranging Sourcing Plans
Emotional Control
Recruiting Right

- Now Available -
- Lou Adler's new book *Hire With Your Head*
- Half-day In-house Training Workshop
- The POWER Staffing Hiring ToolKit - Templates/Forms
- Audio and Video Tape Training Programs

POWER Staffing Hiring Software

Automates Hiring - Generates Interviews
Prepares Performance Job Specs
Tracks/Evaluates Candidates
• See Our Web Site - www.cja-careers.com •
• Call 1-800-559-2559 for Demo •

Candidate Assessment Checklist

Value All Factors Equally - Don't Globalize Strengths or Weaknesses

Trait - Factor	Description	0-10
Drive, Energy, Initiative, Self-motivation	Get examples of team and individual accomplishments from previous jobs	
Talent and Technical Competence	Look for technical level, ability to learn and ability to apply technical knowledge.	
Managerial, Team and Organizational Ability	Compare size of groups managed, complexity of projects, and quality of staff/team development.	
Experience, Education and Environment	Assess quality of experience by comparing to sophistication of prior companies.	
Thinking and Analytical Skills	Compare job needs to thinking skills from tech, tactical, strategic and multi-function perspective.	
ABC and Interpersonal Skills	Determine pattern in accomplishments. Alone, Belonging or in-Charge.	
Leadership	Persuading, hiring, motivating others. Patterns of implementing significant change.	
Commitment and Responsibility	Get examples of commitment and determine frequency and significance.	
Character, Values and Integrity	Find out source and level of motivation and importance of work to candidate's success.	
Personality and Cultural Fit	Look for flexibility and growth over time. Was first impression different after 30 minutes?	
Overall Summary	Reassess any area not covered. Use multiple techniques to measure each factor.	

Writing Performance Job Descriptions

Prepare a Prioritized List of 4-6 SMART Objectives:
Specific, Measurable, Action-oriented, Result, Time-based

Method	Description	Example
The Big Picture Approach - Ask: *"What will the person hired need to do to be successful?"*	Get measurable objectives for each major factor in the job. Cover - technical needs, management issues, team issues, projects, needed changes and problems.	• Launch three new products within the next 12 months. • In the next 90 days upgrade the planning system for manufacturing.
The Little Picture Approach: *Convert needed skills and "must haves" into actions*	Determine what needs to be done with each skill or experience. Develop, a measurable objective that demonstrates competency.	• Use PCs to develop a new project tracking system. • Have enough experience to design three new products per year.
Benchmark the Best! *Discover traits and abilities of best people now in the job*	Compare the best people already in the job and select traits that best predict success. Avoid the traits of the under performers.	• Ability to work with numbers and details for extended periods. • Initiative in dealing with customer problems and making quick decisions.

Index